In memoriam

Prof. Dr. Volker Rittberger
(1941 – 2011)

Die Schriftenreihe trägt der zunehmenden Beachtung des Themenkomplexes von Religion, Konflikt und Frieden Rechnung. Sowohl in der Wissenschaft als auch in Politik, Friedensarbeit, Medien oder Bildungseinrichtungen wird man mehr und mehr gewahr, welche Bedeutung religiösen Überzeugungen nicht nur für die Entwicklung von Konflikten zukommen kann, sondern auch für die Vermeidung oder Beilegung derselben. Entsprechend breit, interdisziplinär und methodisch vielfältig ist das Spektrum der publizierten Arbeiten. Durch theoretische, empirische oder deskriptiv angelegte Untersuchungen richtet sich die Reihe ebenso an das wissenschaftliche Fachpublikum wie an (friedens-)politische Akteure und die an Frieden und Religion interessierte Öffentlichkeit.

Religion - Konflikt - Frieden
wird herausgegeben von

Dr. Markus Weingardt, Tübingen

Band 5

Roland Czada | Thomas Held | Markus Weingardt

Religions and World Peace

Religious Capacities for Conflict Resolution and Peacebuilding

Nomos

Das dieser Publikation zugrundeliegende Vorhaben wurde mit Mitteln des Bundesministeriums für Bildung und Forschung unter dem Förderkennzeichen 01UG0906 gefördert. Die Verantwortung für den Inhalt dieser Veröffentlichung liegt bei den Autorinnen und Autoren.

Die Deutsche Nationalbibliothek verzeichnet diese Publikation in der Deutschen Nationalbibliografie; detaillierte bibliografische Daten sind im Internet über http://dnb.d-nb.de abrufbar.

ISBN 978-3-8329-6705-5

1. Auflage 2012

Preface

> "Values are not there to serve philosophers or theologians,
> but to help people live their lives and organize their societies.
> So, at international level, we need mechanisms of cooperation
> strong enough to insist on universal values,
> but flexible enough to help people realise those values
> in ways that they can actually apply in their specific circumstances."
> *Kofi Annan*[1]

In his lecture on Global Ethics delivered at Tübingen University, the then Secretary-General of the United Nations, Kofi Annan, raised the question of the existence of "universal values" that can jointly endeavour to meet the enormous challenges faced by mankind in the age of globalisation. This referred primarily to religions. Whilst respecting cultural differences, their basic value systems, characterised by tolerance, openness to dialogue and their quest for peace and justice, should contribute towards finding and realising mutually acceptable solutions for coexistence in security and peace.

Following the terrorist attacks on 11th September 2001, the involvement of religions in inciting and justifying violence has become the focus of public and scientific debate. With recourse to Samuel Huntington, religions were deemed to be the driving forces leading to a "Clash of Civilizations" and threatening the international community with numerous violent conflicts. In contrast, an increasing number of events and initiatives have been held across the world that aim to foster interreligious dialogue and to dismantle foe images, stereotypes and cultural misunderstandings. Nonetheless, the ambivalence of religions which, in addition to having the potential for violence, also have a great potential for peacebuilding and peace promotion, still remains a marginal research topic. The same applies to the question of how religious communities can develop resilience to their political exploitation.

The *German Foundation for Peace Research*, the *Research Network Religion and Conflict* and the *Academic Council of the Osnabrück Peace Forum*. collaboratively developed the idea of holding an international conference to address this major scientific and political desideratum. After all, the challenges faced by mankind at the start of the 21st century – namely future energy supplies, the production and distribution of sufficient quantities of food for an ever-growing world population, the increasing shortage of fresh water and the social and economic consequences of climate change

1 Kofi Annan, lecture on Global Ethics delivered on 12 December 2003 at Tübingen University. Download: http://www.weltethos.org/1-pdf/20-aktivitaeten/eng/we-reden-eng/speech_Annan_eng.pdf (here p. 6).

– can only be met if, in line with the points made in Kofi Annan's lecture, consensus can be achieved on universal values and on an understanding of justice and security based on reciprocity. With their potential for promoting peace, religions can make a major contribution to this consensus.

The questions raised by Kofi Annan in his lecture on Global Ethics offered central points of reference for the international conference on "Religions and World Peace: Religious Communities and their Potential for Peacebuilding and Conflict Resolution", held in Osnabrück – the City of Westphalian Peace – between 20th and 23th October 2010. It consciously and explicitly dealt with the peace-promoting and peacebuilding potential of religions, with the aim of enabling them to take a more active role in academic and public discourse. It was for this reason that the event was directed at academia, interested parties, politicians and the general public alike. The huge response demonstrated that an important new impetus had emanated from the conference: not only for the examination of domestic affairs such as social integration, violence prevention and cross-cultural understanding, but also for questions of international significance, such as crisis and violence prevention, conflict resolution and sustainable peace consolidation on a global scale. We are therefore especially grateful to the German Federal Ministry of Education and Research for generously sponsoring the conference. We also appreciate the cooperation of the associations of protestant and catholic academies in Germany, the German section of Religions for Peace, the United Nations Association of Germany, the German Commission for UNESCO, the University of Osnabrück and the City of Peace Osnabrück. Further thanks go to the initiators of the conference, Hans-Jürgen Fip, former lord mayor of Osnabrück, and the late Professor Volker Rittberger, who most unfortunately passed away in November 2011 and to whom this volume is dedicated. We owe special gratitude to Janina Sentner and Lena Förster for managing the conference and getting this book published.

Osnabrück/Tübingen, April 2012

Roland Czada *Thomas Held* *Markus Weingardt*

Inhaltsverzeichnis

I. Introduction

Roland Czada, Thomas Held and Markus Weingardt

The "comeback" or "renaissance" of religion has become a controversial topic under intense public debate. Whether this means an overall decline of secularism and, thus, constitutes a real return of religion to the political arena, or whether it is more a matter of public perception and media coverage, today religion has (once again) advanced to become a relevant and highly regarded factor in international politics. Public perception and debate centre primarily on fundamentalism and violence in the name of religion. There have been, and continue to be, justifications for such a perspective. These range from the establishment of a totalitarian "theocracy" in Iran and the wars waged between Roman Catholic Croats, orthodox Serbs and Muslim Bosnians in the disintegrating state of Yugoslavia to the tyranny of the Taliban in Afghanistan, from the terrorist assaults on the Pentagon and the World Trade Center in September 2001 and numerous subsequent attacks across the globe by the radical Islamic Al Qaida network to, right up to current religiously charged conflicts in Africa, the Near and Middle East and in Southeast Asia.

Against this backdrop, it is hardly surprising that the attention of the media and academia is focused on the *acts of violence* perpetrated by religious fanatics, causing religions to be seen primarily as politically dangerous, destructive and likely to exacerbate conflict. Although "religion seems to be a cause of conflict, as well as of conflict resolution, the effects of religion in both exhorting men to peace and of justifying violence in defense of the "sacred" has been widely noted" (Kratochwil 2005:114). However, research into this ambivalence is still in its infancy, and academic exchange on this topic appears to be underdeveloped (cf. Appleby 2000; Basedau 2009; De Juan/ Hasenclever 2009; Philpott 2007). We know little about the conditions under which conflict constellations develop, and what triggers religious beliefs and religious actions to orientate in a particular direction. Furthermore, even less is known about how the potential for peacebuilding and the resilience to violence within religious communities can be awakened and strengthened.

The question of the significance and effectiveness of religion with regard to the *delegitimisation* and *prevention* of violence springs to mind precisely because at present "religion is perceived as being particularly effective at legitimising violence" (Grieser 2005:182). And yet the media and academia mainly continue to sidestep this issue, or ignore and marginalise it. If religions and religious communities can exert *constructive* influence on political conflicts – not only those of a violent nature – then it would present itself as further developing this potential and harnessing it more effectively for the benefit of peace processes.

Religion and peace

The ambivalent and highly complex relationship between the orientations of religious actors and political patterns of conflict is now widely recognised (cf. Weingardt 2010; Kadayifci-Orellana 2009; Brocker/Hildebrandt 2008; Harpviken/Røislien 2008; Appleby 2000) – and with it, at the same time, the realisation that communities of faith and other religiously oriented actors can contribute to constructive conflict management and have, indeed, done so. In spite of these findings, which are by no means new, for a long time religions played virtually no role in peace and conflict research. It was Samuel Huntington's hypothesis of the "Clash of Civilizations" (Huntington 1993/1996) in particular that drew new attention to the role of "religion". Even if his hypotheses were soon "weighed by academia and found to be too light," (Hasenclever 2003:289; see also Müller 2001), they nonetheless led to greater attention being paid to religion in the academic world. Despite the criticism, however, conflict research adopted Huntington's narrow outlook on the conflict potential of religions. The *constructive* exertion of political influence by religious actors was not intended, let alone theoretically grounded, in this perspective. With regard to the role played by religions, Volker Rittberger and Andreas Hasenclever (2000) approached the problem by differentiating between three schools of thought in the theories of International Relations: *primordialists* (e.g. Huntington 1996, Tibi 1995, Kepel 1991) accord religion, as a central element of culture, a genuinely conflict-creating, or at least conflict-exacerbating, role. *Instrumentalists* (e.g. Senghaas 1998, Meyer 1997, Fuller 1995), on the other hand, do not perceive religion as a source of conflict, and yet stress the risk that can be posed by the radicalisation and instrumentalisation of religion. Finally, *constructivists* (e.g. Hopf 1998, Tishkov 1997, Snider 1996) endeavour to achieve an intermediary role: according to this school of thought, the threat posed by religions does not lie in causing conflicts, nor are they merely a victim of political exploitation. Instead, constructivists view religion as an "inter-subjective structure" (Rittberger/Hasenclever 2000:39) that shapes not only the perception, but also the actions of believers. It follows from this, however, that religious convictions can principally have both a conflict-exacerbating and a conflict-defusing effect, making them *ambivalent* (cf. Appleby 2000).

There is no doubt that, under certain conditions, religions can be called upon to mobilise a considerable potential for conflict and violence. As with secular ideologies, they have a substantial potential to inflate existing interests in a manipulative manner and to literally demonise opponents to gain maximum allegiance and willingness for sacrifice from their followers. And yet such misuse is not a specific feature of religions alone; in the past, secular ideologies have also acted too often as ammunition for the spread of hatred and violence. However, the hitherto neglected empirical observation that religions also have an equally unquestionable strong *potential for peace* is of major interest. Nevertheless, the constructive aspects of religion as contributors to peace continue to form a vacuum in theories of International Relations. It is also the case here that religions are no less suited than secular ideologies to give precedence to working towards *just peace* over the (violent) assertion of their own interests, to view their political opponents as humans despite the differences, and to develop "maximum hope" and enormous constructive powers through faith or spirituality.

This potential has already been apparent on many occasions in various successful peace work activities: in violence prevention and reconciliation work, in nonviolent resistance and in helping to bring about system change, in development policy work in conflict areas or corresponding lobbying in indirectly affected countries, in the constructive management of local conflicts and in brokering international peace treaties. Here, the peace activities of religious actors in all conflict phases should be taken into account. Such activities include the prevention of violence and the avoidance of escalation processes, the de-escalation of conflicts that have already turned violent, and stabilisation and consolidation in post-conflict developments. Commitment is not limited to conflict management in the narrow sense alone, but often also directly connects related aspects of socio-economic conditions and law (legislation, case law and law enforcement).

Numerous case studies on religious peace work demonstrate the enormous diversity of conflicts, actors and approaches (cf. Weingardt 2010). The cultural, religious and political context, type, object, reach, parties and (violent) waging strategies of the investigated *conflicts* vary just as widely as their intensity, duration and evolution. The faith-based *actors* of conflict management belong to various religions and denominations; they act as individuals, groups or (interreligious) institutions, as charismatic leaders or "nameless" activists; they practise various forms of religiousness or spirituality and are also decidedly divergent with regard to their institutional constitution, prominence, political influence or profile and relationship to the conflict. The same applies to their approach, action level, type and method, as well as the measures and mode of action of conflict management, in particular for the importance of religious elements and the degree of escalation or conflict ripeness at the time of *intervention.* These differences between conflict, actor and intervention features make it difficult to define overarching categories. With regard to the significance of religions in terms of peace policy – as opposed to secular or political pacifist forces – the type of *actors* and their approach is of particular interest here.

Some of the contributions to this volume convey a lively impression of the specific peace work undertaken by religious actors. In many other conflict situations, on the other hand, *no* religious potential for peace was, or is, in evidence. The reasons for this are still widely unexplored (cf. Weingardt/Brenner 2010). Peace and conflict research is only gradually turning towards the religious *potential for peacebuilding*, sounding out its possibilities and limitations. Politicians and the media must first follow this change in perspective to be able to make practical use of the lessons to be learned from it. For a long time, they have paid only passing attention to the work and successes of religious peace initiatives, and have failed to take them seriously as relevant political forces. Within the religions themselves, too, there is still a lack of consciousness of their own *responsibility* for peace and peace *competence*. Virtually none of the religious communities' actual commitment to peace, nonviolence and justice complies with the high theological value and claim – emphasised in *all* religions. This is deplorable and should be called for. At the same time, however, it gives rise to the hope that by intensifying dialogue and cooperation between religions, as well as between religions and politicians and, last but not least, academia, new potential for peacebuilding can be tapped and exploited in the future.

The "Religions and World Peace" symposium

The present volume is a compilation of key contributions to the international symposium "Religions and World Peace: Religious Communities and their Potential for Peacebuilding and Conflict Resolution" held in Osnabrück, 20–23 Oct. 2010. Promoting dialogue was a most prominent goal of this conference organized by the German Foundation for Peace Research and financed by the Federal Ministry for Education and Research. Mobilising religion and faith against rather than in favour of violence appears to be a formidable task, facing not only every believer, but also theologians, religious authorities and political actors. If establishing and preserving domestic national and international peace constitutes the ultimate goal and primary objective for politicians, it would seem fitting – in accordance with the spirit of Kofi Annan's lecture on Global Ethics mentioned in the preface to this volume – to involve religions and religious communities in this task.

For this reason, the main concern of the symposium was to facilitate exchange within academia, and between academics, politicians and religions. In line with this, the contributors represented various academic disciplines, positions and methodological approaches, as well as different religions. The keynote and specialist lectures were complemented by practice-oriented workshops and discussions.

The book's first part is devoted to the general issue of the role of religions as peacemakers. In his essay "A Joint Vision for World Peace? Religions as Driving Forces for a Culture of Peace", the eminent theologian *Hans Küng* elaborates on various historical dimensions to shed light upon the ambivalence of peace and violence in world religions. When pointing out the strength of religious communities in fostering peace, he offers a whole range of methods and recommendations to further advance this potential in the future.

In his chapter, *David Little* tackles the discussion of the peacebuilding potential of religions from a political perspective and contextualises the issue within the broader framework of ethno-religious conflicts and nationalist impulses. Religious tolerance and democratic governance are identified as key factors for establishing peace.

As a counterweight to theoretical explanations of religions' potential for peace and conflict, *Jeffrey Haynes* illustrates the actual integration of religious approaches in current peacebuilding practices in the developing world. He thereby focuses on the unique characteristics of faith-based conflict resolution in case studies from Mozambique, Nigeria and Cambodia.

In the following chapter, *Claus Leggewie* develops a post-Westphalian perspective on the relationship between state, society and religion. Recent national issues of religious pluralism and religious governance are also considered and highlight the need for cooperative solutions for the future.

The second part focuses on theological and religious studies using perspectives from Hinduism, Buddhism, Judaism, Christianity and Islam. An overarching explanation of Buddhist understanding and teaching in terms of conflict and peace is provided by *Peter Harvey*. His analysis includes the Buddhist rationale for the causes of conflict as well as solutions to conflict rooted in the Buddhist tradition. Special emphasis is further placed on current Buddhist activist groups such as Sarvodaya Shramadana and Thich Nhat Hanh who have made remarkable strides in advancing peace in Sri Lanka, Vietnam and beyond.

The understanding of peace as a central tenet of the Islamic religion is based on five pillars as interpreted by *Ayse Kadayifci-Orellana*. Also the concept of Jihad, widely known on a superficial basis, is further elaborated on and put into perspective by emphasising the clearly formulated rules of warfare and the humanitarian principles of the Scripture.

Scott Appleby, widely known for his statements on the ambivalence of the sacred, discusses this in his essay on the phenomenon of Christian nonviolence, and how internal resources, contemporary experiences and education all shape Christianity per se and its role in peacebuilding in particular. This includes the question of how Christian reality and peacebuilding activities exercise mutual influence and possess the ability to transform each other.

Joseph Prabhu elaborates on questions of peace and violence in Hinduism with reference to Mahatma Gandhi. As a prominent figure who modernised Hindu traditions, his views and beliefs serve as a basis for Hindu ethics in the 21st century. In contrast to the claims of absolute truth in the monotheistic religions, which are often said to contribute to interreligious conflicts, Prabhu emphasises Gandhi's notion of relative, subjective truth.

Finally, in the third part contributions from a primarily political science-oriented perspective describe the ambivalent relationship between religion and peace from selected topics. *Gerhard Robbers* regards religion in its constitutional context and illustrates how the right to religious liberty contributes to peace and how, vice versa, societal developments in terms of religious coexistence will influence this type of legislative enactment in the future. Secular France despite her laicistic tradition serves as an example of a peace-promoting cooperation between religious communities and the state.

Matthias Basedau, Georg Strüver and Johannes Vüllers point out that, despite the religious diversity in sub-Saharan Africa, and the religious overtones in a number of African conflicts, social science research has only inadequately addressed the question of how and to what extent religion generally influences conflict in Africa. They present an innovative data inventory on religion and violent conflict in all sub-Saharan countries for the period 1990–2008. The data underscore the fact that religion plays a major role in African conflicts. In particular, they demonstrate the ambivalence of religion towards conflict and provide evidence that religion is not infrequently related to peace through numerous interreligious networks and religious peace initiatives.

Preventing the instrumentalisation of religion requires a thorough consideration of how elites and entrepreneurs of violence seek to utilise religious traditions, according to *Andreas Hasenclever*. As a major factor in these processes he identifies the extreme reduction of complexity of religious traditions when war and violence are legitimized. Thus, a solid religious education and public religious debates on these issues could prove as promising means to counter instrumentalisation.

The complexity of the inherent value of human rights and its position within religion on the one side and historic human rights violations in the name of religion on the other is discussed by *Javaid Rehman* with a particular focus on Islam. In the second step, this complexity is distilled to the dynamic of powers, societal relations and issues of governance as determinants of harmful religious ideologies.

In the final paper, *Daniel Philpott* emphasises the valuable contribution of religious communities and religiously motivated forgiveness in transitional societies. In the contemporary age of peacebuilding, faith-based actors have managed to introduce the concept of reconciliation into politics both on an ideological and on a practical level. Religious actors, so he argues, have been enriching the western concept of the "liberal peace".

The contributions compiled here provide an insight into the current state of the art of research into religions' potential for peacebuilding and conflict resolution. At the same time, they highlight the fact that there is still considerable need for systematic research. Although the complexity of the topic places great demands on scientific analysis, there is no shortage of cases of conflict relevant to research in which religious factors and actors have played a constructive peacebuilding role. The religious potential for peace has by no means yet been adequately explored – and is far from having been exhausted in practice.

References

Appleby, Scott (2000): The Ambivalence of the Sacred. Religion, Violence and Reconciliation. Rowman & Littlefield, Lanham (Mass.).

Basedau, Matthias (2009): Religion und Gewaltkonflikt im subsaharischen Afrika: Zur Rolle religiöser Faktoren in Benin und der Elfenbeinküste. In: Bussmann, Margit; Hasenclever, Andreas; Schneider, Gerald (eds.): Identität, Institutionen und Ökonomie. Ursachen innenpolitischer Gewalt (PVS-Sonderheft 43). VS, Wiesbaden, 150-177.

Brocker, Manfred/Hildebrandt, Mathias (2008): Friedensstiftende Religionen? Religion und die Deeskalation politischer Konflikte. VS, Wiesbaden.

Chadwick, Owen (1975): The Secularization of the European mind in the nineteenth century. Cambridge University Press, Cambridge.

Cox, Harvey G. / Jan Swyngedouw (2000): The Myth of the Twentieth Century: The Rise and Fall of Secularization. In: *Japanese Journal of Religious Studies* 27:1/2, 1-13.

Croissant, Aurel/Wagschal, Uwe/Schwank, Nicolas/Trinn, Christoph (2009): Kulturelle Konflikte seit 1945. Die kulturellen Dimensionen des globalen Konfliktgeschehens. Nomos, Baden-Baden.

De Juan, Alexander/Hasenclever, Andreas (2009): Das Framing religiöser Konflikte – die Rolle von Eliten in religiös konnotierten Bürgerkriegen. In: Bussmann, Margit/Hasenclever, Andreas/Schneider, Gerald (eds.): Identität, Institutionen und Ökonomie: Ursachen innenpolitischer Gewalt (PVS-Sonderheft 43). VS, Wiesbaden, 178-205.

Fuller, Graham (1995): The Next Ideology. In: Foreign Policy 98, 145-158.

Grieser, Alexandra (2005): Frieden, Konfliktlösung und Religion: Plausibilisierungsprozesse in modernen Friedensbewegungen. In: Makrides, Vasilios N./Rüpke, Jörg (eds.): Religionen im Konflikt. Aschendorff, Münster, 181-199.

Harpviken, Kristian Berg/Røislien, Hanne Eggen (2008): Faithful Broker? Potentials and Pitfalls of Religion in Peacemaking. In: Conflict Resolution Quarterly 25:3, 351-373.

Hasenclever, Andreas (2003): Geteilte Werte – Gemeinsamer Frieden? Überlegungen zur zivilisierenden Kraft von Religionen und Glaubensgemeinschaften. In: Küng, Hans/Senghaas, Dieter (eds.) (2003): Friedenspolitik. Piper, München, 288-318.

Hasenclever, Andreas (2009): Getting Religion Right – Zur Rolle von Religionen in politischen Konflikten. In: Wilhelm, Jürgen/Ihne, Hartmut (eds.): Religion und globale Entwicklung. Berlin University Press, Berlin, 170-186.

Hildebrandt, Mathias (2005): Einleitung: Unfriedliche Religionen? Das politische Gewalt- und Konfliktpotential von Religionen. In: Hildebrandt, Mathias/Brocker, Manfred (eds.): Unfriedliche Religionen? Das politische Gewalt- und Konfliktpotenzial von Religionen. VS, Wiesbaden, 9-35.

Hopf, Ted (1998): The Promise of Constructivism in International Relations Theory. In: International Security 23, 1, 171-200.

Huntington, Samuel P. (1996): Der Kampf der Kulturen. Die Neugestaltung der Weltpolitik im 21. Jahrhundert. Europaverlag, München/Wien.

Kadayifci-Orellana, Ayse S. (2009): Ethno-Religious Conflicts: Exploring the Role of Religion in Conflict Resolution. In: Bercovitch, Jacob/Kremenyuk, Victor/Zartman, I. William (eds.): The Sage Handbook of Conflict Resolution. Sage, Los Angeles, Calif., 264-284.

Kepel, Gilles (1991): Die Rache Gottes. Radikale Moslems, Christen und Juden auf dem Vormarsch. Piper, München/Zürich.

Kippenberg, Hans G. (2008): Gewalt als Gottesdienst. Religionskriege im Zeitalter der Globalisierung. Beck, München.

Kratochwil, Friedrich (2005): Religion and (Inter-)National Politics: On the Heuristics of Identities, Structures, and Agents. In: Alternatives 30, 2, 113-140.

Meyer, Thomas (1997): Identitätswahn. Die Politisierung des kulturellen Unterschieds. Berlin: Aufbau Verlag.

Müller, Harald (2001): Das Zusammenleben der Kulturen. Ein Gegenentwurf zu Huntington. Fischer, Frankfurt am Main.

Nipkow, Karl Ernst (2003): God, human nature, and education for peace: new approaches to moral and religious maturity. Ashgate, Farnham.

Philpott, Daniel (2007): Explaining the Political Ambivalence of Religion. In: American Political Science Review 101:3, 505-525.

Rittberger, Volker/Hasenclever, Andreas (2000): Religionen in Konflikten – Religiöser Glaube als Quelle von Gewalt und Frieden. In: Politisches Denken. Jahrbuch 2000 der Deutschen Gesellschaft zur Erforschung des politischen Denkens. Metzler, Stuttgart, 35-60.

Senghaas, Dieter (1998): Zivilisierung wider Willen. Der Konflikt der Kulturen mit sich selbst. Suhrkamp, Frankfurt.

Snider, Lewis W. (1996): Growth, Debt, and Politics: Economic Adjustment and the Political Performance of Developing Countries. Westview Press, Boulder.

Taylor, Charles (2007). A Secular Age. The Belknap Press of Harvard University Press, Cambridge.

Tibi, Bassam (1995): Krieg der Zivilisationen. Hoffmann & Campe, Hamburg.

Tishkov, Valery (1997): Ethnicity, Nationalism and Conflicts in and after the Soviet Union: The Mind Aflame. Sage, London.

Weingardt, Markus A. (2010): Religion Macht Frieden. Das Friedenspotenzial von Religionen in politischen Gewaltkonflikten. Bundeszentrale für politische Bildung, Bonn.

Weingardt, Markus A./Brenner, Verena (2010): Verpasste Chancen. Hindernisse für religiöse Friedensinitiativen. Nomos, Baden-Baden.

II.
Religions as Resources for Peacebuilding

A Joint Vision for World Peace? Religions as Driving Forces for a Culture of Peace

Hans Küng

Recalling the Peace of Westphalia, it is by no means obvious that religions should play a particular role in peacebuilding. After all, the Peace of Westphalia was drawn up by political powers, not by religions and even without religions. The religious powers at the time had rather been overstretched and their resources largely exhausted. It was not the papacy that led the way out of the devastation of war. On the contrary: the religious dispute over the one and only truth, fuelled repeatedly by the papacy, was a main element of the Thirty Years' War. And it was only by keeping religious convictions out of view that peace became at all possible. The papacy had shown itself as being unable to establish peace. Christendom in general had lost credibility, so that from then on, it was demoted as a religious, cultural, political and social force within Europe. Christendom itself indirectly brought about the process of detachment from religion, the process of secularisation, which was to decisively shape the new era, the modern age.

The Peace of Westphalia structured Germany according to the principle of parity of the two religious denominations, whilst at the same time giving recognition to the reformists. Pope Innocent X protested against the peace through his nuncio, but to no avail. The vested rights of the denominations, marked out at that time, prevailed in essence through to the 20th century. This is also the case for the independence of Switzerland and the Netherlands from the German Empire, having been recognised by the peace treaty at that time.

A new political constellation emerged in Europe around the mid 17th century. The Roman Catholic supremacy of Spain, which had become rich as a result of conquests and was now exhausted by too many wars, withdrew from the concert of great European powers at the end of the century. Germany (because of the Thirty Years' War) and Italy (vulnerable due to the struggle between the city-states, was plagued by invasions from great powers) had become irrelevant players in world politics. The papacy, which had been excluded as an international authority due to the Peace of Westphalia, was not replaced by a new supranational institution. The offensive power of Protestantism also appeared to be broken. The age of denominations was in fact replaced by the age of monarchical absolutism: the new supremacy was the France of Cardinal Richelieu and Louis XIV. This era ended with the French Revolution in 1789.

In the aftermath of the wars in Afghanistan, Iraq and Palestine, we may wonder whether we are once again on the brink of such a shift of emphasis, a new political constellation. Although the United States may well remain the strongest world power, they have lost their all-determining status. Alongside Europe, India, China and other emerging nations must be taken into account in matters concerning global financial issues and this is reflected in the expansion of the G-7 or G-8 to the G-20. We are heading towards a multipolar world. To be able to shape this new constellation peacefully, it is useful to take a look at the past.

A look at the past: learning from our mistakes. Why is there still no joint vision for peace in the Balkans?

1. Political failure: Serbs, Croats and Bosnians (including the only autochthonous and inherently highly tolerant Muslims) – all of whom are southern Slavs ("Jugo-slavs") who speak the same language – coexisted peacefully for a long time, often interlinked by marriage, in the Balkans, an area as a whole dogged by conflict historically. Following the collapse of communist rule, a real federal solution to their problems could have been found.

But the first fatal error occurred in the first phase. Despite the ethnic-religious differences, the EU and the USA, in the face of the Serbian invasion in 1991, wanted to preserve a centralised Yugoslavian state at all costs. The European great powers and the American President lacked the ethical will to oppose the genuine threats of aggression posed by the Serbian war criminals, Milošević, Karadžić and Mladić.

In the second phase, however, it was the exact opposite. In the wake of massive Serb aggression, the second fatal error was to immediately grant Croatia and Slovenia diplomatic recognition as sovereign states. The Federal Republic of Germany (having been pressurised in part by the Vatican) did just that, resulting in two negative effects: firstly, it divided EU foreign policy. Whilst Germany formally advocated the independence of Croatia and Slovenia, France and Great Britain effectively supported the interests of Serbia. Secondly, multi-ethnic, multi-religious Bosnia-Herzegovina was at the mercy of Serbian war criminals.

The third fatal error then occurred during the third phase: in colonial style, arbitrary frontiers were drawn for Bosnia that de facto recognised "ethnic cleansing", granting areas occupied by force to the invaders, contrary to applicable international law. And what was the result of this political drama? A country ravaged by years of cruel war and, even after the Dayton Agreement in 1995, continued enmity between the three ethnic groups with three complex state apparatuses and diplomatic missions, as well as the uncertain fate of the artificial diplomatic product of Bosnia-Herzegovina.

2. Failure of the Church: A lack of a joint vision for peace in the Balkans. The various religions and denominations were clearly not to blame for this. Instead, blame can be apportioned to the policy of not only the Yugoslavian constituent states, but also of interested European great powers. But the failure of religion and the Church should not be overlooked. The governing bodies of the Church had had fifty years from the end of the Second World War to clarify the situation, accept culpability and seek forgiveness, paving the way for political peace and reconciliation of the peoples.

But as I was able to affirm in the 1984 lectures I delivered in the then the peaceful cities of Zagreb, Belgrade and Dubrovnik: although a formal meeting was held every year between Croatian Catholic bishops and Serb Orthodox bishops, there was no admission of guilt by the Catholic-Croatian Ustasha state which massacred tens of thousands (some claim hundreds of thousands) under the Nazi Protectorate without any protestation by Pius XII or the Archbishop of Zagreb. Nor was the first Slav Pope John Paul II willing to visit the graves of the Ustasha victims, meaning that no visit was ever paid to Serbia. The Serb Orthodox bishops were equally unwilling to confess their blame for the many murders committed by Serbian Chetniks. When approached about it at the time, everyone told of the crimes committed by the other side, and remained silent about their own, similar to the Germans and French in the past.

The failure of political and religious authorities (Islam arrived on the scene of the conflict at a relatively late stage) therefore explains why it was not possible to agree upon a joint vision for peace in the Balkans. Such a vision would have succeeded only if, firstly, one had refrained from aspiring to a Serb-dominated Yugoslavian centralised state again and, secondly, if a multistate solution had not been sought, i.e. if attempts had been made to achieve a federal model, as also discussed for Yugoslavia at the start of the latest conflict. A federal model, such as that realised by the United States of America in 1776, built on the sovereignty of the people, separation of powers and the principle of federal states; and which was also realised by the Swiss cantons in 1848 – following a civil war. Other states have followed suit, and others would be well advised to practise federalism to prevent the break-up of the country – for example, Spain or Belgium.

This joint vision for peace unites maximum diversity with minimum union. In other words:

- the highest degree of autonomy of the different ethnic and religious groupings with regard to language and education, the economy, administration and academia, the media, customs and tradition and, in general, culture and religion;
- but also the necessary degree of union: one government, one army, one currency and one foreign policy.

A look at the present: exploit religions' potential for peace for the non-escalation or de-escalation of political conflicts

As human phenomena, religions – like music, art and culture in general – are ambivalent. Day in, day out, there are news reports about the conflict potential of religions.

Conflicts in Latin America (Columbia, Central America), Africa (Rwanda, Somalia, Nigeria, Sudan/Darfur) or Asia (Sri Lanka, Kashmir, Burma, Tibet) are shaped by religion or ignited by it in very different ways.

But there is far too little media coverage about religions' potential for peace. Dr. Markus Weingardt, employee of the Global Ethic Foundation and co-organiser of the Religions and World Peace Symposium, demonstrated on the basis of 40 well-documented case studies and supplementary case examples how frequently, and the extent to which, religions play a part in conflict management and peace processes (Weingardt 2010).

The important elements of such constructive peace work by religions, and hence for the realisation of a joint vision for peace, are:

1. *Violence prevention*: It was not Christians but Muslims who recognised where the propaganda inciting hate and violence was leading in Rwanda at the start of the 1990s, long before the escalation that ultimately unleashed an indescribable massacre. Around one million people were killed in just 100 days in 1994. Based on this early insight, they held programmes at their Muslim schools with the aim of sensitising young people and making them unreceptive to the propaganda – based on explicitly religious arguments. As the UN Special Investigator Christian P. Scherrer also noted, the result was that the Rwandan Muslims were the only section of the population that almost collectively refused to join in the violence. Furthermore, they provided a great deal of emergency assistance and helped many in trouble to escape, regardless of their tribal or religious affiliation.

2. *Human rights work:* Religious organisations and institutions are also crucial in human rights work. They are usually involved in networks throughout the country, enabling them to gain first-hand information to which many journalists have no access. And they are considered to be reliable sources that can be trusted. One example is the Fray Bartolomé de Las Casas Human Rights Centre established in Mexico by Bishop Samuel Ruiz Garcia. Founded in 1995, it documents human rights violations in the troubled province of Chiapas, organises civil peace camps for national and international observers and carries out intensive PR work. For instance, the Centre publicises the situation of the repressed and disadvantaged population, and puts pressure on politicians.

3. *Public statements*: Of particular note in this respect is the Declaration of a Global Ethic presented at the Parliament of the World's Religions in Chicago (September 1993). In it, over 200 representatives of religions were able to agree on a joint fundamental ethic comprising the two fundamental ethical principles (the principle of humanity and the principle of reciprocity), as well as the four basic standards of humanity (you shall not kill, steal, lie or commit sexual immorality). Of additional importance to Muslims, however, are the fatwas, such as those issued by the Grand Ayatollah Ali al-Sistani in Iraq, one of the highest-ranking and esteemed Shia clerics. In 2004/2005,

he used the religious legal opinion based on the Qur'an to condemn violence, regardless of who commits it and against whom it is applied. Regrettably, such statements are barely noticed by the public and the media – as was the case with the Topkapi Declaration by European Muslims in 2006 and the "Letter of 138" Muslim scholars from around the globe (an invitation to enter into dialogue in response to Pope Benedict XVI's polarising speech in Regensburg in 2006).

4. *Nonviolent resistance*: In conflict situations, nonviolent resistance is often initiated or led by religious actors. The overthrow of the Philippine dictator Ferdinand Marcos in 1986 was primarily thanks to the efforts of the Catholic Church, particularly the priests and Catholic followers in grassroots communities, i.e. where the theology of liberation played a major role: they focused on a nonviolent path in a place where weapons were at the ready and civil war was in the air.

5. *"Good deeds"*: Although they are not spectacular, "good deeds" can be highly effective in supporting and fostering political negotiations – in the background, away from the public and media glare. Such deeds include financial or material assistance, laying on transport for mediators or the provision of neutral negotiating venues, courier services, arranging contacts, and other things besides. Although these are minor acts, they can nevertheless play a vital role, without which many a peace process would have floundered. Special mention must be made here of the decades-long activities of the Quakers, one of the historic Christian "peace churches". Their hallmarks are visible not only in Kashmir and the Nigerian/Biafra conflict (in the 1960s), but also in the East-West conflict and the Middle East conflict.

6. *Mediation*: Occasionally, religious actors undertake the actual mediation of conflicts. The Mozambican Civil War claimed around one million lives and displaced six million refugees in the 1980s. After an attempt at conciliation by the United Nations had failed, the conflict was thought to be quite unresolvable. However, the Mozambican bishop, Jaime Gonçalvez, and representatives of the Catholic lay movement, Sant'Egidio, still managed to bring together the warring parties and to draw up a comprehensive Peace Accord that put a sustainable end to this bloody civil war in 1992 after two years of negotiations.

Furthermore, the peace accord signed in Guinea in 2010, paving the way for the first democratic elections in the country for over fifty years marked by violence and civil war, was also brokered by Sant'Egidio (incidentally, a decidedly Christian mediator in a country that is 90% Muslim).

7. *Holding political office and functions*: In some cases, religious representatives do not just mediate, but also directly assume political office and functions. In Benin, Archbishop Isidore de Souza was chairman of the National Conference which – following increasing unrest in the country – paved the way for a nonviolent transition from the then Marxist-Leninist system to a democracy in 1989/90. For lack of a respected, honourable and competent leader, he agreed to assume the office of "transi-

tional president" for a few years. Respected by all, he therefore made a substantial contribution to preventing a power vacuum from forming and a breakdown into civil war or anarchy.

8. *Development work*: The achievements of religious work in development cooperation deserve mention here. If people are given the opportunity to earn an honest living, avoiding poverty, they are less receptive to the temptations of violence through looting, rewards, protection money or other phenomena of war economies. They are only willing to lay down their arms again if they have viable alternatives and prospects. Faith-based services such as Misereor and Brot für die Welt, or the Buddhist Sarvodaya Shramadana movement in Sri Lanka, and many others, contribute in this way towards violence prevention, de-escalation and reconstruction in conflict regions. Mention should also be made at this point of microcredits, granted not just by the well-known Grameen Bank of the Nobel Peace Prize-winner Muhammad Yunus, but also by such institutions as the Ecumenical Church Loan Fund ECLOF, which has been in operation for years.

9. *Reconciliation processes:* Finally, of course, the central importance of religious actors in reconciliation processes must be mentioned. Cross-faith initiatives are often important here. In Sierra Leone and Nigeria, Bosnia-Herzegovina and several other countries, Interreligious Councils are important actors in reconciliation, as well as in mediation and violence prevention. One such example is the Acholi Religious Leaders Initiative, known as ARLPI, which performs exceedingly valuable work at the regional level in Northern Uganda.

In Cambodia, the Buddhist monk Maha Ghosananda established peace and reconciliation work following the Khmer Rouge's reign of terror, acting as a pioneer and role model for the whole civil society development of the country in the past thirty years and giving a voice to the most important concerns in politics and society.

The outstanding importance of the Nobel Peace Prize-winner Desmond Tutu in overcoming apartheid in South Africa and as head of the Truth and Reconciliation Commission is well known. Despite some difficulties, the Commission has nevertheless made a vital contribution to the largely nonviolent course of the transformation processes.

These are just some of many examples of how religious actors have contributed in a wide variety of conflicts and contexts. We have to agree with Markus Weingardt's conclusion: religions have tremendous potential for peace! And they do not just theorise about it, they successfully take action, too. Religious actors possess experience and specific skills that enable them to bring about constructive intervention in many conflicts where secular actors have failed.

A look to the future: religions contribute to a joint vision for global peace in areas of conflict

1. Religions can promote a paradigm shift in minds, a change of mentality: After the Second World War, a new paradigm of international relations took root and finally spread throughout the whole OECD world. Yet at the turn of the third millennium, this new paradigm had not advanced further, but was increasingly showing signs of having reversed: just think of the historical implications for the world caused by the guilt of the second Bush administration, which was supported by Great Britain under Tony Blair and opposed too softly by the other European powers.

This new paradigm, post-WW2, generally implies a policy of regional understanding, rapprochement and reconciliation rather than the contemporary national interest, power and prestige policy (as in the Treaty of Versailles). France and Germany took the lead here after the Second World War, and the churches played a major role: at grassroots level, for example, the Catholic Pax Christi movement in both countries; at the political level, particularly Pastor Frank Buchman's Protestant movement "Moral Rearmament" in which he acted as an intermediary between Adenauer and Schuman. For concrete political action, including in the Middle East, Afghanistan, Kashmir, Sri Lanka and Africa, understanding and reconciliation necessitate cooperation, compromise and integration in place of the previous confrontation, aggression and revenge.

A vision for peace built on this, and the new overall political constellation associated with it, obviously requires a change in mentality that goes far beyond day-to-day politics:

- A new mind-set is required. It is not enough to simply establish new organisations.
- National, ethnic, religious diversity must no longer be understood as a threat, but at least as a potential for opportunity.
- Whilst the old paradigm always required an enemy or even arch enemy, the new paradigm no longer needs an enemy, but partners, rivals and often also opponents. Economic competition takes the place of military confrontation at all levels.
- After all, it has been shown that national wellbeing is not promoted by war in the long run, but by peace; it is not fostered by working against and in parallel to one another, but with each other.
- And because the differing interests are mutually satisfied, policy can be pursued that is no longer a zero sum game in which one party wins at the cost of the other, but a win-win game.

It goes without saying that politics have not become any easier in the new paradigm. Instead, it remains the – now, of course, nonviolent – "art of the possible". If democratic politics is to function, it cannot be founded on "post-modern" arbitrary pluralism. Instead, it requires a social consensus founded on basic values, basic rights and basic responsibilities.

Religions play an important role in the search for such a consensus and in promoting such a change in mentality. Humaneness and human dignity, solidarity and justice, sincerity and nonviolence – all these aspects are applied and founded in the various religious traditions. Religious communities must reflect upon this and practise it themselves. Then they can, as an influential social force, indeed contribute to the paradigm shift required to achieve sustained world peace.

2. Religions can raise awareness of the ethical foundation for a joint vision for peace: Religions could, but should not attempt to impose their own specific Christian, Jewish, Islamic or other ethic on members of other religions or on the non-religious. What they could and should do, however, is to show how many basic values, basic rights and basic responsibilities they have in common with other religions. Today's societies need a basic ethical consensus, and if peace is to be achieved, this basic consensus must be supported by all social groups, by both believers and non-believers alike, by members of various religions and followers of philosophies or ideologies.

This ethical consensus, which a democratic system must not force but must require, does not mean a joint ethical system ("ethics"), but a common ground of elementary values and standards, rights and responsibilities, a joint "ethic": a human ethic, in other words. It is just as a fair game of football is not possible without an elementary set of rules, nor is social interaction in a school class, company, political community or nation. And just as global rules are required in football today, they are also needed for the most important aspects of society. A human ethic, or global ethic, is required. A global ethic is not a new ideology or "superstructure". Instead, it combines the joint religious-philosophical resources of mankind that are not imposed by law of which we are to be made aware.

In the various religious and ethical traditions of mankind, the following joint ethical traditions can be determined: first of all, the Golden Rule formulated by Confucius, five hundred years before Christ: "What you do not wish to be done to yourself, do not do to others!". This rule of reciprocity, of mutuality, is established in the principle of humanity, true humaneness. "Every human being, man or woman, white or coloured, rich or poor, old or young, should be treated humanely, that is, not inhumanely or brutal." In addition, there are four incontestable instructions in all major cultures: the commitment to being part of a culture of nonviolence and reverence for life ("You shall not kill! – Have respect for life!«), justice and solidarity ("You shall not steal! – Deal honestly and fairly!"), truthfulness and tolerance ("You shall not lie! – Speak and act truthfully!") and the equal rights and partnership of man and woman ("You shall not commit sexual immorality! – Respect and love one another!").

At the same time, according to the St. Gallen political scientist, Alois Riklin (1995), the global ethic is "person-oriented, institution-oriented and results-oriented." As such, the global ethic does not aim only to achieve a collective responsibility that could possibly exonerate the individual (as if only "the circumstances", "history" or "the system" were to blame for certain grievances). It aims in particular at the individual responsibility of every single person in their place in society and, especially, at the individual responsibility of political leaders. Committing freely to a joint ethic does not, of course, exclude, but includes, being supported by an international legal framework which, under certain circumstances, can be brought to bear in the case of genocide, crimes against humanity, war crimes and aggression. In recent times, the International Criminal Court in The Hague has been used when a Contracting State has been unable or unwilling to punish the crimes committed on its territory in one of its own courts.

3. Religions should promote nations' self-criticism, not impede it: Thankfully, the "leaden" years of the Bush administration, of reverting to the old paradigm, are over. Since 2009, the United States of America has a new President, Barack Obama. However, the new President certainly does not have an easy time, being encumbered by the two wars bequeathed to him by his predecessor, who was also partly responsible for the world economic crisis, an oil spill in the Gulf of Mexico, a gigantic deficit of billions and a reactionary, completely uncooperative opposition party. Today, it must be said that the "war against terror" led to the "terror of war", the catastrophic consequences of which are now almost impossible to ignore:

- The war in Afghanistan was unnecessary, and leaves the USA and its allies without a withdrawal strategy and without any hope of being able to defeat the Taliban, the warlords and the drug dealers. Only negotiations, not an increase in troops, can solve the problem. Negotiations are required with the Afghan tribal chiefs and the moderate Taliban, as well as an arrangement with the major neighbouring powers of Pakistan, Iran, China and India.
- The war in Iraq, built on monstrous lies and waged under the violation of international law, leaves as its legacy a country that is politically unstable, is in severe economic need, is beset with social misery and is religiously fragmented. Following the withdrawal of US troops, the solution cannot be to have a continued American presence in Iraq either. The solution lies in facilitating understanding – neglected in all these years – between Sunnites and Shiites, between secularist and Islamist Shiites and, of course, between these groupings and the Kurds. Concerns were raised at the recent Middle East synod in the Vatican that less than 300,000 of the 1.2 million Christians who once lived there remain. However, this blame cannot be apportioned to Saddam Hussein, but – in addition to civil war (Lebanon), discrimination (Saudi Arabia) and threat (Hamas, Jihad) – above all to the invasion by the Christian President George W. Bush.
- Israel's occupation of the Palestinian Territories from 1967, supported by the USA in violation of all UN resolutions, and the ongoing spread of Israeli settlements

have caused considerable damage to the moral and political credibility of the Jewish state after the Holocaust and have heightened both Israelis' insecurity and the misery of the Palestinian people.

- The completely unjustified Israeli invasion of Lebanon (2006) and the utterly disproportionate military intervention in Gaza (2009) causing more than 1300 deaths, most of them civilians. According to the UN investigation report, this was motivated by the intention to destroy the infrastructure and crimes against humanity, and was carried out with the consent of the USA and without any effective protest by Europeans, further contributing to the destabilisation of the Middle East. Furthermore, it alienated the real friends of Israel. I have always considered myself to be counted among them.

But of course a new way of thinking is also required in German politics upon which the Churches must also clearly and unequivocally make their voices heard, as was rightly the case with Bishop Margot Käßmann regarding Afghanistan at the beginning of 2010. Restlessness in the German population is constantly growing in the face of a war that, for a long time, was not allowed to be called a "war" which, after ten years, has still not achieved its primary objectives and which has become more prolonged and bloody than was initially anticipated. Suddenly, without the population having a say in the matter, the pacific German nation has become a warring nation for which it must pay an as yet unforeseeably high human and financial cost. Due to "total solidarity" with the USA, German soldiers became increasingly implicated in the hostilities of this war, and may possibly be condemned to being present and involved in disputes in the Hindu Kush for years to come, where German soldiers are supposedly being defended against impending attacks.

Even non-pacifists are questioning what German soldiers are actually doing in Afghanistan, why German frigates are stationed in Djibouti and at the Horn of Africa, and whether German soldiers are also to unreservedly support wars against Somalia, Syria, Iraq and Iran in the future.

As one of the great German statesmen told me back then at a pivotal time in German history, "If we send German troops to Afghanistan, these troops won't be able to get out for years, if not decades." Advocates of this new military-oriented Berlin foreign policy believe that Germany would be 'marginalised' if it refused to become engaged in Afghanistan. I put this to him, and his response was that "Germany is too large and too powerful to become 'marginalised.'"

In the current debate on the German Federal Armed Forces, it seems to me that it is not enough to simply juggle with figures concerning troop numbers, military expenditure and sites. We must first agree upon the objectives and, first and foremost, the limitations of German military deployments across the globe. After all, no one appears to want German soldiers to be deployed in the case of future conflict on land, at sea and in the air anywhere between the North Pole and the Antarctic, or from the

North Sea to the South Seas. What is, therefore, the point of such deployments, and where are the limitations? The essential question remains: how should we be engaged on the international arena? And should we simply continue in this style in the "war on terror"? Are there not any more constructive approaches that can be used in times of conflict?

These are all questions about which clear statements would be desirable from religious communities: constructive, peace-oriented responses. These need not be final solutions; religious communities need not and cannot take on the work of politicians, quite the opposite: they should attentively and critically accompany and observe politics, measure it against their religious-ethical values and then – where necessary – make themselves heard loud and clear. Religious communities should make others feel uncomfortable. As a leading employee of the Ecumenical Council of Churches said recently, "Being the Church of Peace means being the Church of Resistance."

4. Religions should urge constructive, peaceful solutions: With regard to the Eastern territories lost by Germany, the Protestant Church in Germany assumed an exemplary leading role with its Ostpolitik Memorandum, which contributed to preventing a clash with the Soviet Union and paved the way to a peaceful solution through dialogue. If a "culture clash" with Islam is to be prevented across the globe and, particularly, in European countries, once again dialogue is the only way to find constructive solutions. Such dialogue requires that:

- on the one hand, the Christian-laical majority population in European countries does not only pass on "law and order" to other religious groups as the only regulatory instrument, but shows them at least tolerance, if not respect, which should be based on sound religious knowledge;
- on the other hand, the religious minorities, in particular, Muslims and their organisations, should continue to endeavour to become integrated. In the process, they must, above all, fully agree to the free democratic basic order and, in particular, equality between men and women, as guaranteed by the Constitution, and women and girls' rights to self-determination.

This dialogue will not bear fruit if it is limited to only mutual pleasantries and fails to challenge the other religion. It goes without saying that such criticism must also include self-criticism, if it is to be credible. The peace researcher Dieter Senghaas rightly warns Europeans and Westerners in general to always bear in mind their own record of conflict in history. It took many a battle until it was finally recognised that really all human beings are born free and equal in dignity and rights, before tolerance, freedom of religion, equality of the sexes and much more were generally acknowledged!

If dialogue is to develop into concrete solutions, negotiation processes will be unavoidable, processes generally involving rights that may be uncomfortable for both sides. But any one-sided obtrusive insistence upon rights blocks the process of dialogue, and is counterproductive. In a society in which the law is over-stretched, constant legal dispute threatens its coherence. Rights and responsibilities go hand in hand. Religiously substantiated rights in particular need to be perceived with discernment. In today's often complex cases of conflict, we should endeavour to seek differentiated solutions to the issues in dispute.

How significant it would be if the three Abrahamic religions, which all have peace as a central aspect of their message (Shalom, Salaam, Eirene, Pax, Peace), were to go on the offensive in building peace. Consider the impact in the Middle East, in particular, if the three religions were to use all means available to them today, including the media, to help clarify misunderstandings between Jews, Christians and Muslims, to help deal with the traumatic memories of Israelis and Palestinians, to break down enemy stereotypes, to deal with guilt conflicts socially and individually, and to eliminate hate and destruction. And in so doing, they should concentrate on what they have in common – despite their major "dogmatic" differences – particularly when it comes to our ethic.

5. Religions should choose a path between secularism and clericalism: The self-interest of individuals and social groups, which can easily turn into pure egoism, does not suffice as a basis for life in the long term. A high standard of living is no substitute for a meaningful life in the long run. It is often for this very reason that many people find themselves in life crises and experience loss of orientation, in the search for a sense in life, standards and values. Just as with absolutised belief, absolutised reason is also capable of releasing destructive energies, which have had a devastating impact in non-religious or pseudo-religious ideologies. If today many Muslims show dissatisfaction with not only the Marxist-materialistic aspect, but also some cultural aspects of the Western technological modern age and revert to the traditions of their religion, this is based on such – truly not unjustified – anxieties. This gives rise to a new challenge to be overcome by Muslims and Christians together!

"The liberal, secular state is built on conditions it cannot guarantee itself" (Böckenförde 1991:112) are the eagerly cited words of the constitutional law expert Ernst-Wolfgang Böckenförde (Böckenförde 1991:112). Indeed, although the ideologically neutral state may not decree a meaning of life or legally stipulate supreme values, it must require them if its own mechanisms are to function at all and its laws be obeyed. As I have already explained, the democratic state needs an elementary ethical consensus supported by all social groups and to which all religions, philosophies and world-views should contribute – in Islamic countries, of course, predominantly Islam and in countries shaped by Christianity, Christendom. There should, therefore, be an elementary consensus, not a "strict" or total consensus, but merely a consensus of overlapping elementary binding values, incontestable standards and personal basic attitudes, namely "overlapping consensus" (Rawls 1971:387).

In such a situation, a religion would not, on the one hand, become a slave to ethically fruitless ideological secularism; seen from a global perspective, this is an exception in

Western and Central Europe and amongst American elites. On the other hand, however, religion would not strive once again for a pre-modern clerical dominance over secular areas, as concealed behind the Pontifical-Roman call for "the truth", in which the absolute ruler thinks he can dictate "unerringly" from birth control to euthanasia. Instead, a religion will execute, inspire, motivate and possibly also correct "secularity", "world affirmation", from this very belief:

- If, for example, a majority (of any size whatsoever) spoke out in favour of legitimising torture or forcibly repressing a minority of any kind, then religions must defend the inalienable dignity of all people and protest;
- If in a certain country superrich potentates unscrupulously exploit the population, or, if in a modern economic system in a globalising world individual managers dismiss thousands of employees and approve payments in the millions for themselves, then religions may, and should, urge social justice;
- If a power or superpower thinks it is able to practise unilateralism, violate international law, ignore the UN and wage a preventive war to achieve its hegemonic goals, then religious leaders must join forces in favour of peace and against war.

Politics, business, law, academia, education for individuals and society essentially require a moral framework, which I call the human or global ethic. And all religions are able to make a major contribution to this ethic. The religions' Holy Scriptures, although frequently misused, can give such a "global ethic" a solid ground and a convincing substantiation.

I would like to close with this plea:

- First of all, a plea to academia: continue to deal with the conflict potential of religions, but even more so with their all too frequently neglected potential for peace! Not only conflict research, but also peace research in its actual sense in particular should be promoted!
- Next, a plea to the politicians: take note of peace actors within religions, include them in peace processes! But also keep reminding religious communities of their responsibility for peace!
- A plea to the media: report critically about religions, but practise press freedom in press responsibility: by all means, criticise all violations and misuses, but also stand in awe of the sacred, as expressed by the founding fathers of religions, worshipped by millions upon millions. Report more and more about the successful contributions religions have made to peace processes, even if it is less sensational than reporting about bloody conflict!
- And finally a plea to the religious communities themselves: appreciate your potential for peace, use all of your resources, competencies and connections, and place peace at the top of your own agenda! Positive criticism concerning others is equally as important as self-criticism. And interreligious dialogue should not stop

at words, but should lead to concrete cooperation. In the Middle East conflict, in particular, we are in urgent need of the constructive impulse of religious communities.

My vision of peace in the world is founded on a three-fold unswerving hope:

- that every religion has a powerful future potential, based on its spiritual and ethical richness,
- that all religions can gain greater common ground in understanding and cooperation, and
- that all world religions will join forces to make an indispensable contribution to a more peaceful and just world.

References

Böckenförde, Ernst-Wolfgang (1991). Recht, Staat, Freiheit. Studien zur Rechtsphilosophie, Staatstheorie und Verfassungsgeschichte. Suhrkamp, Frankfurt.

Rawls, John (1971): A Theory of Justice. Harvard University Press, Cambridge.

Riklin, Alois (1995): Politische Ethik. In: Kramer, Helmut (ed.): Politische Theorie und Ideengeschichte, WUV-Verlag, Vienna, 81-104

Weingardt, Markus A. (2010): Religion Macht Frieden. Das Friedenspotenzial von Religionen in politischen Gewaltkonflikten. Bundeszentrale für politische Bildung, Bonn.

In-depth literature

Küng, Hans (1990): Projekt Weltethos. Piper, München.

Küng, Hans (1997): Weltethos für Weltpolitik und Weltwirtschaft. Piper, München. Licensed edition: Wissenschaftliche Buchgesellschaft, Darmstadt 1997; pocket edition: Piper, München 2000.

Küng, Hans and Kuschel, Karl-Josef (eds.) (1998): Wissenschaft und Weltethos. Piper, München. Pocket edition: Piper, München 2001.

Küng, Hans; Picco, G. and Weizsäcker, R. v. (et al.) (2001): Crossing the Divide. Dialogue among Civilizations. Seton Hall University, South Orange. German edition: Brücken in die Zukunft. Ein Manifest für den Dialog der Kulturen. Eine Initiative von Kofi Annan, S. Fischer, Frankfurt 2001.

Küng, Hans (ed.) (2002). Dokumentation zum Weltethos. Piper, München.

Küng, Hans (2002): Erkämpfte Freiheit. Erinnerungen. Piper, München.

Küng, Hans and Senghaas, Dieter (eds.) (2003): Friedenspolitik. Ethische Grundlagen internationaler Beziehungen. Piper, München.

Küng, Hans (2006): Wozu Weltethos? Religion und Ethik in Zeiten der Globalisierung. 2nd edition. Herder, Freiburg.

Küng, Hans (2007): Umstrittene Wahrheit. Erinnerungen. Piper, München.

Küng, Hans; Leisinger, K.M. and Wieland, J. (2010): Manifest Globales Wirtschaftsethos. Konsequenzen und Herausforderungen für die Weltwirtschaft;

Manifesto Global Economic Ethic. Consequences and Challenges for Global Businesses. dtv, München.

Küng, Hans (2010): Anständig wirtschaften. Warum Ökonomie Moral braucht. Piper, München.

Religion, Nationalism, and Conflict: An Update

David Little

Considering the "empirical evidence and explanatory approaches" regarding the connections between religion and conflict and religion and peace, I shall summarize an approach to nationalist conflicts I began to develop in the 1990s and update how that approach looks at present in the light of ongoing empirical research in the area of "ethnoreligious conflict".

I began consideration of the subject as an employee of the United States Institute of Peace (USIP) starting in 1989. It was around that time that increased attention was directed at what was variously known as "religious" or "ethnoreligious nationalism". The reason for the new interest, of course, was the demise of the Former Soviet Union and the consequent collapse of the Cold War. Countries long subjected to Soviet and Soviet-like control, such as the Former Yugoslavia, opened the door to the fervent expression of nationalist impulses. At the same time, examples of nationalist conflict which have occurred in Sri Lanka, Sudan, Israel/Palestine, Northern Ireland, etc. were there all along, but were either unnoticed or not seen for what they were because of the distorting lenses of the Cold War.

At the same time, the influence of religious and ethnic factors on post-Cold War nationalist conflicts went not only in the direction of violence and antagonism, though that was certainly there. In a powerful way, leaders of religious and ethnic groups also helped to guide the national transition from authoritarianism – whether communist as in East Germany and Poland, or anti-communist, as in South Africa and the Philippines – toward greater democracy and ethnic and religious tolerance. The fact that religious and ethnic ideals are capable of encouraging both "constructive" and "destructive" forms of nationalism is of importance for the following considerations.

The original purpose of the USIP study was to determine the role of religion, both negatively and positively, in nationalist conflicts. It was decided to examine comparatively a range of cases that were diverse regionally, religiously and ethnically. Under the direction of my associates and me, a working group of experts convened conferences and monitored research on seven cases: Ukraine, Sri Lanka, Lebanon, Tibet, Sudan/Nigeria, and Bosnia. These investigations yielded three published case-studies: Ukraine: The Legacy of Intolerance (Little 1991); Sri Lanka: The Invention of Enmity (Little 1994), Sino-Tibetan Co-Existence: Creating Space for Tibetan Self-Direction (Little and Hibbard 1994),[1] and provided the basis for later work at Harvard.

1 See also Little, David (1999): Religion and Ethnicity in the Sri Lankan Civil War. In: Robert I. Rotberg (ed.): *Creating Peace in Sri Lanka: Civil War and Reconciliation*. Brookings Institution Press, Washington DC, 41-57.

In particular, the project posited two objectives: One was to determine the degree to which religious and ethnic *intolerance*, as defined by international human rights instruments, and especially by the *UN Declaration on the Elimination of All Forms of Intolerance and of Discrimination Based on Religion or Belief* (DEID), contributes to violence associated with nationalist struggles, as well as how far its opposite, the encouragement of religious and ethnic *tolerance,* helps to mitigate such violence. The other objective was to clarify the sources and causes of tolerance and intolerance including, in particular, the role of religion.

To be exact, tolerance, as understood in human rights documents, means encouraging and safeguarding four particular provisions. Intolerance means violating one or more of these provisions, namely:

- Freedom of conscience, religion or belief, subject only to limitations protecting public safety, order, health, morals or the fundamental rights and freedoms of others.[2]
- Protection against discrimination "by any State, group of persons or person on the grounds of religious or other [fundamental] beliefs". This provision prohibits "any distinction, exclusion, restriction or preference based on religion or belief and having as its purpose or as its effect nullification or impairment of the recognition, enjoyment or exercise of human rights and fundamental freedoms on an equal basis."[3]
- Protecting the right of minorities "to enjoy their own culture, to practice their own religion, and to use their own language."[4]
- Protecting against "religious [...] hatred that incites to discrimination or violence."[5]

In understanding the relation of fundamental religious, ethnic or other beliefs to the meaning of tolerance and intolerance, it is necessary to distinguish two types of intolerance: belief as target and belief as warrant. The first sort of intolerance occurs when the beliefs of an individual or group are singled out for oppression or persecution, as for example in the case of Jehovah's Witnesses or members of the Bahá'í faith who in some countries are the targets of extensive abuse. The implication is that tolerance in

2 International Covenant on Civil and Political Rights (ICCPR) art. 18; cf. Declaration on the Elimination of All Forms of Intolerance and of Discrimination based on Religion or Belief (DEID) art. 1 par. 1.

3 DEID art. 2 par. 1 and 2.

4 ICCPR art. 27; cf. Universal Declaration of Human Rights (UDHR) art. 27 par. 1.

5 ICCPR art. 20 par. 2; cf. UDHR art. 7, ICCPR art. 20 par. 2 stated in full prohibits religious hatred "that incites to discrimination, hostility, and violence." However, unlike discrimination and violence which refer to overt, legally definable acts, hostility is an attitude or emotion and as such is notoriously hard to police. For that reason it tends to be bracketed in the application of art. 20. See, for example, a report on hate speech coauthored by Asma Jahangir, former Special Rapporteur on Freedom of Religion or Belief, A/HRC/2/3, 20 September 2006, 15.

this first sense would mean to refrain from treating religious or ethnic groups in this manner.

Intolerance as warrant occurs when individuals or groups are singled out for oppression or persecution not because of their beliefs but because of the beliefs of those carrying out the oppression or persecution. Thus, some prominent Sinhala leaders in Sri Lanka have held (typically on ethnoreligious grounds) that members of the Tamil minority, simply by virtue of not being Sinhala, are disqualified for equal citizenship. By contrast, tolerance in this second sense would mean overcoming such exclusionary ethnic ideals. This distinction turns out to be very important in empirically refining the incidence of tolerance and intolerance in different settings.

In 1999, I moved to Harvard where I continued to develop my work in this field. I broadened and refined my understanding of nationalism and its relation to religious and ethnic considerations, adding new cases like Iraq and Burma, and making use of new theoretical and historical studies such as Faith in Nation: Exclusionary Origins of Nationalism (Marx 2003) and Chosen Peoples: Sacred Origins of National Identity (Smith 2003). I also expanded my exposure to social scientific studies in the field, developing both appreciation for as well as some reservations about the work of Paul Collier, James Fearon and David Laitin, Ted Robert Gurr and Jonathan Fox, among others.

In addition, I devoted special attention to the more constructive contributions of religious leaders to tolerance and peace. Working with the Tanenbaum Center for Interreligious Understanding, I helped to edit a volume on religion and peacemaking, Peacemakers in Action: Profiles in Religious Conflict Resolution, which bears some interesting implications for the study of nationalism (Little 2006). The book consists of the stories of sixteen religiously-motivated peace activists, fourteen men and two women from Jewish, Muslim, and Christian communities from El Salvador, Northern Ireland, Bosnia and Kosovo, Sudan, Nigeria, Ethiopia, Sierra Leone, South Africa, Israel and Palestine, Afghanistan, and West Papua, New Guinea. In the context of nationalist conflicts, these individuals consistently and self-sacrificially exemplify a commitment to what I have come to call "liberal nationalism." That is, in inventive and heroic ways, they give themselves to the advancement of ethnic and religious inclusiveness based on the rights of equal freedom and tolerance for all citizens, along with an insistent emphasis on the priority of nonviolence as a means of dealing with group antagonism and conflict within as well as across borders.

Religion, Nationalism, and Intolerance[6]

Nationalism is best understood as that special set of political beliefs and patterns associated with the conjunction of "nation" and "state". If a "nation" or "people" is taken to be a community defined by a common historical and cultural identity,[7] and a "state," at least in its modern form, is that set of officials and institutions responsible to govern the inhabitants of a given territory on the basis of a monopoly of legitimate and effective coercion,[8] then nationalism refers to the belief in national or popular identity as the basis of state legitimacy. As Anthony Marx puts it, nationalism is "a collective sentiment or identity, bounding and binding together those individuals who share a sense of large-scale political solidarity aimed at creating, legitimating, or challenging states" (Marx 2003:6). As such, it rests on the idea of a nation imagined "as a deep, horizontal comradeship" (Anderson 1998:7).

We emphasize that the word "nation" is a synonym for "people" or "tribe," conveying the idea of an extended "birth community" from the Latin *natio* (nativity, native). The tie between birth and national identity is thus always salient in conceptions of the nation. However, we also emphasize that nationalism is a modern phenomenon – the term did not appear until the 19th century. That is because it is only in connection with the modern state that the idea of nation "as a deep, horizontal comradeship" makes sense. Only the modern state could gain an effective monopoly of legitimate coercion by means of modern techniques of supervision and enforcement, as well as the capacity to consolidate and regulate political, economic, and cultural life, thereby facilitating the making of "mass societies" within tightly regulated territorial boundaries.

Accordingly, a "nationalist conflict" is a contest – sometimes violent – between two or more groups claiming the "right to rule" within a given territory based upon competing conceptions of nationhood. In short, nationalist conflicts are contests over which national ideal will prevail in a given nation-state. Such conflicts are often described as "ethnic", "religious" or as "ethnoreligious," because it is assumed that the competing ideals of nationhood are shaped or strongly influenced by considerations of ethnic and/or religious identity. Consequently, as indicated earlier, nationalist conflicts typically involve the problem of ethnic and religious intolerance.

Building on the relation of the idea of nationalism to the coalescence of nation and (modern) state, and taking into account the possible influence of religious and ethnic factors on notions of nationhood or peoplehood as the basis for state legitimacy, and

6 The following comments are adapted from the Introduction to Little, David (2006): Religion and Nationalism in Iraq. Harvard University Press, Cambridge, 3-7.

7 For a more elaborate version of the same idea, see MacCormick, Neil (1999): Nation and Nationalism. In: Beiner, Ronald (ed.): *Theorizing Nationalism.* State University of New York Press, Albany, 191.

8 Max Weber's famous definition of the modern state in H.H. Gerth and C.Wright Mills, eds., *From Max Weber: Essays in Sociology* (New York: Oxford University Press, 1958), p. 176.

finally, recalling the variable implications of all this for tolerance and peace or intolerance and violence, we may suggest the following table as a graphic sketch of the suggested approach:

Table: Relationships among Religious Tolerance, State, and Nation

Type of Nationalism (Legitimacy of the State)		Regime Type (Character of State)	
	Inclusive Definition of the Nation	**Liberal-Nationalism** *(high levels of democracy and high levels of religious tolerance)*	**Tolerant, Non-Democratic Nationalism**
	Exclusive Definition of the Nation	**Intolerant Democratic Nationalism**	**Iliberal-Nationalism** *(low levels of democracy and* low levels of religious tolerance)

The general notion is that under the impulse of nationalism, nation and state coalesce in different ways, with variable consequences for the incidence of violence. The assumptions are that ethnic and/or religious values, along with a variety of "external influences"[9] are indispensable in constructing the ideals of the nation, and that ethnic and religious attitudes vary as to how tolerant (inclusive) or intolerant (exclusive) they are and further, that national ideals, in legitimating the state, also vary as between supporting constitutional democratic states and states that are non-democratic for being weak, predatory or authoritarian in character. States are of course understood to be the product of their own specific "external influences", and are considered to exert their own reciprocal influence on the ethnic and religious values that make up the legitimating national ideals; indeed, the interaction between nation and state is probably best described as "synergistic" so as to avoid reductionist or simplistic theories of social causation.

But the critical idea is that the point of convergence on the table between the type of state and the degree of ethnic/religious tolerance associated with national ideals determines the *kind of nationalism* – whether *liberal* (high degree of national tolerance combined with a strong constitutional democratic state) or *illiberal* (high degree of national intolerance combined with an non-democratic regime (of a weak, predatory, or authoritarian type) – and its *relation to the probability of violence.* The supposition is that as the conditions of a given nation-state move toward the upper left-hand corner of the table, in the direction of liberal nationalism, the likelihood of violence will decrease. Contrariwise, as conditions move toward the lower right-hand corner, in the

9 The notion of "external influences" regarding both the state and nation refers to the complexity of historical and international conditions that must be taken into account in order to understand the character and performance of given nation-states in particular times and places.

direction of illiberal nationalism, the likelihood of violence will increase. This approach obviously leaves open the possibility of a wide range of different combinations of national ideals and state type with variable implications for the incidence of violence, as well as a broader range of causal factors bearing on the incidence of violence than has been elaborated.

Here we build on the work of Jack Snyder (Snyder 2000; Mansfield and Snyder 2005). Snyder focuses on the conditions under which nations in transition from authoritarianism to democracy restrain or encourage violence. Violence is mitigated, according to him, by means of "thick versions" of liberal or constitutional democracy, which make up what Snyder calls "civic nationalism" (or sometimes "liberal nationalism" which is the term we choose). It consists of an ample set of preconditions for "a stable, productive, peaceful society" (Snyder 2000:316-317). These are "a certain degree of wealth, the development of a knowledgeable citizenry, the support of powerful elites, and the establishment of a whole panoply of institutions to insure the rule of law and civic rights. The findings of this book suggest that only thickly embedded liberal polities are well insulated from the risk of developing belligerent, reckless forms of nationalism in the course of democratization" (Snyder 2000:316, 318).

Conversely, "democratization in weakly institutionalized settings often plays into the hands of nationalist demagogues and swaggering populists" (Snyder 2000:319). Of special worry in this regard is what Snyder calls "ethnic nationalism" ("illiberal nationalism" in our terms). Here appeals are made to "common culture, language, religion, shared [history], and/or the myth of shared kinship" and they are typically employed "to include [and] exclude members from the national group" (Snyder 2000:319).

Snyder is particularly attentive to the predictability of intolerance and violence in relation to illiberal democracies and weak states, precisely because the institutions of restraint associated with "thickly embedded liberal polities" are missing or badly enfeebled. Under those conditions exclusionary "outbidding" is politically very effective. That is where leaders and elites outdo one another in making "legitimacy bids" favoring one religious or ethnic group and demeaning others, with great political benefit. Such an outcome, especially in a society with scarce opportunities, wealth, and resources in turn readily fuels violence. A good illustration is the connection between the ethnic conflict in Sri Lanka and the distinctly illiberal form of democracy that has existed there since independence in 1948. It was exactly the unsavory combination of electoral democracy, unconstrained by adequate minority protection and other critical constitutional restraints, with the insistent chauvinism of the majority Sinhala ethnic group that led to a form of "majoritarian dictatorship" and eventually to civil war (Little 1994).

Snyder's conclusions may be extended to include predatory and authoritarian states. While the term "predatory state", introduced in a recent book by Larry Diamond, appears to share some of the characteristics and effects of non-democratic states, its key distinguishing feature is the widespread existence of corruption (Diamond 2008). Diamond's description bears importantly on our concern with the potential for violence of nation-states that deviate from the standards of a tolerant constitutional democracy:

> "The predatory society is the inverse of the civic community. [...] There is no real community, no shared commitment to any common vision of the public good, and no respect for law. Behavior is cynical and opportunistic. Those who capture political power seek to monopolize it and the rents that flow from it. Thus, if there are competitive elections, these become a bloody zero-sum struggle where everything is at stake and no one can afford to lose. People ally with one another in the quest for power and privilege, but not as equals [...] 'Corruption is widely regarded as the norm,' political participation is mobilized from above, civic engagement is meager, compromise is scarce, and 'nearly everyone feels powerless, exploited, and unhappy'[...]
> Very often, social fragmentation is reinforced by ethnic, linguistic, and other forms of identity cleavage that keeps the oppressed from collaborating and enables the privileged to rally ready political support. All too often, predatory elites mobilize ethnic tension or nationalism in order to direct public frustration and resentment away from their own exploitative behavior. Yet ethnic tensions and nationalist resentments have an independent origin, which is why elites often find such success when they inflame them. From Nigeria to the Congo, from Columbia to Kosovo, from Serbia to Sudan, ethnic violence, nationalist bloodletting, and civil war have been heavily mixed up with the corruption of cynical elites" (Diamond 2008:298).

Our central contention that the violence potential rises as weak or predatory states combine with increasing degrees of national intolerance also applies to authoritarian states (Zakaria 2003). Nazi Germany's combination of extreme authoritarianism and extreme national intolerance yielded exceedingly high levels of violence, at home and abroad, and thereby exemplified illiberal nationalism in its paradigmatic form, though there are other smaller scale examples such as Serbia under Slobodan Milosovic.[10] While the connection needs to be explored empirically, authoritarian states appear to draw life from ethnic or religious intolerance as a way of justifying the degree of violence required to maintain power.

The diagram assumes, it should be emphasized, that there are degrees of national tolerance and intolerance, which can be measured. It similarly assumes that states in the real world conform to a greater or lesser degree to what it means to be a constitutional or a non-democracy (a weak, predatory or authoritarian state), and that the degree of conformity can also be measured.

10 In contrast to weak states, authoritarian states typically enforce patterns of ethnic and religious relations by means of a high degree of effective coercion. Insofar as those patterns are also characterized by a high degree of intolerance, as in Nazi Germany, the level of violence in such a society would be judged to be very high, even though the levels of interethnic and interreligious violence may not be as high as in weak states.

For example, authoritarian states vary from dictatorial forms, like Nazi Germany, to more paternalistic forms, like present-day Singapore, with important consequences for the violence potential score. Singapore is unquestionably an authoritarian regime, with pervasive, if subtle, forms of coercive repression (Diamond 2008:209). But by maintaining a system where the government "cater[s] to the welfare of all citizens", takes into account both "its mass base to which it remains highly responsive" and the society's "elite[s] whom it works hard to co-opt" (Diamond 2008:209, 211), Singapore does not rely on anything like the degree of coercion that was characteristic of Hitler's Germany or other strictly dictatorial regimes. Undoubtedly, an important part of the reason for the reduced violence potential is that "the regime has forged a national consciousness across the Chinese/Malay/Indian divide" by ensuring racial balance in electoral procedures and other measures (Diamond 2008:212).

Empirical Findings and Explanations

The approach sketched out above draws on case studies of places like Bosnia, Sri Lanka, Sudan, Iraq, and Burma, conducted at first under the auspices of the USIP project and then later at Harvard, as well as on the findings of Jack Snyder and Larry Diamond, cited earlier, in regard to the connection of nationalist conflicts and democratization.

The essential argument has two parts. First, that "liberal nationalism", consisting of a robust, well-entrenched form of constitutional democracy especially dedicated to the protection of rights of conscience, religion or belief of all citizens, including minorities, and of a society made up of groups strongly committed to ethnic and religious inclusivity and tolerance, has the best chance of reducing violence in favor of a durable peace. Second, that "illiberal nationalism", consisting of forms of government variously at odds with constitutional democracy – whether non-democracies of a weak, predatory, or authoritarian type, and of a society made up of groups strongly committed to ethnic and religious exclusivity and intolerance, is most likely to foster higher degrees of violence. It is believed that variations in commitments to national ideals of tolerance and inclusivity and of variations in the institutionalization of constitutional democracy will affect the levels of violence in any given society. This "theory", if it can be called that, connects the rise and fall of ethnoreligious violence to the dynamics of nationalism, or the conditions under which "nation" and "state" are conjoined.

Further empirical work by Ted Robert Gurr lends considerable support to this approach, though his work also suggests some important loose ends that need to be attended to.[11]

Gurr's study published in 2000, significantly entitled Peoples versus States: Minorities at Risk in the New Century, and reconfirmed in his 2004 study, Ethnic Conflict in World Politics, concludes that since around 1995 "more effective international and domestic strategies for managing ethnopolitical conflict" and majority-minority relations have been developed. This trend is described as a "global shift from ethnic warfare to the politics of accommodation". Among the 275 minorities studied, more and more of them are turning to participatory politics and abandoning armed violence, thereby reversing a long-standing pattern. We may mention two principles Gurr identifies as comprising what he calls an "emerging regime of managed heterogeneity".

"The first and most basic" is "the recognition and active protection of the rights of minority peoples: freedom from discrimination based on race, national origin, language, or religion, complemented by institutional means to protect and promote collective interests". This principle implies "the right of national peoples to exercise some degree of autonomy within existing states to govern their own affairs" (Harff and Gurr 2004 278). According to Gurr, it has been signaled by the recent movement in human rights thinking from exclusive concern with individual rights to the protection of group rights, enunciated with special force in the documents of the Organization of Security and Cooperation in Europe.[12] In a large number of cases armed rebellions have been significantly modified or pacified by autonomy agreements, mainly concluded in the nineties, as for example in Northern Ireland, Moldova, Nicaragua, Bosnia, Ethiopia, and Bangladesh (Gurr 2000:196-206).

Secondly, political democracy "in one of its European variants" is "widely recognized as the most reliable guarantee of minority rights". "It is inherent in the logic of [constitutional] democratic politics that all peoples in heterogeneous societies should have equal civil and political rights. Democratic governance also implies acceptance of peaceful means for resolving civil conflicts". By a ratio of 20 to 7, according to

11 Gurr's work as it bears on the relation of religion and ethnic conflict has been refined and elaborated on by Jonathan Fox, e.g. *Ethnoreligious Conflict in the Late Twentieth Century: A General Theory* (Lanham, MD: Lexington Books, 2002). Fox's findings generally confirm Gurr's conclusions in regard to the bearing of state structure on the incidence of ethnic conflict. For example: "Two key factors in determining whether religious elements in a secular society will engage in protest or rebellion are repression and democracy. Democracies generally permit freedom of religion, thus creating an environment in which minority religions are comparatively free from restrictions. The environment also allows, and often encourages, religious movements to pursue their social agenda in a peaceful manner...However, in autocratic and repressive societies, these forms of peaceful political activity are generally not possible and rebellion is the only avenue for pursuing a political agenda. (p. 188).

12 See, in particular, "Document of the Copenhagen Meeting of the Conference on the Human Dimension of the CSCE" (Copenhagen, 29 June 1990), arts. 30-41. In *Documents of the Human Dimension of the OSCE*, prepared by Dominick McGoldrick (Warsaw, 1995).

Gurr, democratic governments have been particularly successful in working out negotiated settlements (Gurr 2000:204). By contrast Gurr also emphasizes, as we would expect, that authoritarian governments "exhibit [a] pattern of high discrimination and pervasive restrictions on minorities" backed by an extensive use of coercion to quell protest and riots, all of which increases "the likelihood that challengers will respond with open rebellion" (Gurr 2000:167). At the same time, he adds – again, as we would predict – that the more extreme and intimidating the amount of force used, "the less likely the chances for open rebellion" (Harff and Gurr 2004:104-105). Under "highly effective" authoritarian regimes, it appears, one extreme form of ethnoreligious violence replaces another.

However, as to the causal connections between constitutional democracy and peace, Gurr partially takes back his second conclusion: "The proposition that democracy inhibits ethnic rebellion has only qualified support" (Gurr 2000:163). In one respect, his comment is not surprising. Jack Snyder also stresses the instability of periods of transition to greater democracy, and particularly the potential for increased ethnoreligious violence at that time. For Snyder, it is only entrenched and comprehensively developed forms of constitutional democracy that can successfully inhibit ethnoreligious violence. Moreover, Gurr's claim that "in the Third World, regimes with a mix of democratic and autocratic features are somewhat better able to contain ethnopolitical conflict than new Western-style democracies" seems plausible in part, given the obvious need to adapt democratic governments to local circumstances.

Still, two cases I am familiar with – Sri Lanka and Sudan – raise serious questions about the effectiveness of Gurr's mixed system of authoritarianism and democracy as recipe for satisfactory ethnoreligious peace in transitional societies. In Sri Lanka, increasing authoritarianism, accompanied by an extensive use of arbitrary force in quelling rebellion and in dealing with minorities has only intensified, it seems, ethnoreligious grievances and divisions in that society. The same applies to Sudan. In the light of these two cases at least, it will be necessary to explore much further than Gurr has done the right balance of national ideals and regime type in transitional societies.

Conclusion

We may draw three main conclusions. One is that, at bottom, nationalism is best understood as the coalescence of nation and state around the modern idea of political legitimacy. A nation, defined as a "people" espousing a distinctive common identity and aspiring to political autonomy on the basis of a sense of "deep, horizontal comradeship", presents itself as justifying a political authority intended to preside over the inhabitants of a sharply circumscribed territory. Another is that religion and ethnicity assume prominence – variously, and along with other important influences – in shaping the character and ideals of the nation and the organization of the state. At the same time, religion and ethnicity are themselves reciprocally influenced by the character and practice of the state.

A third conclusion is that because religious and/or ethnic ideals play such a constitutive part in the dynamics of nationalism, the issue of religious and other forms of tolerance and intolerance becomes extremely salient in relation to the occurrence or mitigation of violence. Where effective constitutional democracies combine with a high degree of national tolerance – examples of "liberal nationalism" in our terms – a very low incidence of violence is predicted. Conversely, where illiberal democracies or weak, predatory, or authoritarian regimes, strongly lacking the characteristics of constitutional democracy, combine with a high degree of national intolerance – examples of "illiberal nationalism" in our terms – a high incidence of violence is predicted.

If this approach is well-founded, then studying the complex interrelations of religion, nationalism and intolerance in the way outlined above will have important implications for future research.

References

Anderson, Benedict (1998): Imagined Communities: Reflections on the Origin and Spread of Nationalism. Revised edition. Verso, London.

Diamond, Larry (2008): The Spirit of Democracy: The Struggle to Build Free Societies throughout the World. Henry Holt & Co, New York.

Fox, Jonathan (2002): Ethnoreligious Conflict in the Late Twentieth Century: A General Theory. Lexington Books, Lanham.

Gerth, Hans Heinrich and Mills, C. Wright (1948): From Max Weber: Essays in Sociology. Oxford University Press, New York.

Gurr, Ted Robert (2000): Peoples versus States: Minorities at Risk in the New Century. USIP Press, Washington DC.

Harff, Barbara and Gurr, Ted Robert (2004): Ethnic Conflict in World Politics. 2nd ed. Westview Press, Cambridge.

Little, David (1991): The Legacy of Intolerance. USIP Press, Washington DC.

Little, David (1994): Sri Lanka: The Invention of Enmity. USIP Press, Washington DC.

Little, David and Hibbard, Scott W. (1994): Sino-Tibetan Co-Existence: Creating Space for Tibetan Self-Direction. USIP Press, Washington DC.

Little, David (ed.) (2006): Peacemakers in Action: Profiles in Religion and Conflict Resolution. Cambridge University Press, New York.

Little, David and Swearer, Donald K. (2006): Religion and Nationalism in Iraq. Harvard University Press, Cambridge.

Mansfield, Edward D. and Snyder, Jack (2005): Electing to Fight: Why Emerging Democracies Go to War. MIT Press, Cambridge.

Marx, Anthony W. (2003): Faith in Nation: Exclusionary Origins of Nationalism. Oxford University Press, New York.

Smith, Anthony D. (2003): Chosen Peoples: Sacred Sources of National Identity. Oxford University Press, New York.

Snyder, Jack (2000): From Voting to Violence: Democratization and Nationalist Conflict. Norton & Co, New York.

Zakaria, Fareed (2003): The Future of Freedom: Illiberal Democracy at Home and Abroad. W. W. Norton, New York.

Peacebuilding in the Field. Religious Approaches, Best Practice and Constraints

Jeffrey Haynes

In recent years, religion has made a remarkable return to prominence. Confounding the expectations of secularists, religion has a strong – perhaps growing – significance as a strong source of identity for millions of people. Religious individuals and faith-based organisations, as carriers of religious ideas, play an important role in many societies, both as a source of conflict and as a tool for conflict resolution and peacebuilding. Religious hatreds and differences are central to many recent and current conflicts. Religious actors can also play a constructive role in helping resolve conflicts and build peace, via early warnings of conflict, good offices once conflict has erupted, as well as advocacy, mediation, and reconciliation.

The influence of religion in this regard is often linked to the multiple impacts of globalisation. Globalisation – characterised by its often destabilising economic, political, cultural and technological effects – can affect groups of religious believers by undermining associated traditional value systems. A consequence is that many people are now said to feel both disorientated and troubled and in response (re)turn to religion to try to deal with associated existential angst (Norris and Inglehart 2004). Such people may find in religion a source of comfort, serenity, stability, and spiritual uplifting. Some may experience new or renewed feelings of identity that not only help provide believers' lives with meaning and purpose but also can in some cases contribute to inter-religious competition and conflict (Carlson and Owens 2003).

Globalisation leads to greatly increased interaction between people and communities. As a result, encounters between different religious traditions are increasingly common but not always harmonious, which can lead to what Kurtz labels 'culture wars' (Kurtz 1995:168). The reason, he contends, is that various religious worldviews encourage different allegiances and standards in relation to various areas, including the family, law, education and politics. Increasingly, it appears, conflicts between people, ethnic groups, classes, and nations are framed in religious terms. Such religious conflicts often seem to 'take on "larger-than-life" proportions as the struggle of good against evil' (Kurtz 1995:170). Such conflicts can seriously affect a country's chance of development.

This paper examines how religion can encourage both conflict and peace in the developing world, and offers brief examples – from Mozambique, Nigeria and Cambodia – of religious peacemakers who have recently made significant attempts to reconcile previously warring communities and achieve social cohesion, crucial foundations, more generally, of progressive human development.

Religion and conflict

According to the eminent Roman Catholic theologian Hans Küng,

> "the most fanatical, the cruelest political struggles are those that have been colored, inspired, and legitimized by religion. To say this is not to reduce all political conflicts to religious ones, but to take seriously the fact that religions share in the responsibility for bringing peace to our torn and warring world" (quoted in Smock 2004).

This highlights the fact that conflicts can have religious roots, whereby religious differences drive accompanying hatred and violence. The implication is that religions and faith communities can be effective as "angels of peace" as well as "war mongers". This is the *ambivalence* of religion; the relationship of the world religions to violence is ambiguous.

Holenstein explains that "All great God-narratives are familiar with traditions that legitimise force in certain circumstances, claim victims in the battle for their own beliefs and demonise people of other religions" (Holenstein 2005:10). Yet this is not the whole story for there are also "sources that proclaim the incompatibility of violence with religion, demand sacrifices for peace and insist on respect for people of other religions." (ibid.) The upshot is that, while we can assume that for the present and for some time to come, religion will persist in being a component in some – but not all – political conflicts, it becomes ever more necessary to bolster, to build up, their "civilising" and peacebuilding aspects and to undermine, to reduce, any propensity for conflict and negation of peacebuilding.

The ambivalence of religion in this regard is clear when we focus upon recent and current religious involvement in large-scale conflicts. For example, mass violence in Africa, Asia and other parts of the developing world is increasingly associated with serious social conflicts, some of which involve religious tensions. Focusing upon Commonwealth countries, many of which are also developing countries, Barringer notes that religious tensions are very often linked to other issues (Barringer 2006:2). These include: 'ethnicity, culture, class, power and wealth, played out both within' countries, for example Nigeria, Fiji, Cyprus, Sri Lanka, and between them, for example India and Pakistan. Turning to the Middle East and North Africa (MENA), we can easily agree that stability and prosperity are key goals, central to the achievement of peace and the elimination of poverty in regional countries. On the other hand, the region is home to many persistent conflicts and many have clear religious connotations: for example the conflicts between Israel and the (mostly Sunni Muslim) Palestinians and between the former and Lebanon's Shia Hezbollah. There are also intra-Muslim conflicts in the region, for example between Shia and Sunni Muslims in Iraq and between the governments of (mainly) Shia Iran and (mainly) Sunni Saudi Arabia. In Egypt, additionally, the country's minority Christian Copts have endured long periods of what can only be described as persecution (Fox 2008:237-238). In sum, such conflicts draw attention not only to the fact that the Middle East is the emblematic birthplace of the three monotheistic world religions (Christianity, Islam, and Judaism) but also that there is a legacy not only of shared religious wisdom but also of sometimes intense religious-political-societal conflicts. This implies a complex relationship that not only impacts on all regional countries, but also on some far away from the region, including the Philippines which has seen growing numbers of Islamic extremist groups, as well as various western countries, including the United States, the United Kingdom and Spain, all of which have experienced Islamist bombing outrages in the last decade.

A key to eventual peace in the MENA may well be the achievement of significant collaborative efforts among different religious bodies, which along with religious and secular organisations from outside the region, including both Europe and the United States, may eventually succeed in developing a new model of peace and co-operation to enable the region to escape from what often seems an endless cycle of religion-linked conflict. It is important to note that in the MENA religion is obviously intimately connected *both* to promulgation and prolongation of conflicts *as well as* to attempts at their reconciliation. This implies that religion's contribution to conflicts in the region is ambivalent: it can play a significant, even a fundamental role in contributing to conflicts in various ways, including how they are intensified, channelled or reconciled. On the other hand, it can play an important role in seeking to resolve conflicts and build peace. This dualistic role of religion is of course not limited to the MENA but is also present in many other conflict areas, for example in Asia (notably Bangladesh, India, Pakistan and Sri Lanka) and sub-Saharan Africa (for instance Nigeria, Sudan and Uganda).

These introductory comments are not intended to "prove" that religion is invariably associated with conflict. This is because religion can also play a significant role in attempts to resolve inter- and intra-group clashes and help build peace. Bartoli notes that "all religious traditions contain references in the form of didactical stories, teachings or even direct recommendations as to how the faithful should act in order to achieve harmony and peace within himself or herself in the first place" (Bartoli 2005:5-6). Appleby points out that, following Johnston and Sampson's "Religion, the Missing Dimension of Statecraft" (1994), numerous relevant journal articles and books now focus on how religious actors can play a role in ending conflicts and building peace (Appleby 2006:1). Summarising an initial set of findings regarding religious peacebuilding and faith-based diplomacy, Appleby avers that:

- Religious leaders are uniquely positioned to foster nonviolent conflict transformation through the building of constructive, collaborative relationships within and across ethnic and religious groups for the common good of the entire population of a country or region.

- In many conflict settings around the world, the social location and cultural power of religious leaders make them potentially critical players in any effort to build a sustainable peace.
- The multigenerational local or regional communities they oversee are repositories of local knowledge and wisdom, custodians of culture, and privileged sites of moral, psychological and spiritual formation.
- Symbolically charged sources of personal as well as collective identity, these communities typically establish and maintain essential educational and welfare institutions, some of which serve people who are not members of the religious community (Appleby 2006:1).

Religious peacemakers, conflict resolution and peacebuilding

Individuals and faith-based organisations from a variety of religious traditions are increasingly active in attempts to end conflicts and to foster post-conflict reconciliation between warring parties in various parts of the world (Bouta, Kadayifci-Orellana and Abu-Nimer 2005; Smock 2006). This is a phenomenon gaining increased attention, although it is not a new one. Religious individuals, often as representatives of faith-based organisations, have for decades carried out mediations, striving to help resolve conflicts. Examples include: Mediation undertaken by the Quakers and financed by the Ford Foundation in the Nigerian Civil War, 1967-70; the work of the World Council of Churches and the All Africa Conference of Churches in mediating a cessation to the Sudan conflict in 1972; efforts made by John Paul Lederach (Professor of International Peacebuilding at the University of Notre Dame) in Nicaragua in the 1980s; and the recent work of the Imam of Timbuktu in mediating various West African conflicts (Conflict and Resolution Forum 2001). This suggests that to focus single-mindedly on conflicts within and between religions not only oversimplifies causal interconnections between religion and conflict, in particular by disregarding important alternate variables, but also leads to an underestimation of attempts emerging from various religious traditions helping to resolve conflicts and to build peace. The point is that, when successful, religion's role in helping resolve conflicts and build peace is a crucial component in helping to advance human development more generally.

"Religious peacemakers" are religious individuals or representatives of faith-based organisations who attempt to help resolve inter-group conflicts and build peace (Appleby 2000, 2006; Gopin 2000, 2005; Ellis and ter Haar 2005). According to Appleby such people are most likely to be successful when they: (1) have an international or transnational reach, (2) consistently emphasise peace and the avoidance of the use of force in resolving conflict, and (3) have good relations to different religions in a conflict situation, as this will be the key to a positive input from them (Appleby 2006:1-2). It can be argued that world religions share a broadly similar set of theological and spiritual values and views and that this should – at least potentially – underpin their ability to provide positive contributions to conflict resolution and peacebuilding. Practical effects in this regard have increased in recent years, with growing numbers and types of religious peacemakers working to try to build peaceful coexistence in multi-faith societies, while advocating reconciliation and fairness in a world that often seems characterised by social and political strife and economic disparity (Bartoli 2005).

The salience of religious peacemakers to conflict resolution and peacebuilding may be increasing and in some cases becoming more effective, demonstrated in the following:

- Faith-based organisations are increasingly active and increasingly effective in attempts at peacebuilding.
- Faith-based organisations have a special role to play in zones of religious conflict, but their peacebuilding programmes do not need to be confined to addressing religious conflict only.
- Although in some cases peacebuilding projects of faith-based organisations very closely resemble peacebuilding by secular non-governmental organisations, the various religious orientations of these faith-based organisations typically shape the peacebuilding they undertake.
- These organisations' peacebuilding agendas are diverse, ranging from high-level mediation to training and peacebuilding-through-development at the grassroots.
- Peace can often be promoted most efficiently by introducing peacebuilding components into more traditional relief and development activities (Smock 2001:1; Smock 2006).

Overall, faith-based organisations of various kinds have increasingly engaged in peacemaking activities in recent years. Many recent and contemporary conflicts are located in the regions of the developing world and it is therefore unsurprising that peacemaking efforts tend to focus on inter-group conflicts there. Faith-based initiatives are credited with contributing positively to peacebuilding in four main ways, by providing: (1) "emotional and spiritual support to war-affected communities"; (2) effective mobilisation for "their communities and others for peace", (3) mediation "between conflicting parties", and (4) a conduit in pursuit of "reconciliation, dialogue, and disarmament, demobilization and reintegration" (Bouta, Kadayifci-Orellana and Abu-Nimer 2005:ix). Characteristically, these activities tend to be rather narrowly focused on specific conflicts, inevitably constraining prospects for wider and more comprehensive impacts. In particular, there are two problems that limit the effects of such efforts: firstly "there is often a failure of religious leaders to understand and/or enact their potential peacebuilding roles within the local community", and secondly many religious leaders lack the ability to "exploit their strategic capacity as transnational actors" (Appleby 2006:2). As a result, as demonstrated by the three case studies that follow in the next section, their impacts tend to be limited and effects mixed.

Conflict resolution and peacebuilding in action: Mozambique, Nigeria and Cambodia

All religious peacemakers seek to help rebuild good community relations and encourage the development of peaceful and constructive relations between previously warring communities. Next, we briefly examine religious peacemakers in action in three developing countries: Mozambique, Nigeria and Cambodia. First, we look at the work of the Catholic lay organisation Sant'Egidio in Mozambique, instrumental in bringing that country's civil war to an end in 1992. Second, we examine the individual efforts of two religious leaders – one Muslim, one Christian – in Nigeria. Finally, we switch focus to Cambodia, highlighting a Buddhist leader, Maha Ghosananda, whose efforts to help resolve the country's deep-seated societal conflict and build peace has been notable. Overall, the examples indicate that religious peacemakers *can* make a difference, an improvement to an existing situation characterised by conflict. This is a way of saying that left to their own devices, it is very likely that conflicting groups would fail to reach a *modus vivendi* and potentially relapse into conflict with, in each case, destabilising effects on regional and international stability and peace. This reflects a situation which, as Mozambique's president Joaquim Chissano, reminds us: "Conflicts, particularly violent conflicts between and within states in other parts of Africa, and in the world in general, are also a danger to our peace and tranquillity. Helping other peoples keep and maintain peace is also a way of defending our own peace" (Harsch 2003:16).

Increased interest and activity in faith-based peacemaking is connected to the increasing role of non-governmental organisations, civil society actors, and religious groups that have recently and collectively increased peacemaking efforts. For example, a Christian non-governmental organisation, Pax Christi, was instrumental in negotiating a (short-lived) peace deal between the Lord's Resistance Army and the government of Uganda in 2006 (Simonse 1998). Soon after, peace was over and conflict resumed.[1] Whenever a peace deal cannot be maintained it shows that peacebuilders – religious or secular – are not magicians, able to force acceptance of peace, in circumstances where one or both parties are not sincere in their stated ambitions to end a conflict.

More generally, large-scale violence in many African countries is often associated with social conflicts, with religion and/or ethnicity characteristics. Numerous regional countries – including Liberia, Sierra Leone, the Democratic Republic of Congo, Côte

1 Reliable Security Information – The Lord's Resistance Army (LRA): http://www.globalsecurity.org/military/world/para/lra-3.htm (last accessed 22.3.2012).

d'Ivoire, Liberia, Nigeria, Sierra Leone, Burundi, Rwanda, Angola, Sudan and Mozambique – have been beset with serious political violence, with a proliferation of armed conflicts and numerous deaths of local people, most of whom were civilian non-combatants. In addition, as Harsch notes, millions more "succumbed to war-related epidemics and starvation" (Harsch 2003:1). In all such cases, conflicts were informed by a variety of issues, including religious and/or ethnicity factors.

Many conflict resolution and peacebuilding missions are set up to monitor peace agreements between established armies holding separate territories. But they often discover that success is hard to find, not least because they are not necessarily well suited to deal with such conflicts. In particular, many recent conflicts in Africa have been civil wars or insurgencies, with multiple armed factions and with grievances often fuelled by poverty, inequality and other development issues. Moreover, even when peace accords *are* successfully negotiated, it is not always the case that all political and military leaders are able or willing to fully control their followers. In some countries, such as Sierra Leone and Liberia, local fighters, who profited from the chaos of war, saw more advantage for a time in continuing to fight than to lay down their arms (Harsch 2003:14).

Mozambique: the role of Sant'Egidio in conflict resolution and peacebuilding

Do faith-based organisations have more success than non-religious entities in helping to resolve conflicts and put peace back on the agenda? While the evidence is mixed in this regard, it is the case that in some African conflicts faith-based organisations have met with success (Appleby 2006). Perhaps the most illustrative case of this type of peacemaking was the mediation by the Catholic organisation Sant'Egidio, credited with playing a key role in ending the civil war in Mozambique in 1992.

Sant'Egidio is a prominent example of a religious group active in faith-based peacemaking. It is an international Catholic non-governmental organisation (NGO) that takes part in attempts at peacemaking in various conflicts in many parts of the world.

Originally, its principal focus was to serve the needs of the urban poor in Italy (Bouta, Kadayifci-Orellana and Abu-Nimer 2005:71). Founded in 1968 in Italy, Sant'Egidio has grown and now has more than 50.000 members in over 70 countries.[2] Sant'Egidio is a church public lay association, formally recognised by the Catholic Church but with an autonomous statute. This means that its membership is "lay" – that is, not professionally religious – although its adherents have a clear religious motivation, forming an important part of its negotiation activities. Sant'Egidio began its activities over four decades ago with charity, humanitarian action and de-

2 Community of Sant'Egidio Website: http://www.santegidio.org/index.php?pageID=2&idLng=1064> (last accessed 22.3.2012).

velopment cooperation to the fore. These were concerns formed on the basis of spirituality and shared principles, including prayer, communicating the gospel, solidarity with the poor and dialogue with other religions (Appleby 2006:10). However, despite its avowedly religious orientation, Sant'Egidio's conflict resolution and peacebuilding activities have focused more on "non-religious" conflicts than on "religious" conflicts, and more on the international level than on the national or local level.

During the early 1980s Sant'Egidio became engaged in various international dialogues. The aim was trying to prevent or to reduce tension between conflicting groups and seeking to mediate between them. Since then Sant'Egidio has played an active peacebuilding role in several African countries beset with civil war including: Algeria, Burundi, the Democratic Republic of Congo, Côte d'Ivoire, Mozambique and Sierra Leone. It has also been active elsewhere including: Colombia, Guatemala, and Kosovo. In each case, the country was beset with serious conflict between polarised groups; in some cases, conditions were exacerbated by the fact that the effectiveness of the central government to administer had diminished significantly (Smock 2004).

One of the clearest success stories of Sant'Egidio's peacemaking efforts occurred between 1989 and 1992 when the organisation was extremely influential in resolving the civil war that had ravaged Mozambique since the mid-1970s. The Catholic Archbishop of Beira, Don Jaime Goncalves, was familiar with Sant'Egidio and its work from the time he had spent in Rome, years before. Following well intentioned but eventually unsuccessful efforts to end the war emanating from the international community, Archbishop Goncalves thought Sant'Egidio might succeed in bringing the government together to peace talks with the rebels of the Mozambican National Resistance (RENAMO) insurgents. He was right: The effort took months but eventually Sant'Egidio not only contacted the RENAMO leadership but also encouraged Mozambican government officials to agree to meet with them (Bouta, Kadayifci-Orellana and Abu-Nimer 2005:71-72).

Sant'Egidio was successful in its efforts because both RENAMO and the government perceived Sant'Egidio as an organisation characterised both by a welcome neutrality and a compassionate outlook, with but one interest in Mozambique: To end the civil war and promote peace. That is, Sant'Egidio was understood to have no political or economic agenda; throughout the negotiations this perception was bolstered as the organisation demonstrated a position of both even-handedness and neutrality (Smock 2004). As far as the Mozambican government was concerned, as an NGO, Sant'Egidio could set up a meeting between RENAMO and the government without it meaning that the RENAMO rebels would be regarded as an entity with the same status as the ruling regime. But Sant'Egidio also had a second important asset, namely the "humble awareness of its own shortcomings in orchestrating international diplomacy, which caused it to seek out the special expertise of governments and international organizations" (Smock 2004:1). The nucleus of Sant'Egidio's mediation team was the Archbishop of Beira, Don Jaime Goncalves, an Italian socialist parliamentarian and former diplomat, and two key leaders of Sant'Egidio. These efforts were complemented not only by the United Nations but also by ten national governments, including those of the United States, Italy, Zimbabwe and Kenya. Once peace negotiations were successfully completed in 1992, the United Nations assumed responsibility for the implementation of the peace agreement. Mozambique is now both peaceful and enjoying relatively strong economic growth (of 4.5 percent in 2009).[3] There have been several national level elections, won by the ruling FRELIMO party. RENAMO serves as the main political opposition to the government.[4]

In conclusion, the mediation work of Sant'Egidio in Mozambique illustrates how faith-based organisations with relevant skills can offer a unique ability to mediate between previously warring factions. They do this by building on a reputation for neutrality and compassion and by utilising not only their own skills but also those of other institutions, in an initiative which, in the case of Mozambique, brought the battling parties together and brought the civil war to a close (Bouta, Kadayifci-Orellana and Abu-Nimer 2005:72-73).

Nigeria: seeking accommodation between religious communities

Nigeria has a population of more than 150 million people, divided between Muslims, Christians and followers of traditional African religions. There are roughly the same number of Muslims and Christians in Nigeria (each between 40 and 50 percent), with the remainder – a diminishing minority – comprising followers of traditional religions (approx. 10 percent). However these figures are necessarily speculative because the only census since 1963 (undertaken in 1991) failed to ask respondents about religious affiliation. Religious competition between Muslim and Christians is now perhaps the single most significant political issue in the country (Korieh 2005). More generally, since the 1960s, religion has been prominent in the Nigerian civil conflict where missionaries and religious partisans see themselves in a zero-sum game to win souls, sometimes entering into deadly conflict.

Antipathy between them flared in the 1980s, when many Christians believed that the predominantly Muslim North of the country enjoyed a disproportionate portion of

3 U.S. Department of State - Background Note: Mozambique: http://www.state.gov/r/pa/ei/bgn/7035.htm (last accessed 22.3.2012).

4 On October 28, 2009 Mozambique held simultaneous presidential, legislative, and provincial assembly elections. The results were much the same as 2004 with FRELIMO candidate Armando Guebuza winning 75% of the presidential vote and Afonso Dhlakama of RENAMO coming in second with nearly 14%; 9.28% of the votes were won by Daviz Simango of the Democratic Movement of Mozambique (MDM). Of 248 parliamentary seats, FRELIMO won 192, RENAMO 48, and MDM 8 (http://www.state.gov/r/pa/ei/bgn/7035.htm#political, last accessed 22.3.2012).

both political power and economic resources (Ibrahim 1991:135). In 1986, tensions were raised by the government's secret decision to join the Organisation of the Islamic Conference (OIC) with 45 members, within which Saudi Arabia and Iran – with their contending visions of the appropriate Islamic society – strive for diplomatic and political prominence. The Nigerian government's motivation for seeking to join the OIC was probably primarily financial. Economic aid would have been expected from oil-rich OIC member states – yet many Christians feared that Nigeria's membership of the OIC would jeopardise the country's status as a secular state and reduce the status and position of Christians (Korieh 2005). Muslim supporters of the membership bid countered that Nigeria was a member of the Commonwealth, a "Christian" organisation, led by the British monarch who, legally, must be a Protestant Christian (Kukha and Falola 1995). The issue was not settled before a further religious controversy erupted in 1987. Now the point of contention was whether a *Sharia* court of appeal would be allowed in the democratic regime which was scheduled (as it turned out, abortively) to accede to power in late 1992. Muslim members of the Constituent Assembly wanted to anchor *Sharia* law in the Nigerian constitution, while Christians would not countenance such a move. Negotiations on the issue broke down (and were to an extent superseded by other controversies), whilst President Babangida was forced to affirm in October 1988 that Nigeria would remain a secular state despite membership of the OIC.

Tensions between the two communities had already escalated into political violence. In early 1987, and again in May and October 1991, anti-Christian riots broke out in parts of northern Nigeria (Maier 1991). In total, over 3.000 people were killed in Christian-Muslim clashes between 1987 and 1993. The death toll included about one thousand killed in a series of pitched battles in May 1992 when Christian Katafs fought Muslim Hausa and Fulani. Churches were destroyed and both Christians and Muslims killed and injured. The political context of this religious violence was the continuation of the military government, a regime that sought not to encourage public political debates (Maier 2002). As a result, with political parties banned and with no legislature, public anger and frustration among Muslims was channelled into religious issues. In effect, many ordinary Muslims were turned into "fundamentalists" in the sense that they began to perceive their Christian countrymen and women as their chief foes, while many Christians, fearing what appeared to them to be a growing threat from Islam, retaliated.

From the early 1990s, inter-religious violence became a common feature of life in Nigeria, primarily involving Muslim and Christian communities. One of the worst-hit regions was the northern state of Kaduna. Generally, Nigeria has a high level of religious violence that claimed more than 10.000 lives during the 1990s, and Kaduna was the main area where casualties occurred (Haynes 1996:213-221). This led to the founding of the Muslim-Christian Dialogue Forum (MCDF) in 1995, a charity to foster

Christian-Muslim dialogue. It was the result of the combined efforts of two former enemies – a Christian pastor, James Movel Wuye, and a Muslim Imam, Muhammed Nurayn Ashafa, both esteemed members of their religious communities. They served as joint national coordinators of MCDF, based in Kaduna. Both made the decision to turn away from similar paths of violence and militancy. Instead, they embraced non-violence, reconciliation, and the advocacy of peaceful relations between their communities, and sought to encourage others to join them in this goal (Moix, n/d).

Three years earlier – in 1992 – relations between the two men were very different: each tried to have the other killed in a clash in Zangon Kataf, Kaduna state. Christian killers murdered Ashafa's uncle, believing that the latter was Ashafa himself; Muslim assassins hacked off Wuye's arm and left him for dead. Discovering their mistakes, both men saw the events as a signal from God and henceforward started to work together as peacemakers. They founded MCDF and in 1999 co-authored a book, "The Pastor and the Imam: Responding to Conflict", which describes their experiences and illustrates the Bible's and the Qu'ran's commitments to peace. A few years later, in 2003, both were enrolled as students at the School for International Training (SIT), and as participants in the peacebuilding institute held every June at SIT's Vermont campus (Wuye and Ashafa 2005)

Ashafa and Wuye wrote in their book that,

> "Religion today, instead of serving as a source of healing sickness, hunger, and poverty, and stimulating tranquility and peaceful co-existence among human beings, is used to cause sadness. It is bringing pain instead of relief, hatred instead of love, division instead of unity, sadness instead of joy, discrimination and destruction instead of accommodation and development. This is especially true between some adherents of Islam and Christianity. Nigeria has its own share of this negative phenomenon. Its ethnic-religious conflict has become a matter so serious and devastating that it can now be seen as a harbinger of the danger of a crisis such as those that have engulfed the former Yugoslavia, Rwanda and Liberia" (Wuye and Ashafa 1999:1).

In March 2003, the MCDF and the US Institute of Peace jointly promoted a five-day dialogue workshop in Kaduna seeking to help address the aforementioned issues. Participants came from Christian and Muslim communities, with one youth leader from both faiths chosen to take part from 30 of Nigeria's states. The reason to focus on the youth at this event was taken in recognition that both Muslims and Christians from this age group have been responsible for much of the religious violence in Nigeria in recent years. More generally, the forum sought to add to the work of the Nigerian Inter-Religious Council, a body comprising older, senior religious leaders that has consistently condemned Nigeria's religious violence.[5] Following the Kaduna forum, plans were made to organise further inter-faith gatherings in other parts of Nigeria.

5 United States Institute of Peace – Religion and Peacemaking: http://www.usip.org/programs/centers/religion-and-peacemaking (last accessed 22.3.2012).

When the workshop started, each side was adamant that the other was to blame for religious violence in Nigeria. When it concluded, participants agreed on a 17-point consensual declaration containing various recommendations, including that:

- both Christians and Muslims should love each other unconditionally as brothers and sisters
- both communities should show good will to each other at all times
- it was important to inform members of each religious community more comprehensively about the beliefs and tenets of the 'other' faith, and
- it was necessary to cooperate with the government in order to hand over for justice those people who continue to use religious violence contravening of the existing law (Crawley 2003).

In sum, this Nigerian case shows that when interfaith dialogue is skilfully organised and pursued it can encourage erstwhile religious enemies, including those who have personally been involved in a conflict, to work together towards peaceful accommodation. This does not necessarily mean, however, that religious conflicts more generally are dealt with via such initiatives. This may be because conflicts that appear to evolve around real or perceived religious differences, as in Nigeria between Muslims and Christians, are also concerned with human development issues, such as poverty – and these of course would require sustained and devoted attention from the government in order to resolve them.

Cambodia: conflict resolution and the legacy of Khmer Rouge rule

In Cambodia, Theravada Buddhism had to contend with serious attempts to eradicate it in the 1970s.[6] During five years of misrule by the Khmer Rouge, the communist regime tried energetically to exterminate religion in the country – including Theravada Buddhism, the country's leading faith[7] – while killing millions of Cambodians as a central facet of state policy (Poethig 2002). Pol Pot, leader of the Khmer Rouge, was an individual who was strongly influenced by the French Revolution from the years he had spent working in France. In addition, he had revolutionary goals inspired by both the Russian and Chinese revolutions. He wanted to create a new society and a "new person" by destroying the three main foundations of the old one. First, there was the western, largely French-influenced, modern culture of the elite. Anyone speaking French (or another western language, such as English) was considered to be part of the modern elite which had to be destroyed. The second source of Cambodia's culture was

6 'Theravada Buddhism' is often shortened in this section to 'Buddhism'.

7 An estimated 95% of Cambodians are Theravada Buddhists: https://www.cia.gov/library/publications/the-world-factbook/geos/cb.html (last accessed 22.3.2012).

Buddhism, epitomised by the country's thousands of Buddhist monks – the *sangha* – which collectively had much societal clout and authority. The *sangha* not only controlled and led religious ceremonies but were also responsible for much of the country's education system. The third source was folk culture, traditionally passed on by the elderly, which was characterised both by interaction with the spirit and the individual history of each village (Wadlow 2007). This was, for Pol Pot, an egregious source of "tradition" that had to be excised in order for a new, revolutionary Cambodia to be born.

The Khmer Rouge killed one in five Cambodians – an estimated 1.5 million people – during their five years in power, the result of a systematic programme of execution, starvation and forced labour. Following an international outcry, a Vietnamese military invasion ousted the Khmer Rouge in 1979. The Vietnamese were faced with a completely disorganised and traumatised society and, following the invasion, Cambodia experienced a lengthy period of political instability. A small number of Buddhist monks survived the Pol Pot years within Cambodia; many did so by casting off their monks' robes and replacing them with civilian clothes. The Vietnamese put these few monks into positions of leadership, while members of the *sangha* who had gone into in exile – mainly in Thailand, Europe or the USA – were not trusted by the Vietnamese. It was not until 1992-93 that exiled monks began to return – when the United Nations took over the administration of the country in the shape of the United Nations Transitional Authority in Cambodia (UNTAC) (Stuart-Fox 2006).

During the UNTAC period, Cambodia became a major focus of concentrated peacebuilding activities. An initially hesitant state gradually began to acknowledge the continued cultural, social and religious salience of Buddhism to millions of Cambodians, recognising its popular appeal and allowing Buddhism a renewed national voice. This occurred at several levels, including the popular level, where an initiative known as the Dhammayietra, whose central tenet was compassion and non-violence, was established. The message of the Dhammayietra – usually translated as "pilgrimage of truth" – was the hope of peace to rebuild the war-torn country.

A Buddhist monk, Somdet Phra Maha Ghosananda, was the chief originator of the Dhammayietra in 1992. Maha Ghosananda is known to many as "the Gandhi of Cambodia". He was a six-time Nobel Peace Prize nominee who died in March 2007. He hold the office of the Supreme Patriarch of Cambodian Buddhism for two decades, having been elected by the country's Buddhist monks in 1988. The years between 1965 and 1978 Maha Ghosananda spent in an isolated forest monastery in southern Thailand, devoted to meditation in silence. It was necessary for him to spend time in this environment in Thailand as settings of comparative tranquillity did not exist in Cambodia, where monasteries are located in towns and villages, implying much daily interaction with local people.

In 1978 Maha Ghosananda was told about the large number of Cambodian refugees fleeing Cambodia for Thailand as the Vietnamese troops brought the Khmer Rouge regime to an end. In response, he left his forest monastery in order to try to assist the Cambodian refugees, many of whom were collected in camps on the Thai-Cambodian frontier. During the next 15 years (1978-1992), he worked with refugees on the frontier, helping them to meet their physical, moral and spiritual needs.

Maha Ghosananda returned to Cambodia in 1992, along with a small number of monks who had been living in refugee camps in Thailand, in common with thousands of Cambodian refugees. The idea of the Dhammayietra drew centrally on a practice of the Buddha. He divided each year into periods of retreats (which usually took place in the rainy season, a time of restricted mobility because of climatic conditions, during which he would teach his assembled followers) and other periods of the year, more amenable to travel. At this time, the Buddha, accompanied by his followers, would walk from village to village not only teaching but also caring for the sick. The practice is underlined in words attributed to the Buddha: "Go forth, and walk for the welfare of the many, for the happiness of many, out of compassion for the world, for the profit, for the welfare, for the happiness of gods and mankind. Expound the *Dhamma* (teachings). Live it in its spirit and its letter."[8]

The Dhammayietra – typically an annual 45-day walk of some 650 kilometres involving both monks and lay people – focused on areas that were still often violently divided and, in some cases, where landmines were still common. The walks would be efforts to build links between people divided by the years of conflict. Villagers along the way of the Dhammayietra saw it as symbolic of the return of Buddhism and Buddhist monks, as well as an indication that peace was becoming consolidated, despite the continued hardships still widely experienced years after the Khmer Rouge regime and the Vietnamese invasion. The purpose of the Dhammayietra was not only teaching and ritual expression of compassion but also active listening by the monks to popular experiences and fears. Maha Ghosananda expressed the idea of the Dhammayietra in the following way: "Each step is a prayer, each step is a meditation, each step will build a bridge [...] We must find the courage to leave our temples and enter the temples of human experience, temples that are filled with suffering. If we listen to the Buddha, Christ or Gandhi, we can do nothing else. The refugee camps, the prisons, the ghettos and the battlefields will then become our temples."[9]

Overall, the Dhammayietra represents an important initiative of peace and reconciliation that draws on core Buddhist norms, values and teachings. The meaning of

8 Somdech Maha Ghosanda – Life and Death: The controversial words from a French Catholic Priest in Cambodia; Francios Ponchaud about Somdech Preah Maha Ghosananda and Cambodian Buddhism with a responding to him from Bhikkhu Vodano Sophan, a Cambodian Buddhist Monk: http://www.ghosananda.org/ppp_letters.html (last accessed 22.3.2012).

9 Somdech Maha Ghosanda – Life and Death: Preah Maha Ghosananda: http://www.ghosananda.org/obituary_news.html (last accessed 22.3.2012).

these walks was rooted in discourses and practices that gained in significance in the context of what was known as "socially engaged Buddhism" that came to the fore from the early 1980s not only in Cambodia and Thailand but also in other Asian countries, such as Burma, where Buddhism is a significant religious tradition (Haynes 2007b). The idea of an "engaged" interpretation of Buddhist doctrine represents a significant revival of Buddhism in post-Khmer Rouge Cambodia that, Poethig argues, was only possible because of transnational and interfaith formations (Poethig 2002). She points to the fact that socially-engaged Buddhism in Cambodia is often linked to the return of Cambodian Buddhist exiles from Thailand and other regional countries. This development required two simultaneous moves in order to maintain its usefulness. On the one hand, it is represented as an exemplary Khmer Buddhist response to Cambodia's entrenched conflicts, as it forges its discursive identity within the "local" space of the nation. On the other hand, this local space is also "mobile" – and this is where the Dhammayietra acquires both religious and peacebuilding significance. Maha Ghosananda, the leading figure behind the walks instructed walkers to move "step by step" towards peace. The aim was symbolically to reverse what Maha Ghosananda – identified as examples of "dangerous mobility" – including, massive internal and external relocations and refugee flights of the Khmer Rouge era that affected millions of Cambodians, as well as the still serious danger of treading on landmines in many parts of the country – which turns the act of walking itself into a mindful act. As Poethig notes, "it is this discursive move that loosens the Dhammayietra's ties to the nation allowing it to slip across political and religious borders and ally itself with a broad and diverse network of interfaith peace groups that are its transnational public forum" (Poethig 2002:28).

In conclusion, the Dhammayietra has made an important and continuing contribution not only to the revival of Buddhism in Cambodia, following the Khmer Rouge's years of depredation and consequent political instability, but also to the possibility of the country developing a post-conflict harmony and shared sense of purpose and direction. Thanks to people of compassion, such as Maha Ghosananda, there is a chance that Cambodia will eventually return to peace and tranquillity.

The walks sought to focus attention on three major problems: (1) Cambodia is still very divided along political lines, with the Khmer Rouge still active in some parts of the country until recently; (2) the country is disorganised both economically and socially, where the ethos to "get rich quick" has become deeply embedded in recent years, and (3) the country's foundation is a Buddhist order where many young men seek to become monks, which is, however, rather due to secular and material than to spiritual concerns: to be a monk is to ensure that you will be fed each day and receive an education, although there are now few senior, educated elder monks to teach them (Wadlow 2007). Overall, these concerns reflect the fact that Cambodia still faces very important challenges – including, poverty, corruption, and a narrow political base, with many politicians apparently more concerned with making money, sometimes corruptly, than providing a public service (McLeod 2007).

Conclusion

This paper sought to give an overview of the role of religion in conflicts, conflict resolution and peacebuilding in the developing world, with examples drawn from Mozambique Nigeria and Cambodia. Regarding conflict, we saw that inter-religious tensions and competition were often implicated in the "politics of identity". In the second half of the paper we turned to the role of religious individuals and faith-based organisations in conflict resolution and peacebuilding in three countries: Mozambique, Nigeria and Cambodia, involving respectively a Roman Catholic NGO (Mozambique), Protestant and Muslim religious and community leaders (Nigeria), and the efforts of a Buddhist monk, Maha Ghosananda, in Cambodia. While the contexts, issues, and religious faiths and actors differed from country to country, overall they shared a common characteristic: Religious links to conflict typically receive much public attention, while the efforts of religious peacemakers in relation to conflict resolution and peacebuilding tend to get much less attention and publicity (Smock 2004; Appleby 2006). However, the available evidence indicates, and this paper would underline, that the norms, values, and teachings of various religious faiths – Christianity, Islam and Buddhism were highlighted in the paper – can demonstrably inspire and encourage devotees to work towards resolving conflicts and develop peace via utilisation of explicitly religious tenets. Importantly, such positive initiatives can occur in environments where religion itself is seen to contribute to conflict, such as in Nigeria and Cambodia (Haynes 2007a).

Outcomes, however, are variable. Sometimes, faith-based organisations may be instrumental in helping deliver and then sustain peace. More commonly, however, such efforts see partial success – or, put another way, partial failure – and do not unequivocally ameliorate the problem over time (Bouta, Kadayifci-Orellana and Abu-Nimer 2005; Appleby 2006; Smock 2001, 2004, 2006). Nevertheless, this paper provides evidence that, as a result of increased public recognition and support as well as through the development of more effective peacemaking strategies, conflict resolution and peacemaking skills of faith-based organisations and religious individuals can be encouraged to develop further over time, offering the prospect of achieving undoubted potential in the future. Peacemaking ability is likely to develop in this way when, acting under the auspices of a religious group, individuals and groups are seen as reflective of a high moral standing, crucially retaining credibility, and building stature, to the extent that they can be regarded by all parties as apolitical or neutral in conflict situations.

Finally, it is important to remember that peacemaking activities are nearly always narrowly focused on the specifics of a particular conflict, rather than encompassing a wider focus on the bases of societal (let alone global) conflict. In some, probably most cases, it is inevitable that faith-based organisations will enter a conflict situation with their attention primarily on trying to resolve its immediate manifestations. Arguably, however, peacemaking should not only be about the short-term achievement of peace. It should, in addition, aim to develop restorative justice and/or the establishment of what are considered "right relationships" between formerly conflicting groups through acknowledgement of each other's positions and the acceptance of accountability by those acting on behalf of religious communities. Effective medium and long-term peace-making requires that peacemakers look more closely at the structural problems that underlie the conflict, aiming to work towards addressing the important background issues that make future conflict more likely.

References

Appleby, R. Scott (2000): The ambivalence of the sacred: Religion, violence and reconciliation. Rowman and Littlefield, Lanham.

Appleby, R. Scott (2006): Building Sustainable Peace: The Roles Of Local And Transnational Religious Actors. Paper presented at the Conference on New Religious Pluralism in World Politics. Georgetown University, Washington DC.

Associated Press (2008): India eyes terrorist groups after bombs kill 77. Level of sophistication in 13 blasts indicates militants got help, officials say. MSNBC World News South and Central Asia. Available at: http://www.msnbc.msn.com/id/27472626/. Accessed on November 19, 2010.

Barringer, T. (2006): 'Taking faith seriously in International Relations and Development Studies', Paper presented at the conference, 'Governance and the Commonwealth: Civic Engagement and Democratic Accountability'. The Institute of Commonwealth Studies, London, March 11-13.

Bartoli, Andrea (2005): Conflict prevention: The role of religion is the role of its actors. In: New Routes: A Journal of Peace Research and Action 10:3, 3-7.

Bouta, Tsjeard, S. Ayse Kadayifci-Orellana and Mohammed Abu-Nimer (2005): Faith-Based Peace-Building: Mapping and analysis of Christian, Muslim, and Multi-faith Actors. Netherlands Institute of International Relations, The Hague.

Carlson, John and Owens, Erik (eds.) (2003): The Sacred and the Sovereign: Religion and International Politics. Georgetown University Press, Washington D.C.

Conflict Resolution Forum (2001) Faith-Based Peacemaking: The Role of Religious Actors in Preventing and Resolving Conflict Worldwide. Conflict Resolution Forum, Washington D.C.Available at http://www.sfcg.org/Documents/CPRF/CPRFApril2001.pdf (last accessed February 22, 2012).

Crawley, Mike (2003): Two men create bridge over Nigeria's troubled waters. The Christian Science Monitor. Available at: http://www.csmonitor.com/2003/0228/p07s01-woaf.html (last accessed on October 3, 2006).

Ellis, Stephen and ter Haar, Gerrie (2005): Religion and Development in Africa. Background paper prepared for the Commission for Africa. Manuscript.

Fox, Jonathan (2008): A World Survey of Religion and the State. Cambridge University Press, Cambridge.

Fukuyama, Francis (1992): The end of history and the last man. Penguin, Harmondsworth.

Gopin, Marc (2000): Between Eden and Armageddon: The future of world religions, violence and peacemaking. Oxford University Press, New York and London.

Gopin, Marc (2005): World religions, violence, and myths of peace in international relations. In: ter Haar, Gerrie and Busutill, James (eds.): Bridge or Barrier. Religion, Violence and Visions for Peace. Brill, Leiden, 35-56.

Gunaratna, Rohan (2004): Defeating Al Qaeda – The pioneering vanguard of the Islamic movements. In: Howard, Russell and Sawyer, Reid (eds.): Defeating terrorism. Shaping the new security environment. McGraw-Hill/Dushkin, Guilford, 1-28.

Harsch, Ernest (2003): Africa builds its own peace forces. In: Africa Recovery 17:3, 1, 14-16, 18-20.

Haynes, Jeffrey (1995): Religion, fundamentalism and identity. A global perspective. Discussion paper no. 65. United Nations Research Institute for Social Development, Geneva.

Haynes, Jeffrey (1996): Religion and politics in Africa. Zed, London.

Haynes, Jeffrey (2003): Religious fundamentalism and politics. In: Ridgeon, Lloyd (ed.): Major religions of the world: Past, present and post-modern. Curzon, London, 321-375.

Haynes, Jeffrey (2005a): Al-Qaeda: ideology and action. In: Critical Review of International Social and Political Philosophy 8:2, 177-191.

Haynes, Jeffrey (2005b): Islamic militancy in East Africa. In: Third World Quarterly, 26:8, 1321-1339.

Haynes, Jeffrey (2005c): Comparative politics in a globalizing world. Polity, Cambridge.

Haynes, Jeffrey (2007a): Religion and development. Conflict or cooperation? Palgrave Macmillan, Basingstoke.

Haynes, Jeffrey (2007b): An introduction to international relations and religion. Pearson, London.

Holenstein, Anne-Marie (2005): Role and significance of religion and spirituality in development co-operation. A reflection and working paper. Swiss Agency for Development and Co-operation, Bern.

Holenstein, Anne-Marie (2006): Governmental donor agencies and faith-based organisations. Proceedings of the workshop: 'Religion, politics, conflict and humanitarian action. Faith-based organisations as political, humanitarian or religious actors', May 18–19, 2005. The Graduate Institute of International Studies, Geneva, 75-81.

Howard, Russell and Sawyer, Reid (eds.) (2004): Defeating terrorism. Shaping the new security environment. McGraw-Hill/Dushkin, Guilford.

Huntington, Samuel (1993): The clash of civilisations? In: Foreign Affairs 72:3, 22-49.

Huntington, Samuel (1996): The clash of civilizations. Simon and Schuster, New York.

Ibrahim, Jibrin (1991): Religion and political turbulence in Nigeria. In: Journal of Modern African Studies 29:1, 115-136.

Juergensmeyer, Mark (2000): Terror in the mind of God: The global rise of religious violence. University of California Press, Berkley.

Juergensmeyer, Mark (2005): Religion in the new global order. The Role of Religion in the New Global Order." In Rob Rieman, ed., Europe: A Beautiful Idea?

Nexus Institute, Netherland.

Kamrava, Mehran (1993): Politics and society in the third world. Routledge, London.

Korieh, Chima J. and Nwokeji, G. Ugo (eds.) (2005): Religion, history, and politics in Nigeria: Essays in Honor of Ogbu U. Kalu. University Press of America, Lanham.

Kukha, Matthew and Falola, Toyin (1995): Religious militancy and self-assertion: Islam and politics in Nigeria. Ashgate, Aldershot.

Küng, Hans (1986) Christianity and World Religions. Paths to Dialogue with Islam, Hinduism and Buddhism. Doubelday, New York.

Kurtz, Lester R. (1995): Gods in the Global Village. Pine Forge Press; Thousand Oaks, London, New Delhi.

Lane, Jan-Erik and Ersson, Svante (1994): Comparative politics. An introduction and new approach. Polity, Cambridge.

Maier, Karl (2002): This house has fallen: Nigeria in crisis. Penguin, Harmondsworth.

Malek, Cate (2004): Identity (inter-group) conflicts. The Conflict Resolution Information Service, University of Colorado. Available at: http://v 4.crinfo.org/CK_Essays/ck_identity_issues.jsp (last accessed on October 25, 2005).

Marty, Martin E. and Appleby, R. Scott (eds.) (1993): Fundamentalisms and society: Reclaiming the sciences, the family, and education. University of Chicago Press, Chicago.

Marty, Martin E. and Appleby, R. Scott (eds.) (1994): Fundamentalisms observed. University of Chicago Press, Chicago.

Marty, Martin E. and Appleby, R. Scott (eds.) (1995): Fundamentalisms comprehended. University of Chicago Press, Chicago.

McLeod, G. (2007): IN SIGHT: Profile in Political Courage. Cambodian Information Center. Available at: http://www.cambodia.org/blogs/editorials/2007/08/in-sight-profile-in-political-courage.html (last accessed on January 4, 2008).

Moix, Brigitte (n/d). Peace is Divine, Preach It. Mission statement. The Muslim-Christian Dialogue Forum, Kaduna, Nigeria

National Commission on Terrorist Attacks (2004): The 9/11 Commission report: Final report of the National Commission on terrorist attacks upon the United States. W. W. Norton and Company, New York.

Norris, Pippa and Inglehart, Ronald (2004) Sacred and Secular: Religion and Politics Worldwide. Cambridge University Press, Cambridge, UK.

Poethig, Kathryn (2002): Movable peace: Engaging the transnational in Cambodia's Dhammayietra. In: Journal for the Scientific Study of Religion 41:1, 19-28.

Rosen, David (2005): Religion, Identity and Mideast Peace. The 10th Annual Templeton Lecture on Religion and World Affairs. Available at: http://www.fpri.org/enotes/20050923.religion.rosen. religionidentitymideastpeace.html (last accessed on May 25, 2006).

Simonse, Simon (1998): Steps towards peace and reconciliation in Northern Uganda. An analysis of initiatives to end the armed conflict between the Government of Uganda and the Lord's Resistance Army, 1987-1998. Report of a consultancy commissioned by Pax Christi Netherlands.

Smock, David (2001): Faith-based NGOs and international peacebuilding. Special report no. 76, United States Institute of Peace. Available at: http://www.usip.org/pubs/specialreports/sr76.html (last accessed on February 4, 2006).

Smock, David (2004): Divine intervention: Regional reconciliation through faith. In: Religion, 25:4. Available at: http://www.global.ucsb.edu/orfaleacenter/luce/luce08/documents/Divine%20Inter-vention,%20Regional%20Reconciliation%20through%20faith--harvard%202004.pdf (last accessed on February 22, 2012).

Smock, David (ed.) (2006): Religious Contributions to Peacemaking. When religion brings peace, not war. United States Institute of Peace, Washington DC.

Stuart-Fox, Martin (2006). Buddhism and politics in Laos, Cambodia, Myanmar and Thailand. Paper presented at the Cambodia, Laos, Myanmar and Thailand Summer School, Asia Pacific Week 2006, Australian National University.

Tokatlian, Juan Gabriel (2006): The partition temptation: Iraq to Latin America. Open Democracy – Free Thinking for the World. Available at: http://www.opendemocracy.net/democracy-protest/ partition_temptation_4140.jsp (last accessed on December 13, 2006).

Wadlow, Rene (2007). Walking for peace in Cambodia. Available at: http://www.buddhistchannel.tv/index.php?id=6,3888,0,0,1,0 (last accessed on December 24, 2007).

Wuye, James and Ashafa, Muhammed (1999): The Pastor and the Imam: Responding to conflict. Ibrash Publications, Lagos.

Wuye, James and Ashafa, Muhammad (2005): The Pastor and the Imam. Nigeria: From rivalry to brotherhood. In: New Routes: A Journal of Peace Research and Action 10:4, 23-26.

Politics and Religious Diversity

Claus Leggewie

The significance and explosive nature of the issue of religion in global politics has re-emerged in recent years. During the long process of secularisation, the religious dimension seemed to have disappeared, particularly from international relations, which was also reflected in diplomatic training and policy advice – we had all become realists. And realists are primarily interested in disputes concerning territories, raw materials and minorities or, put in more general terms, economic interests and strategic objectives, even if religious elements were always conspicuous in regional conflicts, such as in Lebanon and Northern Ireland. The India-Pakistan conflict has been as religiously impregnated as that between the Tamils and the Singhalese, as has been the crisis in the Middle East; furthermore, religious antagonisms were also involved in the disintegration of Yugoslavia.

The assessment of the religious dimension changed at the end of the Cold War when the influential political scientist Samuel P. Huntington and others sensed that culture clashes and religious wars erupting across the globe would oust economic and strategic considerations. Religious currents, once renowned for their mitigating and peace-building efforts in the secular world of states, were now suspected of escalating and radicalising global conflicts. Two frequently overlooked features of religious practice play a role here: the absoluteness of the faith claim that makes conflicts appear indivisible, and the expansion of the time horizon by believers' typical expectation of the hereafter. Although religious militancy can lead to martyrdom on the one hand and altruism on the other, or from war to peacebuilding, both ultimately arise from the desire to devote oneself wholeheartedly to the Holy One, possibly sacrificing one's own life (and, in extreme cases, that of others) in the process.

What makes the pendulum swing in one direction or the other is evidently contingent upon the historical and social context. Furthermore, secularisation and sacralisation are by no means mutually exclusive; in fact, the two coexist. And this is precisely where the conflict potential could lie: the devout can feel as though they have their backs to the wall; the secular can be ridden with self-doubt, possibly even perceiving a kind of phantom pain when comparing their state with the staunchness demonstrated by those with religious faith.

After the Peace of Westphalia had depoliticised religion (see Küng in this volume) and the modern order of states became organised on the basis of the peaceful coexistence of religious denominations, now social movements are emerging as political religions again, "post-Westphalian" as it were, simultaneously against states, alongside states and with states. The fact that world religions emerged prior to the world of nation states is relevant here. The (Holy) Spirit, as well as money, is a cross-border medium and, just as businesses are the engines of global markets, religions can be engines of globalisation. Here, they have the advantage of being anchored in the local environment, whilst also being able to speak for humanity as a whole.

Just as the modern age did not disappear in the postmodern era, church-state relations also continue to exist in the post-Westphalian era. However, they are being loosened up by a deregulated 'religions market' in which conversion and mutual missionary work are the order of the day, and mainstream churches and parochial organisations face competition from a fashionable, flexible form of spirituality. A "hot" experience-based and often miracle-orientated search for God takes the place of "cold" theologically-scientifically based doctrine. Religious centres and areas are supplanted by multinational diaspora networks. Examples of this include the "Shiite renaissance" and the advance of Evangelical and charismatic currents in mainstream Protestantism in the United States, from where it extends into the Catholic, Muslim and Orthodox spheres of influence in Central and South America, West Africa and Eastern Central Europe.

Religious dimensions are consequently becoming discernible as the norm in international relations and even if they are not the primary trigger of international and multinational conflicts, they can no longer be viewed as secondary or even marginal, as they were in the Cold War era. At that time, two secular ideologies of the West stood face to face: liberalism and Marxism. The turning points were the proclamation of the Islamic Republic of Iran in April 1979 and the Soviet invasion of Afghanistan, destined to fail from the start, which anticipated the end of bipolarity. "Don't worry, America can't do a damn thing against us," proclaimed Ayatollah Khomeini, who also called the Soviet Union a devilish power and predicted it would perish in the Hindu Kush. Since then, the Intifada and the Palestinian regional war have become international, and terrorist groups now operate on the world stage in the name of religion.

The principle of separation, where people are organised into nation states, essentially affirmed by even Islamic republics – the primacy of the political over the religious – is radically contested by Jihad International (most notably Al Qaeda), which completely negates and circumvents the nation state model. The unworldliness of religious transcendence is radicalised in the foreign policy arena, where the salutary checks and balances of a political society are lacking and there is no *Leviathan* (in other words, a state monopoly on the use of force) to be feared. An anti-political triumph over *realpolitik* is called for here, and the battle zones of religious intolerance are the megacities of the Global South.

The violent enforcement of conflicts is fostered wherever a strong religious sense of unity is combined with exclusive ethnic identities; disintegration of the state, democratic shortcomings and bad governance increase the tendency for conflict, as does a region's geostrategic exposure. The accumulation of these factors suspends the ambivalence of the sacred; the potential for conflict mediation and peacebuilding from religious teachings and practices are invalidated and religious envoys promoting ecumenism and coexistence are discouraged.

Nevertheless, there are examples of how the peacebuilding role of religions can be effective on the international stage, such as the commitment of the Roman Catholic Community of Sant'Egidio and the Protestant Church in South Africa. Here, religious individuals, communities and organisations have promoted the creation and safeguarding of peaceful conditions in the event of political conflict. They were able to do so because church organisations act as advocates, mediators, observers and educators extending beyond ethnic groups and national frontiers, and promote international communication. Thus, they occasionally take the place of defunct and failed state structures; churches, mosques and temples lend themselves as neutral locations.

Secular peace activists also use the resources and reputations of religious organisations which, in turn, can draw on the continued high degree of dedication of their members. Examples can be found in virtually all of the large religious communities, primarily in Christian ecumenical churches, but also amongst Buddhists and interdenominational groups. In concrete terms, they are involved in the preparation, establishment and supervision of ceasefire and peace agreements, in establishing democratic structures in transformation societies and in arranging methods for investigating crimes against the state and genocides both in and out of court. As international non-governmental organisations, national and international churches and religious groups are intervening in the diplomatic process in an increasingly professional manner.

It is, then, no coincidence that they engage in fields and with agendas in which national and conventional international policy has been inadequate: in the North-South conflict between rich and poor, in global environmental and climate protection, and in the protection of human rights and minorities. It is also no coincidence that the values base organisations give to foreign policy is frequently of a religious clerical provenance. This also remains recognisable in completely secularised settings, such as the United Nations.

Under such circumstances, religious *ancillary foreign policy* is therefore certainly desirable. The fact that the associated moralisation of politics is beset with problems is, of course, demonstrated by the influence of evangelists on United States foreign policy. This led to the radicalisation of the already Manichean move to fight *evil em-*

pires after 2001, and conditioned development aid, the fight against AIDS and human rights policy in a Christian manner. Middle East policy – where Christian Zionism is probably more influential than the Jewish lobby – was particularly affected by this.

With this in mind, it is all the more remarkable that the German head of state openly speaks up on behalf of Christians in Turkey. Considering the ambivalence of faith-based policy in the USA, which is responsible to a large extent for the transatlantic alienation, and the interest-led Confucianism in China's global policy that denies freedom of religion in the interior of the country, there is no reason why this moderation of religious claims should be renounced, even if the exceptional historical position of Europe should come to the fore even more clearly. Western democracies had good reason for deciding that their policies should no longer be enlightened by divine revelation. Although their constitutional norms may spring from certain traditions, such as Christian-Jewish roots, they do not blend with these roots to such an extent that they can be used in cultural battle against other traditions.

How to defuse internal social religious conflicts

Global pluralism also changes the religious landscape in the interior of Western immigration societies, which become multi-religious and, in this respect, "Americanised". This brings with it a stricter separation of the state and religion, along with a more uninhibited presence of many religions in the public realm, the erosion of religious oligopolies in favour of a horizontal, more sectarian than church-like coexistence of religious communities, greater popular piety, more intensive and subjective religious practice and politicised religious lobbies involved in domestic and foreign policy.

In particular, the islamisation of the Arab-Islamic diaspora in Europe challenges the established relationship between the State and the Church, if Muslims wish to codify the power relationship within the family, in education and sexuality (just like the Jehovah's Witnesses) to their religious perspective. Claims and forms of religious instruction and training of theologians do not fit in well with laicist secularism or church constitutional law arrangements; at present, they amount to Islam becoming a church-like institution or to a general privatisation of religious instruction.

Of late, the fiercest and most controversial cause of national populist unrest has been sparked by the construction of representative mosques. Minarets and cupolas signify decades of immigration history – and their failures; they demonstrate the presence and self-confidence of Muslim immigration in Europe: those who build intend to stay. Hence self-images of the majority and, equally, public images of the Islamic minority are changing; the issues under debate are the position of Muslims in German society and the significance mainstream society wishes to accord it.

Two fronts are involved here: those who keep a cool head with regard to the currently rampant fear of Islam and those who want to foster a European secular Islam. The first front is for Article 4 of the German Basic Law, which guarantees the freedom of faith and the undisturbed practice of religion, to which German Muslims emphatically refer. It should be noted that Article 4 does not indicate that anyone is allowed to build anything anywhere. A modern European religious condition requires all mosque builders, all city and municipal administrations, all mayors and all local residents become involved in shaping the urban or rural environment, i.e. in urban planning. A mosque must, in its widest sense, "fit into the broad picture."

Conflicts involving the construction of mosques are actually conflicts of recognition. Such conflicts – and this is the crux of religious sentiment and convictions – appear to be indivisible, often making them unresolvable. With such conflicts, it is not a matter of seeking compromise, based perhaps on material compensation for disadvantaged building projects, but of the extremism of an unbending conviction that turns particularly aggressive when neither side has any escape route. Conflicts appear to be insurmountable when there is not only disagreement in the matter – which is commonplace in religious disputes, particularly in pluralist communities, and of central importance to the ability of modern societies to develop – but also when opponents cannot even agree on the mediation process because they categorically reject the opposing position and would prefer, literally at times, to see them eradicated.

Unless one wishes to maintain this polarisation, possibly having to succumb to dire consequences – there have already been arson attacks on mosques in the Netherlands, Austria and Germany following verbal attacks – endeavours must be made to transform indivisible conflicts into divisible ones, i.e. to change the "either – or" into a "more or less." The 'ill wind' behind conflicts involving the construction of mosques could consequently be that, ultimately, coping with them successfully contributes more to social integration than the superficial consensus of interreligious dialogue or countless open days. "Integration by conflict" is the admittedly difficult message behind modern sociology, tested on urban complexity, where cross-cultural conflicts are the normality, and cross-cultural relationships do not merely start with the immigration of other religions. Each peacefully settled and successfully resolved conflict further progresses society as a whole.

This message is difficult because it demands a lot from all those involved. Muslims claim freedom of religion – for this they do not only have to accept secularisation and religious pluralism in diaspora and from there in the core Islamic countries, but also to learn that this can cause a gain for their own (religious) convictions. At this point starts the "second front," In light of the terrorist attacks and honour killings committed by Islamists in the name of Islam, and in view of the racism rampant amongst young people, Muslims are well advised to not only distance themselves rhetorically from religiously motivated violence and discrimination ("That has nothing to do with Islam!"), but also to conduct a self-inspection of those elements in Islam that need reviewing, just like the earlier irreconcilability of Christianity and Judaism with the modern age. These include the disregard for women's and gay rights, the dogmatism of a literal text interpretation, insistence on a religious monopoly and the rejection of freedom of speech and artistic expression.

However, the current climate of opinion confirms an unholy alliance between Islamic fundamentalists and critics of Islam, both of whom claim to know the "true Islam", by which they allege that Islam as such cannot be reformed and cannot *per se* be incorporated into Western secular societies. Such a perception is paranoiac to the extent that it implies Islam as a whole has paranoid traits.

Designs play an importance role here. In order to promote harmonious relations within the community, the height of the minaret could be reduced, i.e. the architecture and planning permission can be adapted to the prevailing circumstances and compromises could be struck by, perhaps, refraining from broadcasting the call of the muezzin over loudspeakers. These are examples of building bridges so that it is no longer a matter of "do or die," but literally a matter concerning metres, decibels and the number of parking spaces available. As the example of the Islamic Forum in Penzberg shows, architecture plays an important role: not only should it make the owners feel comfortable, it should also contribute towards the understanding and modernisation of society. To enable the "all or nothing" of a religiously overloaded territorial conflict to actually be converted into a modest gain for all, neutral instances are then also required that civilise the contextual disagreement of the "struggle of faith" by shaping it. "Shape" is given not only through architectural designs, but also through legislation, political compromise and cross-cultural mediation. Such mediation promotes empathy and removes radicalisation.

Outlook

The question was where political-religious disagreements are heading within national and global frameworks. Are they a source of cooperation in managing urgent future problems or do they contribute to the violent destruction of future foundations? It would be a huge step forward if interreligious dialogue (including agnostics, sceptics and atheists) was based on "the actual matters in hand" rather than on political-religious dogmas. Technical and medical progress has raised pivotal questions of life and death about which religious communities are expected to form opinions. Furthermore, the dramatic decline of biological diversity and climate change puts pressure on religions to "uphold the integrity of creation."

On the other hand, there could be further progress if religions were to return to their "core business" after a phase of overpoliticisation, in other words, if they primarily facilitated experiences of religious immersion and transcendency. At the same time, today, faith is a matter of individual choice. Just as the existence of atheists or agnostics was improbable three hundred years ago, the balance has now shifted so that in the West it is now more likely to be the default that someone who believes in a God (or several gods), has to justify their position. "I don't believe in God" is the standard phrase, and those who believe have to explain whether he or she is of sound mind. When dealing with an experience of death, the writer Julian Barnes said "I don't believe in God, but I miss him," and this example shows that the individual, buffered against transcendency, also has questions that need answering. Religion has always tried to seek answers from experiences of suffering, evil and mysteriousness, thus it was a "place of fulfilment" (Charles Taylor).

Finally, this allows the acceptance of religious identity as just one of a number of possible identities, in addition to public and private existence as a citizen, family member, neighbour and follower of any number of pastimes and interests. Religious people would take themselves more seriously if they no longer had to take religion so seriously. If people are not only different in terms of religion, and are permitted to be so, and of course also in every other respect, then multicultural societies are about such group affiliations which may be left to one's own free will. The core of multiculturalism understood along these lines is thus individual self-determination. Such claims can be found in all cultures and religions, which is why the West must "change its cultural spots" and renounce the associated claims to hegemony.

III.
Religions as Peacemakers?
Perspectives from Theology and Religious Studies

Resources for Peacebuilding in the Jewish Political Tradition

Ben Mollov

This paper will offer an overview of resources for peacebuilding based on the Jewish political tradition with emphasis on the modern period. Although explicit contributions to peacebuilding from a religious perspective in general and Judaism in particular are a relatively modern endeavor, biblical and Talmudic insights aiming at promoting conflict management and peacebuilding will serve as the point of departure of this paper. Important interpreters of this tradition have identified numerous biblical examples of peacebuilding emphasizing the promotion of empathy along with pragmatic approaches to managing conflict. Also the Jewish role in serving as a mediating force in world affairs from its biblical foundations will also be addressed.

To be sure, as all of the monotheistic religions carry the potential for promoting both peace and violence, exclusivism or inclusivism, Judaism is no different. Thus any discussion of resources emanating from the Jewish political tradition must also include reference to exclusionary trends. Given the fact though that the same biblical passages often can and have been interpreted by Jewish sages in different ways which reflect either moderation/reconciliation or conflict between parties, a clear "ambivalence of the sacred" exists in the Jewish tradition.

This being said, a major focus of this paper will be on resources emanating from the Jewish political tradition and experience in the modern period as articulated by several prominent thinkers: Daniel J. Elazar, Martin Buber and Hans J. Morgenthau.

The study of religion and peacebuilding, along with the emerging field of conflict management, is a relatively recent endeavor. Important landmark works such as "The Ambivalence of the Sacred" (Appleby 2000) and "Between Eden and Armageddon: The Future of World Religions, Violence, and Peacemaking" (Gopin 2000), have focused our attention on the capacities of religions to both facilitate peacebuilding while also fostering militancy in the name of the absolute truth. Additional works, such as Johnston and Sampson (1994) and Fox and Sandler (2004), have pointed to the emerging importance of the religious factor in statecraft and international relations as a whole. Samuel Huntington (1993, 1996), focusing on the paradigm of inter-civilizational conflict in the wake of the cessation of the Cold War, offers a central framework for appreciating the contours of emerging cultural conflict between civilizational units, often rooted in religious identity and worldview as a central axis of international conflict today. He also refers to the need for civilizations to find common ground between them as a means of moderating conflict (Huntington 1996:320).

Against this background, this paper will address: (1) Aspects of militant tendencies within Judaism; (2) resources for peacebuilding within the earlier and modern Jewish political tradition with emphasis on the contribution of several important thinkers highly relevant to this endeavor, partly connected to the German-Jewish heritage; and (3),this paper will also offer some insights concerning the deeper dynamics of the Arab-Israeli conflict, with emphasis on its inter-civilizational/cultural dimension, and connect efforts to navigate this conflict towards more peaceful avenues, based on the contribution of the thinkers and efforts of some contemporary Jewish Israeli actors on the ground whose work will be explored.

Exclusive vs. Inclusive Tendencies within the Biblical and Rabbinic Traditions

This section is not meant to serve as an exhaustive description or analysis of exclusive and inclusive tendencies within the fundamental Biblical and Talmudic periods of the Jewish tradition, but to point to some specific tendencies and examples which can promote either conflict or peacebuilding.

Two themes reflecting the "ambivalence of the sacred", as expressed in both Jewish tradition and experience, refer to the perceived intentions of the "outside world" concerning the Jewish people and their attitude towards non-Jews which can reflect either "exclusive" or "inclusive" tendencies. These tendencies, often accompanied by opposing trends, such as militancy and moderation, are expressed in various periods of Jewish history, in biblical text and among rabbinic interpreters of sacred texts. In the following analysis a number of the more militant expressions will be cited, followed by more moderate approaches that can be a basis for advancing peacebuilding.

In the book of Exodus (15:3) God is described as a "man of war" when, following generations of slavery he brings about the drowning of Pharaoh's Army while freeing the Children of Israel. This victory of mammoth proportions is celebrated in the "song of Moses and Miriam" in the Hebrew Bible (Exodus 15:1-21). It has further been observed that at some points in their earlier biblical history the Jews "were commanded by God to annihilate their enemies in wars of conquest and vengeance" (David and Rosenak 2007:46). Such commands are reflected in biblical verses as those found in Numbers 31, Deuteronomy 20, Joshua 8-12 and I Samuel 15. In a struggle between good and evil, Judaism's message of God's sovereignty over the earth will often accompany the redemption of the Israelites, the Lord's people, from their oppression at the hands of other enemy nations.

However, the championing of the cause of the Jews is certainly not the only or even predominant motif in biblical text. If verses, such as those referred to above, express exclusivist and militant views, they are balanced by other passages which severely temper and even condemn any resort to war, violence and bloodshed; and advocate the adoption of peacebuilding. An important example is the divine command denying King David, a seminal and heroic personality in biblical/Jewish history, the privilege of building the sacred Holy Temple in Jerusalem on the basis of his being a warrior, albeit he only engaged in necessary conflict (Heschel, 1962:61). The honor of building this sacred structure, ordained to be a "house of the Lord", was given to David's son, Solomon, whose mission was to be that of a reconciler. This central venue ultimately serving as a "house of prayer for all nations" in which "enmity between nations will turn to friendship" is perhaps the most significant Jewish interpretation (Heschel 1962:186). While many biblical verses express this aim it is recited repeatedly in the liturgy of Yom Kippur as the most sacred day in the Jewish calendar (Heschel 1962:186).

Furthermore Isaiah's powerful vision is that of a world in which "nation shall not lift up sword against nation nor shall they learn war any more" (Isaiah 2:4). This is to be part of a process in which the nations ascend to Jerusalem, which is ultimately deemed to be the "city of peace". In the Jewish view nations are to accept certain basic human values, rooted in the ethics of divine law, but not required in any way to accept the specific Jewish religion. Thus a kind of "particularist universalism" characterizes the ideal Jewish self-image in which the Jews are called upon to a "Nation of Priests and a Holy People" (Exodus 19:6). According to the important rabbinic Jewish commentator, the "*Sforno*", who lived during Renaissance Italy, the meaning of this injunction is that the Jews are to serve "as an example and inspiration to mankind". Thus an inherent pluralism and "acceptance of the other" exists within the Jewish tradition, with the Jewish people called upon to act as ethical examples and teachers of mankind.

Considerations about the attitudes towards non-Jews continued to be a feature of post-biblical Talmudic and rabbinic discussion: Based on ambivalent wording in the issue of the status of non-Jews, concerning the law of torts for instance, has been treated in different ways by different rabbinical authorities and the law of torts. Time and context also matter as discriminatory attitudes in many religious cultures were not uncommon. However, there is clear evidence that many rabbinical authorities expressed positions supporting the equality of peoples and the possibilities of ultimate reconciliation between the Jewish people and those who have made them their enemies based on an analogy of biblical text and commentary such as the conflict between Jacob and Esau. Further description of such examples has already appeared elsewhere (Mollov et al. 2007; Zohar 2003).

Conflict Management from a Jewish and Inter-religious Perspective

In recent years, in the wake of escalating inter-ethnic and inter-religious conflicts throughout the world important scholarly work has appeared which has highlighted the role that religion can play in seeking to moderate conflict, as opposed to being solely a source for conflict exacerbation. Much of this work emanated originally from

Christian sources. Resources and outlooks from the Christian tradition culled from the Christian tradition emphasizing love and forgiveness have been significantly explored (Appleby 2000; Lederach 1997).

The effort to tap resources within the Jewish religious and political tradition is a relatively new endeavor and essentially a "work in progress." A foundation for these efforts have emanated from explorations of the Jewish political tradition, particularly those of Daniel J. Elazar who was a pioneering figure in this field (Elazar, 1981a, 1981b). Within this context newer efforts to develop particularly Jewish approaches to conflict management have been fostered (Gopin 2000; Mollov and Steinberg 2007; and Steinberg 2000, 2008)

Mark Gopin (2000), for instance has sought to emphasize resources in the Jewish tradition particularly during the Biblical period. He has called our strong attention for instance to prototypical figures such as Aharon the Priest who unrelentingly pursued the cause of peace. Gerald Steinberg has explored rich resources within the Biblical and Rabbinical periods and has suggested that the Jewish tradition expresses a "realist" view of conflict and approaches to conflict management emphasizing the importance of compromise balancing the requirements of justice and peace (Steinberg and Mollov 2007). And efforts have been made to cull rabbinic approaches to conflict management on many levels from those of the family to tribal to intra-communal (Steinberg 2008).

The Challenge of Jewish Sovereignty and Conflict Management

However this task has become more urgent currently as the Jewish people have been challenged to develop more unique strategies that can be advanced from the foundation of a sovereign Jewish state.

The renewal of Jewish sovereignty in the Land of Israel, beginning in 1948, represents a watershed in Jewish history essentially since biblical times. During the approximately 2.000 years of Jewish exile and dispersion, Jews frequently were the object of discrimination and persecution in their host countries. There were alternately periods of both hostility and hospitality. Yet, the Nazi holocaust was the ultimate disaster which had engulfed the Jewish people and which still is a powerful element in the Jewish people's collective identity affecting its perception of the world.

Beginning prior to the Holocaust, the modern Zionist movement which emerged in the 19th century sought to return a lost dignity to the Jewish people as they returned to the Land of the Bible, to which their spiritual and even physical link was never severed throughout the generations. With the establishment of the State of Israel, the Jews became an active collective actor in civilization and international politics. One of the challenges of modern Jewish life is to assure the survival of the State of Israel while attempting to contribute its share to the advancement of mankind and particularly to the cause of peacebuilding (Hertzberg 1997; Landau 2003). This endeavor is deeply predicated on uncovering and further developing the Jewish political tradition. As part of this effort the Jewish people and the State of Israel are challenged to rediscover rich resources in the Jewish heritage which can be the basis of conflict management and peacebuilding.

The next section of the paper – focusing on the modern period – will seek to link some insights emanating from the field of the Jewish political tradition to the emerging field of conflict management as religious communities and completely different civilizations seek to develop relevant tools to "engage" with the "other". The following section will focus on three important thinkers and theorists from different cultural milieus and historic periods in the modern era who were influenced by the Jewish experience and heritage and who are considered part of the Jewish political tradition. Their contributions for developing approaches towards the "other", in the framework of the larger attempt to develop tools within the Jewish political tradition for navigating conflict and developing approaches towards peacebuilding, will be explored. Prior to focusing on these three thinkers, a short background on the development of the Jewish political tradition and newer work on conflict management from a Jewish perspective will be presented.

Background of the Jewish Political Tradition

Approximately throughout the last three decades the field of the Jewish political tradition was pioneered by the late Daniel J. Elazar (Elazar 1981a; Elazar and Cohen 1985). A variety of foci emerged out of the sub-discipline integrating political studies, Jewish philosophy and history as well as other relevant disciplines. Areas of research included the Jewish approach to the ideal government, dynamics of governance in Jewish communities throughout Jewish history and even approaches to Jewish foreign policy. The latter theme has been brought to light as part of an on-going effort by Shmuel Sandler (Sandler 1987, 2007). In addition, the Jewish political tradition has been integrated with the emerging field of conflict management which has yielded scholarly work on Jewish approaches to peacebuilding (Steinberg 2000; Steinberg and Mollov 2007).

Framework and Overview

As noted, this exploration of the Jewish political tradition and its relevance for conflict management will focus on three modern personalities influenced by the Jewish heritage and experience, particularly on how it relates to approaches of managing and/or transforming conflict with reference to the Jewish people and outside actors. Following a brief overview, there will be a focus on each thinker in greater depth, both in terms of their message and background. As a result of this analysis additional resources within the modern Jewish political tradition relevant to conflict management will be identified. Each thinker represents diverse approaches towards the "other" and the exploration of their messages may be of use in the task of further developing resources within the Jewish political tradition relevant to conflict management in general and in particular to the effort of managing conflict between cultures and civilizations.

The three personalities are: (1) Daniel J. Elazar who was a pioneer in the area of federalism and the Jewish political tradition. He articulated the essence of federalism (which he argued was based on the Jewish idea of "Brit" or covenant) in emphasizing social partnership and interaction rather than an agreement on definitions. Elazar was an American born Sephardic Jew who was deeply influenced by the Jewish and American experiences and later in life took up residence in Israel; (2) Martin Buber a product of the German-Jewish heritage, who fled Nazism and also took up residence in Israel championed the belief in dialogue and human transformation. As a powerful champion of the "I-Thou" dialogue he influenced statesmen and scholars with a particular approach to dialogue rooted in the dynamics of Judaism. His philosophy reflecting the possibilities of social partnership can also be a reflection of federalist thinking as articulated by Elazar; and (3) Hans J. Morgenthau who was a German-Jewish refugee to the United States following the rise of Nazism and as the prime theoretician of the discipline of international relations became the foremost exponent of the realist school of international relations, influenced by the lessons of the Holocaust but tempered by the normative political values of the German-Jewish heritage.

Daniel J. Elazar

Daniel J. Elazar (1934-1999) saw the Jewish political tradition and the area of federalism as intrinsically related (Mollov 2009). His background reflected a unique combination of the Jewish Sephardic heritage,[1] the American and later the Israeli experience.[2] Born in the Midwestern United States, with family roots in pre-Israel Palestine, he deeply absorbed both the American and Jewish experiences and values (Mollov 2009). Indeed he believed, along with other Jewish thinkers, that the federalist traditions of the United States had their roots in the Hebrew Bible. While Elazar did not articulate clear assumptions about the nature of the "other", his life's work focused

1 Jews who originated in Asia and the Balkans as opposed to Europe.
2 Elazar was a study in contrasts reflecting an integration of the American, Jewish, Sephardic and to a degree the Israeli experience coming to live in Israel as he did in 1973.

on federalism and the Jewish political tradition whose essence he saw in advancing means of social partnership and workable relationships between groups. Thereby Elazar sought to develop pragmatic tools and approaches for "encountering the other" and finding means in political life to regulate diverse identities and views.

He argued that federalism and the Jewish political tradition were inherently linked through the concept of "Brit" or covenant and asserted:

> "Before its political character had become clear [federalism] had emerged as a theological concept used to define the proper relationship between God and man. The federal theology saw God and man linked by covenant in lasting yet limited union, in a partnership designed to make both partners jointly responsible for the world's welfare while preserving their respective integrities" (Elazar 1971:4).

Elazar's primary message was that the Jewish political tradition emphasized the possibilities of "diversity within unity. He further asserted that the concept of "Brit"/ covenant central to the Jewish political tradition since biblical to modern times "is of great importance because of what it offers in the way of building relationships. The Bible develops a whole system of relationships based upon covenants, beginning with the covenants between God and mankind, which serve as initial political acts" (Elazar 1981b: 9).

In a further expansion of this theme – Elazar presented an illuminating paper presenting a macro-vision for the Jewish world in the new setting of the global village. Anchored in the idea of "Brit" and mutual responsibility, Elazar called for an integration of Jewish civic capabilities, a renewal of Jewish spiritual values and a re-affirmation of Jewish covenantal ties as a core basis of survival. Starting from the idea of "arevut", or mutual responsibility, Elazar extended the motivating spirit of covenant linking the Jewish people to "other peoples of kindred spirit" (Elazar 1996).

In emphasizing the possibilities of "diversity within unity" and mutual responsibility rooted in the Jewish political tradition Elazar's message can serve as an important animating theme in helping to develop bridges between cultures.

Martin Buber

Martin Buber (1878-1965) was a figure of international stature known for his philosophy of dialogue, and as Morgenthau, he was an eminent product of the German-Jewish heritage. Although born a generation earlier than Morgenthau, he was influenced greatly by the German-Jewish enlightenment affecting his worldview as a Jew in affirming a belief in progress and the possibilities for achieving understanding between peoples. However, he fled from Nazi Germany, too, and took up residence in the pre-state of Israel Palestine in 1938.

Although not a formally observant Jew, Buber was steeped in the Jewish sources and literature and became a major interpreter of the legacy and heritage of Hasidism in the Western world. This Jewish religious movement swept Eastern Europe in the 18th and 19th century and emphasized the joyful communion with God and performance of his commandments as a means of achieving unity and redemption (Steinberg and Mollov 2007).

The most well-known contribution of Buber is his classic work "I and Thou" which according to one scholar has been termed a "great statement of Jewish faith" (Buber 1970:35). The essence of Buber's message is that "all living is meeting" and that man meets the world on two levels: "I-It" and "I-Thou". "I-It" is a utilitarian interaction (not necessarily exploitative) – and constitutes the level that most societal and human interactions take place in. Nonetheless, at times man is also capable of engaging his fellow beings on the level of "I-Thou" in which humans can encounter and perceive each other in the "fullness of their common humanity". In such rare but lofty cases, according to Buber, the "eternal Thou" or the presence of God is also revealing itself. Thus human beings and even groups can attain an elevated transcendent character when true encounter and dialogue occurs (Buber 1970).

In the early part of his career Buber was active in the nascent Zionist movement and throughout his life and career he emphasized the humanistic elements and strivings which he considered to be at the core of the Jewish renewal in the Land of Israel. In no way confined to strictly academic pursuits Buber sought to reach out in dialogue to diverse groups in pursuit of peace and understanding. He was most active in furthering inter-religious understanding and was dedicated to achieving understanding between Jews and Arabs throughout his lifetime.

Based on the power of dialogue and its possibilities for human transformation he applied his philosophy to an array of international issues from the Arab-Jewish conflict in Palestine to Cold War relations between the superpowers, and thereby attracted the attention of international statesmen such as former UN Secretary-General Dag Hammarskjöld (Mollov et al. 2007).

Based on Jewish thinking, Buber reminds us that we all share a common link as creations in the divine image and that we can encounter the "other" in a manner which transcends political and social conflict. Indeed, since he believed in human transformation through the process of genuine dialogue, his approach is highly germane to the efforts to bridge inter-civilizational conflict and promote dialogue between civilizations.

Hans J. Morgenthau

Hans J. Morgenthau (1904-1980) was a seminal theoretician of the modern discipline of international relations and probably the foremost expositor of the realist approach to international relations. As a Jewish refugee from Nazi Germany, his own biography reflects the disillusionment which German Jewry, earlier nurtured by the hopes of the German-Jewish enlightenment. Initially growing up as part of the only Jewish family in Coburg in Southern Bavaria, he held idealist tendencies which were crushed by the virulent anti-Semitism, including the rise of Nazi movement which he was exposed to. This provided the background for his development of a realist perspective which affected him both personally and in terms of an academic and political worldview (Mollov 2002).

Morgenthau left Germany in 1935 and arrived in the United States in 1937. He then became a pioneer figure in the development of the discipline of international relations in general and the school of realism in particular. He advanced a particular form of "liberal realism" which combined harsh assumptions about the conflictual nature of the political world and the centrality of power along with the belief in the need to bring about change and take stands on political and public issues based on certain essential values. The Jewish experience and heritage influenced both these elements of his thinking, as was his political activism in both Jewish and general causes. Indeed, both the German-Jewish heritage of "Bildung" (character education) as well as the Jewish prophetic heritage was reflected in his commitment to public service along with his academic pursuits (Mollov 2002).

His seminal book "Politics Among Nations" (Morgenthau 1967) served as a guidebook for effective diplomacy in managing conflict. Both Morgenthau's early experiences in Germany and later political messages reflected the need to contain and counter threats, as well as to raise awareness of the danger which the "other" could pose to international actors in general and to Israel and the Jewish people in particular (Mollov 2002).

The basic message of political realism which he articulated in "Politics Among Nations"[3] which was preceded by "Scientific Man vs. Power Politics" (Morgenthau 1946) was that the world was conflictual in nature and tragedy, and thus an inescapable characteristic of political and social life. He asserted that power is the central currency of international politics and that imperialist or expansionist power can only be met and restrained by superior power.

During much of his extraordinarily successful academic career in the US, Morgenthau was significantly involved in Jewish affairs, particularly that of Israel and Soviet Jewry. He also surprised many with his ardent opposition to the war in Vietnam claim-

3 First edition of 1948.

ing that the war represented a misuse of power and at its worst was a betrayal of the American moral heritage. He called upon academic intellectuals to take principled stands on the pressing challenges faced by society and linked this expectation to the legacy of the Hebrew prophets (Mollov 2002).

Thus we see Morgenthau's continuing realist approach relating to the social world and particularly the lessons which the Jewish people have absorbed; however these are tempered by liberal values which Morgenthau exhibited in a number of contexts particularly the struggle for Soviet Jewry, Israel's struggle for survival, and his vigorous opposition to the War in Vietnam (Mollov 2002).

In sum, at the core of political realism as articulated by Morgenthau, lies the need to restrain the power of a potential adversary and/or maintain viable balances of power among different international actors to maintain national survival and international stability (Morgenthau, 1967). Such a message is also most relevant to a world in which very real threats still exist.

As part of this paper we will now address aspects of the Arab-Israeli conflict in the larger context of inter-civilizational conflict and efforts to ameliorate it.

An Inter-religious, Intercultural Approach to the Arab-Israeli Conflict

When discussing foreign policy elements of the world's Jewish polity, researcher Scott Lasensky contends similarly to Sandler, that the application of the Jewish political tradition "is also highly relevant for the field of conflict resolution and for experts on Arab-Israeli relations" (Lasensky 2005:4). He further suggests that the exploration of this field could be very relevant for developing approaches to preventing a civilizational divide with the Muslim world: "A Jewish grand strategy with respect to Islam and Islamic organizations is therefore urgently needed" (Lasensky 2005:4).

The point of departure of this analysis is the contention that the Arab-Israeli conflict is fundamentally a clash of two parallel civilizations, the Jewish and the Islamic, which sought to renew themselves in response to their particular circumstances in the 19th century on the model and inspiration of an earlier "heroic period" in their histories (Garfinkle 1991; Tessler 2009).

In the Jewish case, the harbingers of the early Jewish Zionist movement, who emerged for the most part from 19th century Russia, protested against their historic persecution in the diaspora. They dreamed of renewing their earlier "heroic period" of the Bible in the Land of Israel. As part of this project, for instance, the Hebrew language was revived and pioneers, inspired by age-old longings of a return to Zion, began the daunting task of immigrating to the Land of Israel to build new and novel institutions.

In the Muslim case, an historic process took place in the 19th century as well. An Arab awakening occurred recalling the former Arab-Islamic empire and its advanced civilization, which arrived at its peak between the 7th and 10th century. The memory of this heroic era inspired the Arab people to seek independence from Turkish rule and from the experience of humiliation from European powers (Antonius 1946).

These two powerful movements, each motivated by their respective narratives, ultimately rooted in religious identity, collided in the 20th century with the focal point of conflict being the Land of Israel/Palestine. Subsequent powerful political, demographic, and global dynamics intertwined with the fundamental clash over conflicting narratives and the respective claims on the Holy Land.[4]

Although there seems to be an insurmountable gap between the parties to the conflict, research and field work has reported on highly innovative approaches to bridge this conflict by means of inter-religious dialogue (Mollov and Lavie 2001; Mollov et al. 2007). Such dialogue has focused on the similarities between Islam and Judaism in terms of practice and structure and served to humanize "the other". Furthermore it has been a means of touching upon the core issues of the conflict in terms of the parties' connection and claim on the same land. Ideally the more elevated and inclusive elements of each religion can be a means of finding transcendent points of contact between the two religiously motivated civilizations (Mollov 2006, 2010).

Indeed a number of important "track two" actors in Israel have found means of advancing small but promising examples of inter-religious dialogue between Israelis and Palestinians. For instance pioneering and consistent work over approximately ten years by the Interfaith Encounter Association based in Israel, has brought together hundreds of Israelis and Palestinians for inter-religious dialogue in which common ground has been found in commonalities between elements of Jewish and Islamic tradition. Other efforts involving dialogue between Jewish and Arab religious educators have also advanced opportunities for relationship building, which is an important means for peace building (Lederach 1997; Saunders 1999). Documentation and analysis of these and other efforts have appeared in the literature emphasizing the important and insufficiently understood contribution of inter-religious dialogue in bridging the Israeli-Palestinian divide (Mollov and Lavie 2001; Stolov 2009;-added Yarden 2009). Furthermore such approaches duplicated on the larger macro level can serve as a new paradigm for "religious diplomacy" in which religious actors engage with each other and core issues of identity and attachment to the same land by both Jews and Arabs can be addressed in a constructive manner (Mollov 2010; Tange 2010). Indeed such efforts exemplify an "inclusive" religious approach as opposed to more militant exclusive approaches, which can serve as a barrier to peacebuilding.

In addition, from a Jewish point of view some innovative approaches to explore how the Temple Mount in Jerusalem could be shared by both Judaism and Islam have emerged. One initiative known as the "God's Holy Mountain" has offered suggestions

4 Furthermore it should be remembered that the earlier "heroic eras" of both Judaism and Islam took place in the absence of the "other".

how the "holy space" might be shared and perhaps ultimately how to realize the Prophetic ideal of the Temple Mount serving as a "house of prayer for all peoples" in the spirit of Isaiah's prophecy.[5]

Conclusion: The Relevance of the Jewish Political Tradition for the Management of Contemporary Conflict

This paper has sought to offer an overview of some of the resources for peacebuilding based on the Jewish political tradition. As noted earlier, the rediscovery and application of the rich Jewish political tradition is a fairly recent endeavor developing generally in parallel to the renaissance of Jewish statehood and the opportunity it holds for the Jewish people to engage as a vital actor in world affairs. While the task of Israel's survival is still an on-going concern for the Jewish people, rich resources can be called up to further the understanding between civilizations in general and to provide innovative means to address the Arab-Israeli conflict in particular.

Beginning from biblical sources reflecting exclusive/militant approaches versus inclusive/peacebuilding approaches in line with insights concerning the "ambivalence of the sacred" (Appleby 2000), there has been emphasis on some of the more modern resources for the task of conflict management. The three thinkers presented above, Daniel J. Elazar, Martin Buber and Hans J. Morgenthau, offer diverse messages, which in combination provide a rich array of powerful tools to advance the task of conflict management in the contemporary era. The vital work of Elazar provides a framework for appreciating the importance of the Jewish political tradition with its central emphasis on the concept and ethos of "Brit" or covenant. The idea is constructed around the dynamic of social partnership involving both man and man and man and God. Rooted in the Hebrew Bible and Jewish history as a whole it allows for "diversity within unity" which is a vital resource for managing the challenge of inter-civilizational conflict. Martin Buber's, seminal work in dialogue based on the I-Thou relationship has important implications for promoting international and inter-civilizational understanding – also in the Middle East – which might be effectively integrated with Morgenthau's realist insights. Indeed, the attempt of such integration has appeared elsewhere (Mollov et al. 2007).

Hans J. Morgenthau emphasized power as a means of survival in a dangerous world, particularly for Israel and the Jewish people, but maintained that power must also be accompanied by a moral awareness, which was partly an expression of the Jewish moral heritage. Power must be used responsibly, but real and objective dangers exist in the clash of civilizations and sometimes hurting stalemates and necessary balances

5 See God's Holy Mountain Website: http://www.godsholymountain.com/English.

of power are a precondition for other means of bridging these divides. Indeed, in the case of the Arab-Israeli conflict "hurting stalemates" reflecting keen balances of power have served as the background for diplomatic initiatives and peace agreements.

Another highly significant thinker, Jonathan Sacks, an important contemporary Jewish rabbinical voice, has articulated a responsible vision for promoting inter-civilizational understanding with both its dangers and opportunities from a uniquely Jewish core. With relevance for the Abrahamic faiths he seeks to find common ground between those faiths and a striving for the common good. Based on classic texts, he reminds mankind that its true vocation is to help improve the world in partnership with God (Sacks 2005). Echoing Elazar's emphasis on covenant he has tapped into uniquely Jewish concepts such as "Tzedaka" (or righteousness) to promote the "dignity of difference" (Sacks 2002) and the common good in this age of inter-civilizational conflict.

Thus, while remaining acutely aware of the real existence of evil and threat in this era, resources for peacebuilding in the Jewish political tradition can offer a responsible basis for survival along with an avenue of hope.

References

Antonius, George (1946): The Arab Awakening: The Story of the Arab Nationalist Movement. Putnam, New York.

Appleby, Scott (2000): The Ambivalence of the Sacred: Religion, Violence, and Reconciliation. Rowman and Littlefield, Lanham.

Buber, Martin (1970): I and Thou: With Prologue and Translation by Walter Kaufman. Charles Scribner's Sons, New York.

David, Joseph E. and Rosenak, Avinoam (2007): Judaism and Peace: Between Responsibility and Identity. In: Yusuf, Imtiyaz (ed.): The Role of Religious and Philosophical Traditions in Promoting World Peace. Konrad-Adenauer-Stiftung, Singapore, 43-90.

Elazar, Daniel J. (1971): The Themes of a Journal of Federalism. In: Publius Vol. 1:1, 3-9.

Elazar, Daniel J. (1981a): Covenant as the Basis of the Jewish Political Tradition. In: Elazar, Daniel (ed.): Kinship and Consent: The Jewish Political Tradition and its Contemporary Uses. Turtledove, Ramat Gan, 21-56.

Elazar, Daniel J. (1981b): The Jews' Rediscovery of the Political and its Implications. In: Elazar, Daniel (ed.): Kinship and Consent: The Jewish Political Tradition and its Contemporary Uses. Turtledove, Ramat Gan, 1-17.

Elazar, Daniel J. and Cohen, Stuart (eds.) (1985): The Jewish Polity. From Biblical Times to the Present. Indiana University Press, Bloomington.

Elazar, Daniel J. (1996): Response: A Reinvented Jewish Polity in a Globalized World. In: Gal, Allon and Gottschalk, Alfred (eds.): Beyond Survival and Philanthropy: North American Jewry and Israel Conference Proceedings. Hebrew Union College Press, Cincinnati; also appears in: Daniel J. Elazar On-line Library, as "Jewish Civilization and Polity in a Globalized World: A New Vision for Organized Jewry." http://www.jcpa.org/djeindex.htm.

Fox, Jonathan and Sandler, Shmuel (2004): Bringing Religion into International Relations. Palgrave-Macmillan, New York.

Garfinkle, Adam (1991): Genesis. In: Rubinstein, Alvin Z. (ed.): The Arab-Israeli Conflict: Perspectives. Harper Collins, New York.

Gopin, Marc (2000): Between Eden and Armageddon: The Future of World Religions, Violence, and Peacemaking. Oxford University Press, New York.

Hertzberg, Arthur (1997): The Zionist Idea: A Historical Analysis and Reader. Jewish Publication Society, Philadelphia.

Heschel, Abraham Joshua (1962): The Prophets: An Introduction. Harper and Row, New York.

Huntington, Samuel P. (1993): The Clash of civilizations. In: Foreign Affairs Vol. 72:3, 22-49.

Huntington, Samuel P. (1996): The Clash of Civilizations and the Remaking of World Order. Simon & Schuster, New York.

Johnston, Douglas and Sampson, Cynthia (eds.) (1994): Religion: The Missing Dimension of Statecraft. Oxford University Press, New York.

Landau, Yehezkiel (2003): Healing the Holy Land: Interreligious Peacebuilding. In: Israel/Palestine, United States Institute of Peace, Peaceworks monographs No. 51. Available at: www.usip.org/files/resources/pwks51.pdf. Accessed on January 2011.

Lasensky, Scott (2005): A System of its Own? Mapping Jewish Foreign Policy and World Politics. Paper presented at the Association of Israel Studies Annual Meeting in Tucson, Arizona, May 2005.

Lederach, John Paul (1997): Building Peace: Sustainable Reconciliation in Divided Societies United States Institute of Peace, Washington D.C.

Mollov, Ben (2002): Power and Transcendence: Hans J. Morgenthau and the Jewish Experience. Lexington Books, New York.

Mollov, Ben (2006): Managing Conflict: Can Religion Succeed Where Politics has Failed? An Israeli Addresses a Global Peace Forum in Malaysia. In: Jerusalem Viewpoints No. 548, November.

Mollov, Ben (2009): Daniel Elazar's Approach to Federalism as Based on the Idea of 'Brit'. In (eds.): Bacon, Gershon; Baumgarten, Albert; Barnai, Jacob; Waxman, Chaim and Yuval, Israel: Essays in Jewish Studies: Volume II History of the Jewish People and Contemporary Jewish Society. World Union of Jewish Studies, Jerusalem, 249-262.

Mollov, Ben (2010): Religious Diplomacy: Jewish Perspectives. In: Quarterly of Institute of International Relations. (Italian Institute for the Study of International Politics), April, 69-83.

Mollov, Ben and Lavie, Chaim (2001): Culture, Dialogue and Perception Change in the Israeli-Palestinian Conflict. In: The International Journal of Conflict Management Vol. 12:1, 69-87.

Mollov, Ben; Meir, Ephraim and Lavie, Chaim (2007): An Integrated Framework for Peacebuilding: Jewish Approaches. In: Friedens-Warte Journal of International Peace and Organization Vol. 82:Issues 2-3, 137-158.

Morgenthau, Hans J. (1946): Scientific Man: vs. Power Politics. University of Chicago Press, Chicago.

Morgenthau, Hans J. (1967): Politics Among Nations. Fourth Edition. Alfred A. Knopf, New York.

Sacks, Jonathan (2002): The Dignity of Difference. Continuum, London.

Sacks, Jonathan (2005): To Heal a Fractured World: The Ethics of Responsibility. Schocken Books, New York.

Sandler, Shmuel (1987): Is there a Jewish Foreign Policy? In: Jewish Journal of Sociology Vol. 29:2, 115-121.

Sandler, Shmuel (2007): Towards a Theory of World Jewish Politics and Jewish Foreign Policy. In: Hebraic Political Studies Vol. 2:3, 326-360.

Saunders,Harold (1999): A Public Peace Process. New York: St. Martin's Press.

Steinberg, Gerald (ed.) (2000): Jewish Political Studies Review (Special Issue, Jewish Approaches to Conflict Resolution) Vol. 12:3 and 4.

Steinberg, Gerald and Mollov, Ben (2007): Jewish Approaches to Peace, Conflict and Ethical Commitment. In: Yusuf, Imtiyaz (ed.): The Role of Religious and Philosophical Traditions in Promoting World Peace. Konrad-Adenauer-Stiftung, Singapore, 169-193.

Steinberg, Gerald (2008): Jewish Sources on Conflict Management: Realism and Human Nature. In: Roness, Michal (ed.): Conflict and Conflict Management in Jewish Sources. Program on Conflict Management and Negotiation, Bar-Ilan University, Israel, pp.10-23.

Stolov, Yehuda (2009): Jewish Religious Narratives on Jerusalem and their Role in Peace Building. In: Konstanze von Gehlen (ed.): Religious Narratives on Jerusalem and their Role in Peace Building Proceedings of an Interreligious Conference, Konrad-Adenauer-Stiftung, 51-61.

Tange, Lennekke (2010): Assessment of Meeting: Dialogue and Further, Nes Ammim Conference Center, Israel. May 26-28, 2010 (Unpublished).

Tessler, M. A. (2009): A History of the Israeli-Palestinian Conflict. Second edition. Indiana University Press, Bloomington.

Yarden, Ophir (2009): Religious Self-Restraint as a Positive Contribution to Easing Tensions in Jerusalem. In: Konstanze von Gehlen (ed.): Religious Narratives on Jerusalem and their Role in Peace Building Proceedings of an Interreligious Conference, Konrad-Adenauer-Stiftung, 63-81.

Zohar, Noam (2003): Text, Power and Responsibility: The Crucial Role of Midrashic Reinterpretation. In: Ben Mollov (ed.): Religion and Conflict Resolution Proceedings of an International Conference held at Bar-Ilan University, May 27-28, 2002. Konrad-Adenauer-Stiftung, 109-116.

Peace and Violence in Buddhism. Perspectives from Theology and Religious Studies

Peter Harvey

As seen in the Sinhala-Tamil ethnic conflict in Sri Lanka, which the government hopes to have ended through military defeat of the Tamil Tiger rebels, Buddhists have not been free of involvement in violence over the centuries, though it has been hard to find cogent support for this from Buddhist teachings. Moreover, Buddhism has some particularly rich resources for use in dissolving conflicts.

A common Buddhist approach to any problem is to analyse the conditions that lead to it, as seen in its teachings on the four True Realities for the Spiritually Ennobled,[1] on the nature and cause of suffering, and the path leading to its cessation. Behind this lies the teaching of Conditioned Arising: that everything in the world, mental or physical, only arises and exists due to supporting conditions. If one knows how something arises, one has the knowledge to help prevent it arising in the future, if it is problematic, or to nurture it if it is beneficial. It is not surprising, then, that Buddhism has various things to say on the factors which lead to war and conflict. In what follows, I will be drawing on the texts of Theravāda and to some extent Mahāyāna Buddhism, and looking at two examples of present-day Buddhist peace activism.

Buddhist analyses of the causes of conflict

A key influence on human action is seen to be spiritual ignorance: an ingrained misperception of the world, a lack of true insight into its changing, painful and insubstantial nature. This is expressed both in attitudes and beliefs, which then condition intentional actions – that is, karma – that then produce future good and bad fruits. The ignorance also feeds into craving, which in turn conditions grasping, whether for pleasures, favoured ways of doing things, or views, theories, opinions and ideologies.

The roots of all suffering in the world are summarised as greed, hatred and delusion that is craving for things, craving to be rid of disliked things, and distorted views, confusion and plain stupidity. These are also seen as at the root of human conflicts. Any of them may overpower someone, leading to the thought "I have power and I want power", and thus to persecution of others (A.I. 201-202), with fear as another cause of

1 Usually translated into English as 'Noble Truths'.

evil actions (D.III.182).[2] Fear shuts down human sympathies and helps create deluded justifications for violence. As Nyanaponika, a German Buddhist monk, said:

> "In war, rulers might chiefly be motivated by greed (for territory, wealth, economic dominance or political supremacy); but to make the war popular among their own people, they will employ hate-propaganda as a false pretext. Delusion, as a motivating factor, was prominent in the religious wars of the past, and in our present time in ideological wars and revolutions. Delusion is likewise dominant in religious, political and racial persecutions within a particular country. In all these cases, delusion produces hate." (Nyanaponika 1978:50).

That said, the Christian observer of Buddhism, Elizabeth Harris, feels that Buddhism:

> "has taught me that the perpetrators of violence are not aberrations within the human race. They are people like me and you, who are caught up in their own prisons of greed, hatred and delusion. [...] They are formed by conditions, by external and internal causal factors." (Harris 2010:114-116).

Perhaps the key delusion, for Buddhism, is self-centredness: the feeling/attitude/gut-reaction "I am" based on the sense that one has a permanent, substantial Self that must be protected at all costs. The Buddha emphasised that no fixed, permanent Self or I could be found, just conditioned mental and physical processes, for nothing in the world is permanent or unconditioned. Accordingly, one can also argue that, as everything lacks an unchanging inherent essence, a "country" is only a changing conventional reality, not something to be defended at all costs. Nevertheless, people invest much of their identity in "my country", "my community", "my religion", or "my gender", and when this "entity" is seen as being threatened or offended, people feel that they themselves are being threatened or offended. So relationship with a group, which in one sense helps take a person out of ego-centric preoccupation, then becomes the basis for a group-wide "ego" that can itself be "offended". The Buddha, though, did not encourage his followers to feel anger at insults, but told his monks that if anyone disparaged him, the *Dhamma* (his teachings) or *Sangha* (the monastic order) they should not be angry, and if anyone praised these, they should not be elated. In either case, this would be a hindrance to clarity of mind. Rather, they should calmly assess and acknowledge the degree of truth, if any, in what was said (D.I.3).

Nevertheless, Buddhists have been involved in wars that have been portrayed as 'defending Buddhism' (Bartholomeusz 2002; Jerryson and Juergensmeyer 2010; Victoria 1997; Zimmermann 2006), though these have typically been more about defending a nation that has come to be semi-sacralised by its association with Buddhism, or defending the interests of Buddh*ists* rather than of Buddh*ism*. As reported by Harris, a Thai monk speaking in 1988 in Sri Lanka at the height of the ethnic conflict there, asked while recognising that many believed Buddhism was threatened in the country:

2 See the abbreviation list at the end of this article.

> "But what do you mean by Buddhism? [...] And in what way do you wish to preserve it? Buddhism is not its institutions, its traditions or even its culture. Rather, it is a spirit and a way of life. To preserve Buddhism is to preserve this spirit in a life of peace, compassion and wisdom." (Harris 2010:105).

The idea that Buddhist values – amongst which non-violence is central – might be defended using violence is certainly problematic, though at various times Buddhists have persuaded themselves that this is appropriate. Lambert Schmithausen suggests that:

> "As for the motives of these explicit exceptions to the norm of not killing, especially in connection with war, I suggest that at least one was the increasing wealth and social, economic and political influence of the Buddhist monasteries. Wandering ascetics have little to defend, but wealthy monasteries can be destroyed or deprived of property and privileges. Hence the tendency to justify forceful defense of their interest by lay followers and rulers." (Schmithausen 1999:62).

Buddhists have occasionally also portrayed their enemies as embodiments of Māra, the Buddhist devil, as did the much-criticised Thai monk Kittivuddho in his portrayal of Communists threatening Thailand in the 1970s (Harvey 2000:260-261).

The Buddha once explained why people, though they wished to live in peace and without hate, did not do so. Due to thinking round and round an issue in a proliferating way, thought focuses on a particular matter, leading on to desire, and thus to dividing people into "liked" and "disliked" – "us" and "them" –, and on to greed, avarice, and thus hatred (D.II.276–77).

The Buddha also often referred to the negative effects of attachment to speculative or fixed views, dogmatic opinions, and even correct views if not directly *known* to be true, or over-generalised from (Premasiri 1972). Surveying the intellectual scene of his day, he referred to "the wrangling of views, the jungle of views". In a world mapped on the radar-screen of one's own side's world-view, only one's own side's *grievances* show up, along with *threats* from the other, very often equally aggrieved side. Grasping at views is dangerous, and can be seen to have led to religious and ideological wars, crusades, bloody revolutions, and gas chambers. Indeed, millions of deaths were caused in the twentieth century by those attached to particular ideologies which "justified" actions which went against basic human sympathies: Hitler, Stalin, Cambodia's Pol Pot, and terrorists of various kinds.

Conflict also arises from attachment to material things: pleasures, property, territory, wealth, economic dominance, or political superiority. As a text cited by the Mahāyāna poet Śāntideva puts it, "wherever conflict arises among living creatures, the sense of possession is the cause", that is, "me and mine" (Bendall and Rouse 1971:20).

Apart from actual greed, material deprivation is seen as a key source of conflict, as seen in the *Cakkavatti-Sīhanāda Sutta* (D.III.58–77; Fenn 1996:100-108). In this is described a line of mythical universal emperors (*cakkavatti*s) of the past. Each is seen as having been a compassionate ruler, who counsels his son on how to rule, like him, according to *Dhamma*, in the sense of justice or righteousness. In one case, the son does all that his father advised, *except* giving to the needy. As a result of this failing, poverty arises for the first time in ages. Consequently, stealing arises. When a thief is caught and is brought before the emperor, he explains that he stole as he was poor. Consequently, the emperor provides him with funds to support his family, set up a business, and be able to give alms. When others hear of this, though, stealing only increases. The emperor therefore makes an example of the next thief by executing him. This then leads to thieves arming themselves and killing those that they rob, so that there are no witnesses (D.III.64–68). Thus, a government which allows poverty to develop is sowing the seeds of crime and social conflict. Systemic poverty threatens law and order and thus inhibits both social cohesion and personal morality (Fenn 1996:107). In today's world, we can certainly see how deprivation within countries feeds unrest and civil wars, and on the international stage, unequal access to resources is storing up trouble for the future.

The bad influence of others – whether of a government or friends – is seen as another factor which may lead to conflict. Thus it is said that when a king acts in a non-virtuous way, this influences his ministers to do likewise, and this influence then spreads to priests and householders, and on to townsfolk and villagers (A.II.74). That is, rot at the top can easily spread downwards through the whole of society.

We can thus summarise the causes of conflict, according to Buddhism, as: greed for material things and pleasures, the thirst for power, the sense of possession and the felt need to defend possessions, material deprivation, fear, hatred, delusion, attachment to views and ideologies, whether religious or political, attachment to various forms of identity, and the bad influence of others.

As Buddhism emphasizes the emotional and psychological roots of conflict, there is scope for a fruitful dialogue with Western psychology and conflict management. Indeed there is much current interaction between Buddhism and psychology, such as work on Mindfulness Based Stress Reduction, and Daniel Goleman's ideas of 'emotional intelligence'. The Sarvodāya Śramadāna movement, described below, draws on conflict management techniques, and John McConnell has written *Mindful Mediation: A Handbook for Buddhist Peacemakers* (McConnell 1995).

On the more political level, Buddhism shares with other perspectives the idea that conflict can be avoided by addressing material deprivation as a contributory cause. It emphasizes being aware of the limitations of one's own side's view of things, and a bearing in mind of the shared problems that all humans have to deal with.

Solutions to conflict

Economic means

In the *Kūnadanta Sutta* (D.I.134–36), the Buddha says that, in a past life, he had advised a king that the best religious 'sacrifice' to organise was to address the fact that his kingdom was being ravaged by thieves and brigands. This situation would not be solved by repressive measures, for those who survived these would continue to cause problems (as often happens in anti-guerrilla measures today). He then gives an alternative plan: granting grain and fodder to farmers, granting capital to traders, and giving proper living wages to those in government services:

> "Then those people, being intent on their own occupations, will not harm the kingdom. Your Majesty's revenues will be great, the land will be tranquil and not beset by thieves, and the people, with joy in their hearts, will play with their children, and will dwell with open houses" (D.I.136).

A key message here is that if a government allows poverty to develop, this will lead to social strife, such that it is its responsibility to avoid this by looking after the poor, and even investing in various sectors of the economy. While Gombrich comments that this passage was meant as a critique of Brahmanical sacrifice, and that he knows of no Indian Buddhist king who did such things as grant capital to businessmen, the spirit of the passage still expresses a Buddhist ideal – and one which is often cited by contemporary Buddhists (Gombrich 1988:83).

Negotiations emphasizing the mutual harm of war

The Buddha is said to have once prevented a war (Dhp.A.III.254-56, J.V.412-14). In a time of drought, the Sākyans (people of the republic from which the Buddha came) and the Koliyans were about to go to war over rights to the use of waters of a river that divided their territories. On learning of this, the Buddha got the Sākyan leaders to see that they were about to sacrifice something of great value – the lives of warrior-nobles – for something of very little value – water. They therefore desisted.

Mahāyāna texts suggest that Buddhists should try to see to it that warring parties are more ready to settle their differences (Luk 1972:89, cf Nhat Hanh 1975:95), and Buddhist monks have often been used by armies to help negotiate peace settlements. In such negotiations, as in others, one aspect of the virtue of "right speech" is surely relevant:

> "Abandoning malicious speech, he abstains from malicious speech; he does not repeat elsewhere what he has heard here in order to divide (those people) from these, nor does he repeat to these people what he has heard elsewhere in order to divide (these people) from

> those; thus he is one who reunites those who are divided, a promoter of friendships, who enjoys harmony, rejoices in harmony, delights in harmony, a speaker of words that promote harmony" (M.I.288).

Reflections to undermine hatred and develop patience

Among the central values of Buddhism are those known as the "divine abidings": lovingkindness, compassion, joy at the happiness of others, and equanimity. Allied to these, there is also the virtue of patience or forbearance. All such values are directly relevant to defusing conflicts and their practice will make these less likely to occur in the first place.

By contrast to the Christian emphasis on not holding ill-will *against* someone, the Buddhist emphasis is on not holding it *within* oneself, due to its harmful effects. As part of the method of developing lovingkindness, the fifth century Theravāda commentator Buddhaghosa gives various reflections, in his *Visuddhimagga*, for undermining hatred or anger (Vism. 298–306). Several of these reflections are in the spirit of: "Whatever harm a foe may do to a foe, or a hater to a hater, an ill-directed mind can do one far greater harm" (Dhp.42). An example is:

> "Suppose another, to annoy, provokes you with some odious act, why suffer anger to spring up, and do as he would have you do? If you get angry, then maybe you make *him* suffer, maybe not; though with the hurt that anger brings, *you* certainly are punished now" (Vism. 300).

That is, when someone attacks or abuses one, truly lasting harm only arises when one reacts with anger or violence. An enemy wishes one to suffer, yet Buddhism holds that allowing oneself to be overcome by anger brings one various sufferings (A.IV.94). Getting angry with others is compared to picking up a burning stick to hit someone with, or throwing dust against the wind: one only suffers oneself, through immediate unpleasant feelings, and future karmic results. While the other person presents the occasion for the response, one's action is one's own, and through it one directly brings harm on oneself. Anger is conditioned by an attack of an assailant, but it is not wholly determined by it. There must always be some co-operating reaction on one's own part: something that one can come to have increasing control over, by developing more self-control and undermining the attachment to "I" and "mine"– though of course one cannot uncaringly *demand* or *expect* such good self-control of others.

In a more concrete way, Buddhaghosa suggests that if another is harming one because of one's *own* anger, the wise thing to do is to put the anger down. Or, again, if one's presence is fuelling another's anger, it is best to get out of the way for a while, so that tempers may cool. He also recommends one to focus only on the good qualities that an offending person has, or remember that all beings must have been a close relative or friend in one of their, and one's own, innumerable past rebirths: so that one should now bear in mind their past kindnesses (S.II.189-90; cf. Bendall and Rouse 1971:21). As past human rebirths might have been in a variety of ethnic groups or cultures, such a reflection seems particularly relevant to situations of ethnic strife between two peoples who view each other as alien "others".

Buddhaghosa also suggests that one should reflect on impermanence, and acknowledge that the mind-states of a person who has harmed one are likely to be different now than when he or she did the harmful act; of course the same applies in conflicts between groups of people. One may also reflect that lovingkindness brings happiness to one (A.V.342), and if all else fails, it is useful to give a gift to, or receive one from, a person for whom one has hostility.

In his *Bodhicaryāvatāra*, Śāntideva says:

> Therefore, even if one sees a friend or an enemy behaving badly, one can reflect that there are specific conditioning factors that determine this, and thereby remain happy." (Bca.vi. 33).

Anger at a fool for harming others is like anger at a fire for burning things (Bca.vi.39). If someone harms one, just look at it as the karmic results of similar harm one has done to others (Bca.vi.42). Moreover:

> "If even this small measure of suffering cannot be tolerated now, then why is anger, the cause of torment in hell, not restrained?" (Bca.vi.73).
> "Indeed, an enemy should be looked on as like a beneficial treasure, for he gives one a good opportunity for practising patience, and should be venerated accordingly." (Bca.vi.107-11).

Forbearance and forgiveness

In accordance with the spirit of the above are passages which recommend the strength and transformative potency of forbearance and forgiveness. In one of these, it is emphasised that calm in the face of anger is not weakness, but real strength (S.I.222). Again, when a Brahmin insults and abuses the Buddha due to a relative becoming a Buddhist monk, the Buddha asks him what he does when a gift he offers is declined. When he replies that the gift remains his own, the Buddha says that he does not want to 'dine' on his 'gift' of anger, so it remains with him as the giver. He then says: "He seeks the welfare of both himself and the other, who, having known the anger of another, mindfully maintains his peace" (S.I.162).

The Buddha also tells the story of a prince who had the chance to avenge the murder of his parents, but desisted, saying:

> "my parents were killed by a king, but if I were to deprive the king of life, those who desired the king's welfare would deprive me of life, and those who desired my welfare would deprive these of life; thus hatred would not be settled by hatred." (Vin.I.348).

Accordingly, the Buddha taught:

> "He abused me, he beat me, he defeated me, he robbed me, the hatred of those who harbour such thoughts is not appeased.
> Hatreds never cease by hatred in this world; only by non-hatred (lovingkindness) do they cease. This is an ancient law." (also at Dhp.3 and 5).

Here one sees that one should not take on the mantle of victimhood, thinking "poor me" or "poor us", so as to nurse malice for those who one sees as one's oppressors.

The English monk Ajahn Brahm reports that in the mid-1970s, as neighbouring countries were falling to Communism, and Thailand was concerned about Thais who were Communist insurgents on its borders, the military and government successfully used a three-part strategy against this:

> 1. Restraint. The military did not attack the Communist bases, though every soldier knew where they were [...]
> 2. Forgiveness. Throughout this dangerous period, there was an unconditional amnesty in place. Whenever one of the Communist insurgents wanted to abandon his cause, he would simply give up his weapons and return to his village or university. He would probably experience surveillance, but no punishments were imposed [...]
> 3. Solving the root-problem. During these years, I saw new roads being built and old roads being paved in the region. Villagers could now take their produce to town to sell. The king of Thailand personally supervised, and paid for, the construction of many small reservoirs with connected irrigation schemes [. . .] The poorest region in Thailand was being cared for by the government in Bangkok, and the villagers were becoming relatively prosperous.
>
> [. . .] By the early 1980s, there were hardly any insurgents left, so then the generals of the jungle army, the leaders of the Communists, also gave themselves up [. . .and] were offered important positions in the Thai government service, in recognition of their leadership qualities, capacity for hard work, and concern for their people! (Brahm 2005:84–87).

That said, Thailand was the base for American planes that bombed North Vietnam, and Thailand sent soldiers to fight alongside the Americans in Vietnam.

Respect for people of different religious traditions

One of the edicts of the third century BCE Indian Buddhist emperor Asoka says that he valued:

> "growth in the qualities essential to religion in men of all faiths. This growth may take many forms, but its root is in guarding one's speech to avoid extolling one's own faith and disparaging the faith of others improperly or, when the occasion is appropriate, immoderately. The faiths of others all deserve to be honored for one reason or another. By honoring them, one exalts one's own faith and at the same time performs a service to the faith of others.

> By acting otherwise, one injures one's own faith and also does disservice to that of others. For if a man extols his own faith and disparages another because of devotion to his own and because he wants to glorify it, he seriously damages his own faith. Therefore concord alone is commendable, for through concord men may learn and respect the conception of Dharma [the religious path] accepted by others. King Priyadarśī desires men of all faiths to know each other's doctrines and acquire sound doctrines."

It is true that in ancient India, Hindu Brahmin priests did not like Asoka's criticism of their use of animal sacrifice, but even many in Hinduism came to criticize this, and it is of note that the majority Hindu but formally secular state of India has on its flag a wheel symbol that was particularly associated with Asoka, who ruled the largest Indian political unit prior to the modern era. We also see that the Buddhist king of Thailand sees himself as the protector of all religions in his land.

The code of monastic discipline and monastic authority structures

While Buddhist monastics have occasionally engaged in or supported violence, the monastic code is very clear that any monk or nun who intentionally kills a human should be expelled from the monastic order. However, while angry speech is against the monastic code, expressing opinions is not restrained by the rule, though it may be by custom and practice. In Thailand, the views of Kittivuddho, cited above, were also widely criticized in the press. In different countries, the situation varies as to whether there is a central monastic authority, backed by the state, as in Thailand, or whether there are various monastic organizations, as in Sri Lanka.

Non-violent reflections on a violent world

Among Buddhist teachings and principles relevant to the use of violence are the following:

i) The first ethical precept, daily chanted by all committed Buddhists: "I undertake the rule of training to abstain from harming any living being". This entails avoiding the intentional harming or killing of any sentient being, whether directly or by the agency of another person. It is the most important of the Buddhist ethical precepts, which are themselves seen as the foundation of the Buddhist path.
ii) The emphasis on lovingkindness and compassion.
iii) The ideal of "right livelihood", which precludes making a living in a way that causes suffering to other beings. Among the specifically listed forms of "wrong livelihood" is "trade in arms" (A.V.177), meaning selling arms, though it is also

said that soldiers who die in combat may be reborn as an animal or in a hell, not in some warrior's heaven (S.IV.308-9).

Given these emphases, can war and similar forms of violence ever be justified? The Buddhist path aims at a state of complete non-violence, based on insight and inner strength rooted in a calm mind. Yet those who are not yet spiritually well-developed, living in a world in which others may seek to gain their way by violence, still have to face the dilemma of whether to respond with defensive violence. Pacifism may be the ideal, but in practice Buddhists have often used violence in self-defence or defence of their country – not to speak of sometimes going in for aggressive violence, like any other group of people.

Having said this, there are a number of textual passages which reflect on war and punitive violence, seeking to subvert the "violence is sometimes necessary" of worldly common sense by a dialogue with the non-violent ideal. In two short discourses (at S.I. 82–3 and 83–5), the Buddha comments on two battles which arise when the evil king Ajātasattu attacks the land of his uncle, king Pasenadi, a "friend to whatever is good". In the first, Pasenadi is defeated and retreats, and the Buddha reflects on his misery: "Victory breeds hatred; the defeated sleeps unhappily. The one at peace giving up victory and defeat sleeps happily" (S.I.83; Dhp.201). This implies that conquest leads to unrest for the defeated, which may lead to hatred and a desire to overcome the conqueror. In the second battle, Pasenadi wins. Capturing Ajātasattu, he spares his life but confiscates all his weapons and army. Here the Buddha comments:

> "The slayer gets a slayer (in his turn), the conqueror gets a conqueror, the abuser gets abuse, the wrathful gets one who annoys. Thus by the evolution of karma, he who plunders is plundered." (S.I.85).

Without justifying defensive violence, this points out that aggression often leads to defensive counter-violence, which can be seen as a karmic result for the aggressor. Such a response happens, whether or not it is justified. Thus aggression is discouraged. Yet Pasenadi, the generally peace-loving defender, is not free of censure. To spare the life of a defeated enemy is surely good, but to leave him defenceless, without an army, is seen as storing up trouble. Pasenadi is portrayed as acting in a limited way according to his emotions and situation. Elsewhere, he laments to the Buddha the preoccupations of his kingly role, which encourages such things as greed and conquest. The Buddha therefore helps him to re-focus his mind on wholesome actions by reminding him that, like everyone else, he will grow old and die, and then experience the karmic results of his actions (S.I.101-02).

Buddhist texts do talk of the ideal *cakkavatti* ruler (A.IV.89-90, cf. D.I.88-9), a type of just and righteous king who rules a large empire without the use of force: he has an army, but potential enemies willingly become his subjects and accept his advice to follow the five ethical precepts (D.III.62). Nevertheless, it seems acknowledged that this is an ideal that requires an exceptional person to fully live up to. Thus Harris holds that in early Buddhist texts:

> "The person who feels violence is justified to protect the lives of others has indeed to take the consequences into account. He has to remember that he is risking grave [karmic] consequences for himself in that his action will inevitably bear fruit. [...] Such a person needs to evaluate motives [...]. Yet that person might still judge that the risks are worth facing to prevent a greater evil." (Harris 1994:47-48).

If violence is then used, it is something that Buddhism may *understand* but not as such *approve of*.

We do have the case, though of the first century BCE king Dutthagāmanī, who in the Buddhist chronicle the *Mahāvansa* is described as making war to drive out a Tamil king who had occupied Sri Lanka, this being in the name of the defense of Buddhism. Here, there is the suggestion that his good intention somehow negated the evil of his involvement in killing. The text says, firstly, that those he killed were wicked, worthless people, and secondly it emphasises that the king went on to do many (non-violent) good deeds. The second of these is in line with Buddhist principles – seeking to dilute one's evil karma with good karma, but the first is a disreputable idea that is best seen as an example of delusion in "Buddhist" guise.

We also find that some Mahāyāna Buddhist texts, such as the *Upāya-kauśalya Sūtra*, contain the idea that killing might sometimes be acceptably if done out of "skilful means", where compassion over-rides the principle of non-violence in cases where violence is needed to stop many good people being killed. They do not, though, say that intention is all that matters. Intentional killing is always seen as problematic, though background motivation may help to counteract the evil of killing for those whose motive is truly compassionate – so compassionate that they are willing to suffer the karmic results of killing in order to help others. Such genuine compassion reduces these results, though. Note that while some Mahāyāna texts are very careful in their description of the conditions under which killing may be validated by compassion, others, such as the *Mahāparinirvāna Sūtra*, do it in a rather loose way, which could then end up being used to "validate" such actions as armed conflict between rival Buddhist groups in medieval Japan. Justifications of violence can be a slippery slope towards dangerous outlooks.

Buddhist action for peace in the modern world

Sarvōdaya Śramadāna as a force for defusing conflict in Sri Lanka

One movement which is a force for social harmony in Sri Lanka, led by A. T. Ariyaratne is the Sarvōdaya Śramadāna self-help rural development movement. This is not a narrowly Buddhist organisation, but has been influenced by the ideals of Mahātma Gandhi and Quakerism. A key aim of the movement is to break down barriers between people, whether based on caste, political party, wealth, age, gender, race or religion. At Sarvōdaya village work-camps, the method is to get all sections of a village actively involved in identifying needs that the village has, for example a metalled road, or a new school, and then working side by side to build these. One particular emphasis is on getting women to speak up and be more active in shaping their world. By the mid-1990s the movement had, since its inception, recruited more than 800,000 volunteers and touched the lives of over 4 million people in promoting the renewal of rural communities. It was even operating in predominantly Tamil areas in the North, becoming the only organisation that was able to work and travel in all parts of the country: even the government could not do this in areas held by Tamil guerrillas (Bond 1995:5). Personnel from Sinhalese and Tamil areas have visited each other's areas, with Tamils visiting Buddhist temples and Sinhalese visiting Hindu ones (Burr 1995:14; Macy 1983:50). Tamils have held prominent leadership positions in Sarvōdaya, and Tamils who work with it see it as a Sri Lankan organization rather than a Sinhalese Buddhist one (Bond 1996:136). At Sarvōdaya work-camps, multi-religious services are carried out, with people of the minority religion of the area always being the first to perform their rituals (Macy 1983:50). Many Buddhist monks are involved in Ariyaratne's lay-led movement, and those in Tamil-dominated areas have sought to help anxious and fearful Tamils contact relatives arrested by the security forces. There are, though, other Buddhist monks in Sri Lanka who express hard-line views against any "concessions" to the Tamils, who they see as unjustifiably threatening the territorial integrity of "Buddhist" Sri Lanka.

During the 1983 ethnic riots, Ariyaratne immediately, but unsuccessfully, asked the President to announce a curfew, and went on to unilaterally set up refugee camps (Burr 1995:14). After the riots, the movement organised a national conference, at which 2.000 religious and civil leaders explored ways to settle the conflict. The conference produced a Sarvōdaya-influenced "People's Declaration for National Peace and Harmony", emphasising "only by non-hatred does hatred cease" and the need for "a friendly dialogue" (Bond 1995:6). A peace march was then proposed from the Sinhalese-dominated South to Tamil-dominated far North, but though thousands began this, it was called off on government advice (Bond 1996:137). Shorter peace-marches followed over the next few years in the central hill-country. The movement also became a key conduit for relief supplies and funds, supplied by Western donors, to refugees (Bond 1995:6-7).

The Sarvōdaya strategic plan for 1995-98 saw the movement as having a role in "national re-integration", addressing problems of poverty and "unachievable lifestyle expectations" which it sees as feeding the ethnic problems, and continuing to aid refugees and orphans. This is in line with its emphasis on basic human needs, both material and cultural, and avoiding both poverty and consumerism. One of its three priorities has been to "play a more assertive conflict-resolution and peace-making role" (Burr 1995:5). Ariyaratne emphasises that the solution to the ethnic conflict lies in education and getting the common people of both communities to unite (Burr 1995:14). He points out that the urge to win at other's expense leads not to a win-lose situation, but to a lose-lose one (Burr 1995:15). In line with this, the movement planned a series of workshops to train 600 Sarvōdaya monks to engage in conflict management and mediation in their villages (Burr 1995:6). At the first of these, it was emphasised that the solution to a conflict needs a careful mapping of it, a neutral description, and sympathy for the needs and interests of all parties. For this, effective, active listening is needed. One also needed to be assertive, rather than aggressive or passive (Burr 1995:10-13).

Thich Nhat Hanh and Buddhist action for peace in Vietnam and beyond

Thich Nhat Hanh, the well known Buddhist peace activist, first emerged to prominence during the Vietnam war. This poet-monk founded the School of Youth for Social Service in 1964, involving 10.000 young people in work to rebuild destroyed villages and resettling tens of thousands of refugees fleeing war-zones (Nhat Hanh 1987:12; Không 1993). They did not take sides, but tried to understand both the Communists and anti-Communists and their sufferings. Both sides attacked them, though, as they thought they were working for their enemies (Nhat Hanh 1987:69).

In 1965, Nhat Hanh founded the Tiep Hien Order, comprising lay-people, monks and nuns, as a vehicle of what he calls "engaged Buddhism" (King 1996:323). For followers in the West, he calls it the "Order of Interbeing", for he emphasises the Mahāyāna Buddhist idea of the inter-related existence of all things (Nhat Hanh 1987:87). The Order's first precept is:

> Do not be idolatrous about or bound to any doctrine, theory, or ideology, even Buddhist ones. All systems of thought are guiding means; they are not absolute truth.

The twelfth precept is:

> Do not kill. Do not let others kill. Find whatever means possible to protect life and to prevent war. (Nhat Hanh 1987:98)

Before the end of the Vietnam war, Nhat Hanh said he would rather have peace at any price, even if it meant the end of Buddhist institutions, buildings and scriptures, for in a peaceful country, Buddhism could be reborn in people's hearts (Sivaraksa and Ginsburg 1992:81).

During the war, anti-war songs and writings were widely circulated by Buddhists, including Nhat Hanh's poem "Do Not Shoot Your Brother", which described "Our enemy" as "hatred ... inhumanity ... anger ... ideology ... the effort to divide us" (King 1996:335). In opposition to the sometimes anti-Buddhist policies of the Catholic-influenced South Vietnamese government, some individuals and groups fasted, others shaved their heads, a few even burnt themselves to death. Others went on strike or boycotted classes. Deserters and draft resisters were encouraged and protected from discovery (King 1996:335-336). When villagers were caught in cross-fire, monks and nuns would help evacuate them, sometimes forming a double line through which they could run.

Many "boat people" fled Vietnam after the war, risking drowning or attacks by pirates in their attempt to find refuge from the new Communist government. In 1976-77, Nhat Hanh and his associates organised an effort to save some of these. He emphasised how people are driven to bad actions both by circumstances and their own unresolved limitations, and that to truly address problems of suffering, one must deeply empathise with both victim and victimiser, such as attacking pirates, as well as reflect on one's own indirect involvement in such situations, due to the deep inter-relationship of reality (King 1996:340-342). To do this requires socially committed action, but this needs to be rooted in non-anger and strong meditative mindfulness of one's body and mind (King 1996:342; Nhat Hanh 1975; Kraft 1992:19).

Nhat Hanh now lives in Plum Village, a Buddhist community in France. He has written over sixty books, and these have a wide circulation in the West, where they help stimulate the practice of Buddhism, especially in an "engaged" form directed at overcoming the sufferings of the world. He and his followers have worked on behalf of political prisoners in Communist Vietnam and to ease the plight of the poor and refugees there, as well as being active for peace on a wider scale. In America, the Buddhist Peace Fellowship, which has been particularly influenced by Nhat Hanh, campaigns against war, particularly the threat of nuclear war to "all sentient beings", and political oppression (Ives 1992:96-97; Kraft 1992:14-16, 23-24).

In his *Being Peace*, Nhat Hanh underlines the relevance of inner peace to outer peace:

> "It is with our capacity of smiling, breathing, and being peace that we can make peace." (Nhat Hanh 1987:9).
> "If we are not peaceful, then we cannot contribute to the peace movement [...] Peace work means, first of all, being peace." (Nhat Hanh 1987:80).

He argues that sitting and walking in meditation is a form of non-violent resistance to the uncontrolled energies of anger etc. in the world (Nhat Hanh 1987:110).

Conclusion

Buddhism thus has strong resources to draw on for conflict resolution, though these resources and related ideals must become more well known and acted on. People such as A. T. Ariyaratne are quietly but firmly reminding their fellow Buddhists of the profoundly non-violent and tolerant spirit of the Buddha. Thich Nhat Hanh and the Dalai Lama have strongly embodied this spirit in both seeking to help their own people and in writings and activities directed beyond their lands.

Among contemporary Buddhist leaders, the Dalai Lama and Aung San Suu Kyi of Burma have been awarded the Nobel Peace Prize, and Nhat Hanh was nominated for it by Martin Luther King. Uniting threads among Buddhist peace activists include: the centrality of non-violence and non-anger against oppressors; the idea of compassion for both sides in a conflict; an emphasis on the avoidance of dogmatic clinging to views, and being open to the perspective of others; the emphasis that peace starts within the individual, and then spreads outwards; and the inter-dependence of all beings.

Abbreviations

A.	*Anguttara Nikāya*
Bca.	*Bodhicaryāvatāra* of Śāntideva
D.	*Dīgha Nikāya*
Dhp.	*Dhammapada*
Dhp.A.	*Dhammapada* commentary
J.	*Jātaka*
M.	*Majjhima Nikāya*
Vin.	Theravāda *Vinaya*
Vism.	*Visuddhimagga* of Buddhaghosa
S.	*Sanyutta Nikāya*

Translations for all of the above except Bca. can be found listed on the website of the Pali Text Society (www.palitext.com). For Bca.: translated by K. Crosby and A. Skilton (1996): *Śāntideva: The Bodhicaryāvatāra*, Oxford and New York, Oxford University Press.

References

Bartholomeusz, Tessa J. (2002): In Defense of Dharma: Just-war Ideology in Buddhist Sri Lanka. Routledge Curzon, London.

Bendall, Cecil and Rouse, W. H. D. (1971): Śiksā Samuccaya: Compendium of Buddhist Doctrine, Compiled by Śāntideva Chiefly from the Early Mahāyāna Sūtras. 2nd edition. Motilal Banarsidass, Delhi.

Bond, George D. (1995): The Sarvodaya Movement's Quest for Peace and Social Awakening. Seventh International Seminar on Buddhism and Leadership for Peace, Department of Philosophy, University of Hawaii, 12 pages.

Bond, George D. (1996): A. T. Ariyaratne and the Sarvodaya Shramadana Movement in Sri Lanka. In: Queen, Christopher S. and King, Sallie B. (eds.): Engaged Buddhism: Buddhist liberation movements in Asia. State University of New York Press, Albany, 121-146.

Brahm, Ajahn (2005): Who Ordered This Truckload of Dung? Inspiring Stories for Welcoming Life's Difficulties. Wisdom Publications, Somerville.

Burr, Ron (1995): Buddhist Conflict Management. Seventh International Seminar on Buddhism and Leadership for Peace, Department of Philosophy, University of Hawaii.

Fenn, Mavis (1996): Two Notions of Poverty in the Pāli Canon. In: Journal of Buddhist Ethics. Vol. 3, 98–125. Available at: http://jbe.gold.ac.uk/3/fenn1.pdf

Gombrich, Richard Francis (1988): Theravāda Buddhism: A Social History from Ancient Benares to Modern Colombo. Routledge and Kegan Paul, London and New York.

Harris, Elizabeth J. (1994): Violence and Disruption in Society; A Study of the Early Buddhist Texts. Buddhist Publication Society, Kandy. Available at: http://www.accesstoinsight.org/lib/bps/wheels/wheel392.html

Harris, Elizabeth J. (2010): Buddhism for a Violent World. Epworth Press, London.

Harvey, Peter (2000): An Introduction to Buddhist Ethics: Foundations, Values and Issues. Cambridge University Press, Cambridge.

Ives, Christopher (1992): Zen Awakening and Society. University of Hawaii Press, Honolulu.

Jerryson, Michael K. and Juergensmeyer, Mark (eds.) (2010): Buddhist Warfare. Oxford University Press, Oxford.

Không, Chân (1993): Learning True Love: How I Learned and Practiced Social Change in Vietnam. Parallax Press, Berkeley.

King, Sallie B. (1996): Thich Nhat Hanh and the Unified Buddhist Church: Nondualism In Action. In: Queen, Christopher and King, Sallie B. (eds.): Engaged Buddhism: Buddhist liberation movements in Asia. State University of New York Press, Albany, 321–65.

Kraft, Kenneth (ed.) (1992): Inner Peace, World Peace: Essays on Buddhism and Nonviolence. State University of New York Press, Albany.

Luk, Charles (1972): The Vimalakirti Nirdesa Sutra. Shambhala, Berkeley.

Macy, Joanna (1983): Dharma and Development: Religion as Resource in the Sarvodaya Self-help Movement. Kumarian, West Hartford, Connecticut.

McConnell, John (1995): Mindful Mediation: A Handbook for Buddhist Peacemakers. Buddhist Research Institute, Mahachula University, Bangkok.

Nhat Hanh, Thich (1975): The Miracle of Mindfulness: A Manual on Meditation. Beacon Press, Boston.

Nhat Hanh, Thich (1987): Being Peace. Rider, London.

Nyanaponika, Thera (1978): The Roots of Good and Evil. Buddhist Publication Society, Kandy.

Premasiri, P. D. (1972): The Philosophy of the Atthakavagga. Buddhist Publication Society, Kandy.

Queen, Christopher and King, Sallie B. (eds.) (1996): Engaged Buddhism: Buddhist Liberation Movements in Asia. State University of New York Press, Albany.

Schmithausen, Lambert (1999): Aspects of the Buddhist Attitude towards War. In: Houben, Jan E. M. and Van Kooji, Karel R. (eds.): Violence Denied: Violence, Non-violence and the Rationalization of Violence in South Asian Cultural History. Koninklijke Brill NV, Leiden, 45–67.

Sivaraksa, Sulak and Ginsburg, Tom (1992): Seeds of Peace: A Buddhist Vision for Renewing Society. Parallax Press, Berkeley.

Victoria, Daizen (1997): Zen at War. Rowman & Littlefield, Lanham.

Zimmermann, M. (ed.) (2006): Buddhism and Violence. Lumbini International Research Institute, Kathmandu.

Peace and Violence in Islam

S. Ayse Kadayifci-Orellana

Prophet Mohammed said: *"Faith is a restraint against all violence, let no Mu'min [a believer] commit violence"*.[1] In another *Hadith*, the Prophet is recorded to have said: "*A perfect Muslim is one from whose tongue and hands mankind is safe, and a true emigrant [muhajir] is one who flees from what God has forbidden*".[2]

However, most of the conflicts today involve Muslims. Human rights abuses, authoritarianism, communal violence and corruption are rampant in many Muslim countries. The monstrous attacks of September 11, 2001 as well as attacks in London, Istanbul, Madrid, and Mumbai, undertaken by groups and individuals in the name of Islam, have shaken both the Muslim and the non-Muslim world. Suicide bombs explode in Muslim contexts such as Pakistan, Iraq, or Afghanistan, killing more Muslims than non-Muslims. Kidnapping or execution of foreigners, including aid workers, or attacks on tourists facilitate the image of Muslims as 'violent' and 'barbarian'.

Consequently Islam, which in fact is derived from the word *slm* (peace), has come to be associated with violence and terrorism and Muslims are stereotyped as backward, barbaric and violent as pointed out by the theory of "Culture Talk" which defines every culture based on its tangible essence. In turn, politics are shaped as a consequence of that essence (Mamdani 2004:17). Islam has become a "foil against which we [the West] could measure our achievements" (Armstrong 1991:39), an existential threat to 'civilized us' and to the possibility of creating the conditions of a 'perpetual peace' (Jabri 2007:139). Accordingly, Muslims are either perceived as 'the other' or they are indiscriminately pigeonholed into categories of radical Muslims-moderate Muslims' or 'bad Muslim-good Muslim' (Mamdani 2004).

While some unsympathetic observers heralded a "clash of civilizations" (Huntington 1996) and argued that Islam is an inherently backward and violent religion, others maintained that Islam is under siege by a group of fanatics and that Islam actually is a religion of peace and tolerance (Ahmed 2003). Recently there have been serious efforts to explore and emphasize Islamic values of peace and conflict resolution in the Quran, as well as deeds and sayings of the Prophet Mohammed, and to apply these principles to current day conflicts (Huda 2010; Abu-Nimer 2003; Kadayifci-Orellana 2003; Funk and Said 2009). These scholars have tried to capture the peaceful role that Muslim

1 Sahih Collection of Abu Dawud. See "A Collection of Hadith on Non-Violence, Peace and Mercy" available at http://www.sufism.org/society/articles/PeaceHadith.htm.
2 Sahih Collection of Bukhari. See "A Collection of Hadith on Non-Violence, Peace and Mercy" available at http://www.sufism.org/society/articles/PeaceHadith.htm.

organizations, theologians, and communities can assume in responding to internal and external sources of violence (Abu-Nimer and Kadayifci-Orellana 2008).

Indeed, despite its current image, the Islamic tradition very clearly emphasizes the importance of peace and justice and since its formative years Muslims have sought ways to live in peaceful and just societies. Muslims, from fundamentalists to the strict adherents of nonviolence, agree that Islam is a religion of peace and that the application of Islamic principles will bring justice, harmony, order and thus peace to the world (Kadayifci-Orellana 2007:85). Although from a theological perspective life in the world often involves conflict, the ultimate objective of life's struggle is peace (Funk and Said 2009:62). In fact, Islamic sources including the Quran and the *Hadith* as well as the practices of the companions of the Prophet are rich in values, principles and examples that emphasize peacebuilding and conflict resolution. Historical records also provide evidence that these values and principles have informed many Muslim leaders, such as Saladin or Caliph Omar, among others, in their conducts towards other states or non-Muslims. This paper will introduce various Islamic principles of peace and conflict resolution employed by various Muslim peace actors.

Contemporary Approaches to Peace and Violence in the Muslim World

Evidently, like the followers of other religious traditions, Muslims have not always lived up to the highest ideals of their religious tradition. Challenged by colonialism, modernization, and globalization, many Islamic thinkers during the last century blamed the decline of Muslim power on a deviation from the *right path of Islam* and called for the reinstitution of Islamic rule (Kadayifci-Orellana 2007). They have reinterpreted Islamic texts to address contemporary problems. Within this context all kinds of resistance movements and leaders adopted *jihad* as an ideological framework, and as a political rhetoric to justify their policies and conduct. This trend continues today as many Muslim leaders – including self-proclaimed ones such as Osama bin Laden – argue that their actions and methods are not only in conformity with Islamic values but required by them.

Today there are conflicting interpretations of violence and peace competing with each other for legitimacy in a world where the social and traditional structures are crumbling and instant, extensive communication mechanisms are creating space for those who did not have an audience previously. These interpretations can be categorized under three headings: "*Offensive Islamic interpretation of war*", "*Defensive Islamic interpretation of war (or Just War perspective)*", and "*Nonviolent Islamic interpretation of war*".

Held mostly by current day militant fundamentalist groups like Al-Qaeda, the offensive Islamic perspective of peace and war holds that Islam, as the only 'true path' to justice, freedom, and peace, should be the religion that governs the world and that Islam should aim to expand its influence through various ways, including offensive wars. Adherents of this approach are convinced that the current economic, political and international system that dominates the world only breeds oppression, injustice, and exploitation, therefore must be removed and replaced by God's governance. In order to achieve that goal, it is incumbent upon every Muslim to "fight" with whatever means they have. In this "*jihad*", offensive wars and even attacks against civilian targets are necessary evils to bring God's rule to earth.

The Just War perspective, which is held by the majority of Muslims, argues that Islam permits war and violence only under certain dire circumstances such as in *self-defense*. This perspective views *jihad* as a comprehensive effort towards the path of God, which requires "utilizing all the physical, mental, and spiritual faculties of human beings", and "includes actual participation in war but only as a last resort, with those non-Muslims who actively oppose and hinder the *deen* [religion] of Allah and wish to subvert it" (Qurashi 1991:58). Thus minor *jihad* or war is permitted purely for defense purposes and aggression is forbidden altogether (Asad 1961). This perspective holds that in the face of oppression and persecution, Islam calls Muslims to defend themselves and to fight in order to establish justice and restore harmony.

Depending on what they consider permissible in a just war, this perspective can be further divided into two categories: "moderate" and "extremist" (Kadayifci-Orellana 2007). The moderate perspective holds that not only the ends but also the means of *jihad* must be based on ethical grounds, and that although war is permitted, it is also limited (Kadayifci-Orellana 2007). According to this view – which is also held by al-Azhar, the most authoritative Islamic institution – the Quran permits Muslims to fight in order to protect their faith, their freedom and their lands and property. Nevertheless, they add that the Quran insists that Muslims must be strong advocates of peace (Khan 1998:5), and if war is necessary, it must be fought as humanely as possible (Tibi 1996:137).

The extremist perspective, on the other hand, holds that Islam permits defensive wars, but adds that Islam allows Muslims to utilize all necessary means to win it. Consequently, all the weapons of the opponent, which could also include nuclear weapons, and those weapons that cannot distinguish between combatants and non-combatants can be employed, as long as the opponent also employs them (Kadayifci-Orellana 2007). Supporters of this perspective do recognize that there is a clearly articulated regulation in the Islamic tradition, but believe that these restrictions can be set aside under extreme conditions (Tibi 1996:133). They further argue that under the current war system, where distinguishing between the civilian and military targets is increasingly difficult, Islam allows all that is "necessary", including suicide (or as they prefer to call "martyrdom") attacks to "defend" Muslims against their enemies.

Conversely, the nonviolence perspective holds that nonviolent struggle is the preferred response to injustice, conflict, and war according to Islam (Kadayifci-Orellana 2005; 2007). Islamic holy texts emphasize values and principles that promote nonviolence and peaceful resolution of conflicts such as patience, forgiveness, and kindness. Although there are verses in the Quran that seem to allow war, there are also stringent rules that govern the use of violence under extreme conditions (Kadayifci-Orellana 2007). Accordingly, if violence cannot discriminate between combatants and non-combatants, it is not acceptable in any form or shape. Since modern technologies of destruction render discrimination virtually impossible, Muslims are not allowed to use violence in the contemporary world (Sa'id 1997:1). Yet, Islam teaches Muslims to fight for justice based on the understanding that human life- as any of God's creations – has a purpose and is sacred. Therefore, being true to Islam implies to utilize nonviolent action as the mode of struggle. Moreover, Islam itself is a fertile soil for nonviolence because of its potential for disobedience, strong discipline, sharing and social responsibility, perseverance, self-sacrifice, the belief in the unity of the Muslim community, and the oneness of mankind (Satha-Anand 2001:209).

From the very inception of Islam the nonviolent Islamic perspective has been an integral part of Islamic practice and today there are many Muslim individuals and organizations that base their work for peace and justice in their communities and around the world quite successfully on this perspective. Many of these actors adopt an approach that takes into consideration the unique social, historical, economic, cultural and political context in which they operate. Their approaches are derived from key Islamic sources such as the Quran and *Hadith*, and build upon historical examples and traditional conflict resolution mechanisms. Many of them also educate their communities through sermons, and/or religious schools (Abu-Nimer and Kadayifci-Orellana 2008). It is vital to recognize the important contributions of these actors and to empower them in their efforts. The next section will introduce various Islamic principles and approaches to peace and conflict resolution employed by Muslim peacebuilding actors in their daily work.

The Islamic Conception of Peace

Despite their unique cultural, political, and social evolution, religion plays an important role in the socio-political life of many Muslim communities and religion is one of the key components of people's identity both as a cultural framework and as a religious creed. For Muslims the Quran is the foremost source of social, political, legal, and ethical frameworks in Islam. Other sources include recorded sayings (*hadith*) and practices (*sunna*) of the Prophet, as well as the conduct of His companions and family members. These sources contain sacred truths that form the basis for Islamic ethics and inform actions of believers. Whenever these sources are silent on an issue, Islamic religious scholars (*ulama*) apply hermeneutical approaches such as rational analysis (*ijtihad*), consensus (*ijma*) or analogy (*qiyas*) to establish Islamic rule and preferences. These sources and tenets create a unified community (*ummah*) and provide Islamic approaches to peace with a common vocabulary, a set of values and principles. To be considered legitimate and authentic, Muslim perspectives on peace, war and the traditions of peacebuilding must be derived from the Quran, *Hadith*, and *Sunna.* As "a powerful constituent of cultural norms and values" they influence individual and social conceptions of peace and have a direct impact on notions of justified war and mechanisms of conflict resolution (Said and Funk 2002:37-38).

Many references to peace in the Quran (e.g. *salam, silm, sulh*) suggest that peace together with "justice" is the central theme in the Islamic discourse (Kadayifci-Orellana 2003:43). Muslims, irrespective of the Islamic tradition they adhere to, agree that Islam is a religion of peace and that the application of Islamic principles will bring justice, harmony, order, and therefore peace (Kadayifci-Orellana 2007:101). Indeed even the word *Islam* is derived from the Arabic word *salam/silm* (peace) suggesting peace through submission (*taslim*) to the will of God and "for the practicing Muslim, the Quranic revelation is understood as a call to integration and wholeness through surrender to the divine" (Funk and Said 2009:61).

The Islamic concept of peace is not limited to a negative understanding of peace that is defined as the absence of war, oppression and tyranny but is viewed as a process in which human beings strive to establish foundations for interacting with each other – and with nature – in harmony and to institute just social, economic and political structures where they can flourish and fulfill their potential. This definition of peace requires a condition of both internal and external order and encompasses both individual and social spheres as "the individual must be endowed with the necessary qualities to make peace an enduring reality, not only in the public sphere but also in the private domain" (Kalin 2010:8). Peace in Islam begins with God, since *as-Salam* (peace) is one of the most beautiful ninety-nine names of God (Q59:23) and this peace is a positive state of safety or security, which includes being at peace with one-self, with fellow human beings, nature, and God (Kalin 2010:8). But peace is not a "mere state of passivity", "it is being fully active against the menaces of evil, destruction, and turmoil, which may come from within or without" (Kalin 2010:8). Similarly, God constantly calls believers to strive to establish harmony, justice and peace on earth and to achieve the "abode of peace" (Q10:25).

Additionally, Prophet Mohammed's *hadith*, his basic attitude towards peace and his diplomatic conduct, can be summarized in his slogan "reconciliation of hearts" that he issued at the capture of Mecca in 630 (Q9:60; Troger 1990:17). He often emphasized kindness, mercy, and forgiveness as opposed to violence or conflict. He is recorded to have said "kindness is a mark of faith, and whoever has not kindness has not faith."

"Coming to terms with adversaries and enemies and the contractual guaranteeing of agreements were corner stones of Mohammed's policy" and he preferred peaceful regulations of conflicts and peaceful resolutions of enmity (Troger 1990:16). During his prophethood, he concluded 23 treaties and agreements between groups and tribes, advocated tolerance, and strictly enforced compliance to treaties. In particular, both the *Hudaybiya* Treaty, signed by Mohammed to end the hostilities with the Meccans, and the Constitution of Medina which contractually regulated relations between Muslims and non-Muslims and ensured peaceful coexistence of people with different ethnic and religious backgrounds are clear practical examples of this.

Muslims also model their behavior according to the companions of the Prophet, family members of His household (particularly the Shia) and some significant Islamic leaders known for their just and righteous behavior. When Jerusalem came under Islamic rule without a battle, Caliph Umar established a system of governance that recognized the importance of Jerusalem for Christians and Jews. He proactively renegotiated the agreement between him and the Christian Patriarch of Jerusalem in order to bring Jews back to the city who were not permitted in Jerusalem during the Christian era before Caliph Umar. He not only brought 70 Jewish families back initially, but invited them to join Muslims in cleaning the sacred sites previously used as garbage sites. Furthermore, he employed 20 Jews for the protection and maintenance of the Holy Sites and these 20 Jews were exempt from the poll-tax.

Salah ad-Din Ayyubi is another exemplary Muslim leader who is often remembered for his just and restrained conduct during and after the war against Crusaders who had killed many Muslims, Jews, and other non-combatants. In addition to following Islamic laws of warfare and combat strictly, he is also well-known for his sense of justice and kindness towards Muslims and non-Muslims alike and for inviting Jews, who were not allowed in the city during the Crusade period, back to the city.

Pillars of an Islamic Conception of Peace

Many values and principles – such as goodness (*ihsan*), pursuit of love, kindness, benevolence, wisdom and knowledge, service, social empowerment, universality and dignity of human life, sacredness of human life, equality, quest for peace and harmony, creativity and innovation, individual responsibility and accountability, patience, collaboration and solidarity, inclusion and participation, diversity and unity among others – inform the Islamic understanding of peace (Abu-Nimer 2003). A closer examination of Quranic verses and the Prophet's *sunna* associated with peace and peacebuilding reveal the centrality of a number of key values and principles. These values and principles, which can be called the pillars of an Islamic conception of peace, include *Tawhid* (the Unity of Being), *Fitrah* (the original constitution of human beings), *adl* (justice), *afu* (forgiveness), *Rahmah* and *Rahim* (compassion and mercy), and *sabr* (patience) (Kadayifci-Orellana 2009). This paper argues that these six values, elaborated below, constitute some of the foremost values in the Quran in terms of building sustainable peace.[3]

1. Tawhid or "the principle of the Unity of God and all being" is a pivotal Islamic principle, referring not only to the all-powerful one God, but also to 'all-Oneness', the One who transcends all duality and plurality, embraces all diversity and multiplicity from which the Islamic understanding of peace is derived (Sharify-Funk 2001:278). It expresses the fundamental unity of all humankind and all life and rejects a vision of humanity rooted in exclusiveness (Q49:3; 5:48; Said and Funk 2001:248). "As the ultimate source of peace, God transcends all opposites and tensions, is the permanent state of repose and tranquility, and calls his servants to the abode of peace (dar al-salam)" (Kalin 2010:9). Tawhid mediates the direct personal relations to the Absolute (which is absolute peace) and the maintenance of harmony with all of God's creation, including other human beings, animals, and the nature that surrounds us (Said and Funk 2001). The Unity of Being – God's one reality – is the source of harmony, order and peace and from the Islamic point of view recognizing the unity of all being.

"By acknowledging God's unity and praising His name, man joins the natural world in a substantive way…" (Kalin 2010:10). Muslims are urged to actively pursue unity and harmony because, according to the original covenant between humans and God, humans have assumed the responsibility of protecting, and taking care of God's creation. Conflict and war between mankind result in the corruption and the ruin of the earth and all that inhabits it. Thus each Muslim must work towards bringing all creatures under the sway of equilibrium and harmony and must aim at living in peace with creation (Chittick 1990:156).

2. Fitrah: The individual responsibility to uphold peace emerges out of the original constitution of human beings (*fitrah*), which, according to Islam, is good and Muslim in character (Said et al. 2002:7). According to the Islamic tradition every human being is created in accordance with the form and image of God and His Divine Names or Qualities, which are manifested in their entirety in the human form (Al-Hakim 1998:5). The Quran states "verily, we have honored every human being" (Q 17:70) and points out that every human being is worth of respect because they are made "in the best of molds" (*ahsan taqwim*) (Q 95:4). This perspective holds that every human being is created innocent, pure, true and free, and is inclined to right and virtue. "Although the Quran occasionally describes the fallen nature of man in gruesome terms, presenting him as weak, forgetful, treacherous, hasty, ignorant, ungrateful, hostile and egoistic

3 Some of these values are also explored in Kadayifci-Orellana "Muslim Perspectives on War and Peace" in *Peace-Building by, between, and beyond Muslims and Evangelical Christians,* edited by Dr. Mohammed Abu-Nimer and Dr. David Augsberger (Lexington Books, 2009.).

(e.g., 14:34; 17:11; 18:54; 22:66; 33:72; 43:15; 100:6), these qualities are eventually considered deviations from man's essential nature (*fitrah*)…" (Kalin 2010:10-11).

"*Fitrah* provides not only the foundational premise for constructive politics of human potential and value maximization, but also a safeguard against dehumanizing "the other" within the context of a conflict situation" (Sharify-Funk 2001:279). It reminds Muslims that, irrespective of gender, religion, race, etc., all human beings are created in the image of God, therefore they are all sacred. Only God knows the heart of a human being, thus he is the only judge, and at any point in life, each individual, no matter what he or she has done so far, has the potential to repent and turn to God. The principle of *fitrah* urges Muslims to separate the individual from his/her actions, and it warns against stereotyping and dehumanizing 'the other.' Therefore, the notion of *fitrah* is critical for the Islamic conception of peace since recognition of the goodness of each and every human being is a precondition for peaceful, constructive and harmonious relations between human beings and human communities irrespective of their religious, ethnic or ideological differences.

3. Al-Adl (justice) is, like *As-Salam* (peace), one of the most beautiful names of God according to the Islamic tradition. God is the Ultimate Judge (*Hakam*) and Absolute Justice. Justice is an integral aspect of the Islamic discourse of peace, since the Quran clearly states that the aim of religion is to bring justice: "We sent aforetime Our messengers with clear signs and sent down with them the book and the balance (of right and wrong), that men may stand forth in justice." (Q 57:25). From an Islamic point of view without justice, there can be no peace "for peace is predicated upon the availability of equal rights and opportunities for all to realize their goals and potentials" (Kalin 2010:8). Muslims are asked to resist and correct the conditions of injustice, which are seen as a source for conflict and disorder on earth (Q 27:52). Therefore justice is the essential component of peace according to the Quranic message. Such an interpretation of the Islamic understanding of peace suggests that justice is the overriding principle (Kadayifci-Orellana 2007).

The Quranic notion of justice includes both economic and social dimensions and is universal and valid for all creatures since it transcends any consideration of religion, animosity, race, or creed. The verses read "O ye who believe! Stand out firmly for justice as witnesses to Allah even as against yourselves, your parents or your kin…" (Q 4:135); "…To fair dealing, and let not the hatred of others to you make you swerve to wrong and depart from justice. Be just for it is next to piety..." (Q 5:8; see also Q 16:90; Q 2:178). The universality of justice for all, not only for Muslims, is critical for the resolution of conflicts and the development of peaceful relations as it calls upon Muslims to be self-reflexive, self-critical, humble and to accept responsibility for one's actions. Clearly, pursuing justice in Islam is not only a responsibility but a divinely ordered command which must be pursued by every Muslim in order to establish the Islamic ideal of harmony and peace.

4. Afu (forgiveness) – considered as an act of *ihsan* (goodness) – is another critical notion in the Islamic understanding of peace. "There is a clearly articulated preference in Islam for nonviolence over violence, and for forgiveness (*afu*) over retribution" (Said et al. 2001:8). The Quran urges believers to forgive when they are angry thereby stressing that forgiveness is a higher value than hatred. (Q 42:37). The verse "The recompense for an injury is an injury equal thereto (in degree): but if a person forgives and makes reconciliation, his reward is due from Allah: for (Allah) loveth not those who do wrong." (Q 42:40) advocates sincere forgiveness as the preferred option to establish God's harmony on earth. Even the Prophet himself was told by God to forgive (Q 7:99).

The Quran states that human life on earth started with an act of forgiveness by God (Q 2:36-38). The Quranic narration of the story of Joseph and his brothers emphasizes how he forgave them and treated them with respect and honor. Also, as the most forgiving, God has constantly forgiven the Children of Israel and indicated that those who seek forgiveness of God should also be forgiving themselves. Also many *Hadith* and *Sunna* emphasize forgiveness. For instance one *Hadith* records: "That person is nearest to God, who pardons, when he has someone in his power, one who would have injured him". Also the Prophet himself forgave all those who persecuted and fought him when he entered Mecca and stated "There is no censure from me today on you (for what has happened is done with), may God, who is the greatest amongst forgivers, forgive you" (al Kubra 1957:93). This attitude of forgiveness was the basis of his reconciliation efforts aimed at establishing peace between the Muslims and the Meccans, (Troger 1990:17).

5. Rahmah (compassion) and Rahim (mercy): Closely related to the principle of forgiveness are the twin values of *Rahmah* and *Rahim*, which are invoked by every Muslim before they take any action by reciting "*Bi Ism-i- Allah al-Rahman al-Rahim*" (i.e. begin in the name of Allah who is compassionate and merciful). The centrality of compassion and mercy is evident in the Quran as almost all chapters start with this recitation and God states "My mercy extends to all things" (Q 7:156). Moreover, according to a famous *Hadith*, God states: "Without doubt My mercy precedes My wrath," which is one of the crucial principles of Islamic thought.

Mercifulness and compassion are key qualities of the Prophets. The Quran refers to the Prophet Mohammed as "Mercy to the World" (Q 21:107), thus, as the messenger of God, he represents Universal Mercy. Again, Moses was declared a prophet after he had shown compassion to the ewe that ran off to the desert and fell down exhausted. He compassionately said: "O hapless one, wither are you fleeing? Whom do you fear?" After he picked her up and carried her back to the flock, God said to the angels: "Saw ye with tenderness my servant treated that dumb ewe? Because he took trouble and harmed not the ewe, but rather had mercy on her, (I declare) be My glory that I will raise him up and make him My interlocutor; I will grant him prophet-hood and send him a book, and as long as the world exists, his name will be spoken" (Kadayifci-Orellana 2011:212-213).

Besides pointing out that God is most forgiving, compassionate and merciful, the Quran asks Muslims to be forgiving and compassionate to all creatures: animals, plants and humans (Q 17:18). As the *Hadith* "God is not merciful to him who is not so to mankind" indicates, especially those seeking God's mercy should be merciful themselves. Thus, a true Muslim must be merciful and compassionate to all human beings, irrespective of their ethnic, religious origins, or gender. Values of compassion and mercy connote that a true Muslim cannot be insensitive to the suffering of other beings (physical, economic, psychological, or emotional), nor can he be cruel to any creature. Thus, torture, inflicting suffering or willfully hurting another human being or another creature is not allowed according to Islamic tradition.

6. Sabr (patience): Another critical value which informs the Islamic conception of peace is patience (*sabr*) because it makes a person capable of finding a positive and successful solution to a problem (Q 39:10; Khan 1998:1). As such it is the opposite of violence. The entire spirit of the Quran is in consonance with the concept of patience as more than 200 verses address it (Khan 1998). God asks believers to be steadfast and promises deliverance to those who endure these difficulties with patience: "And We made a people, considered weak (and of no account), inheritors of lands in both east and west – lands whereon We sent down Our blessings. The fair promise of thy Lord was fulfilled for the Children of Israel, because they had patience and constancy, and We leveled to the ground the great works and fine buildings which Pharaoh and his people erected with such pride" (Q 7:137). In another verse of the Quran all the Prophets declare: "We shall certainly bear with patience all the hurt you may cause us." (Q 14:12-13). Patience in these verses clearly implies a peaceful response or reaction to injustice and conflict, whereas impatience implies a violent response. Yet, the Quran does not ask Muslims to remain passive in the face of oppression and injustice. On the contrary, it asks Muslims to engage in an active struggle (*jihad*) to establish peace, justice and harmony on earth.

The Islamic Conception of Jihad and War[4]

Although peace is a central tenet of Islam there are verses in the Quran that seem to permit war as a legitimate conduct to correct injustice and overthrow tyranny and oppression. Various verses deal with the initiation and termination of hostilities, the

4 1400 years Islamic literature is rich with debates regarding this issue. Various prominent jurists, philosophers such as Ibn Khaldun, Ibn Taymmiyya, Al Ghazali, Al Farabi, among many others dealt with war and peace in Islam. Although acknowledging this vast literature, this paper utilizes only more recent sources and debates.

conduct during war and the nature and duration of treaties (Salmi et al. 1998). For example, the verse Q 2:190 commands "Fight in the cause of Allah those who fight you, but do not transgress limits; for Allah loveth not transgressors" ("fight in the way of Allah against those who fight against you; but begin not hostilities", Pickthall 1930). Another verse states "Go ye forth, (whether equipped) lightly or heavily, and strive and struggle, with your goods and your persons, in the cause of Allah" (Q 9:41).

Based on these verses and the wars the Prophet himself has participated in, Muslim scholars developed a systematic body of legal provisions regarding war and relations with non-Muslims under the title *Siyar*. "Although originally it was applied to the Prophet's conduct in war", *Siyar* was formalized to encompass Islamic laws on the conditions for peace and neutrality in the 8th century by Imam Abu Hanifa in a lecture series entitled "The Muslim Laws of War and Peace" (Troy 1997:45). These lectures were later compiled by his student Shaybani under the title "Introduction to the Law of Nations." Other scholars have also contributed to the development of the *siyar* tradition.

More specifically *siyar* deals with the initiation and termination of hostilities, the treatment of prisoners, relations with non-Muslims, and the nature and duration of treaties. The Siyar tradition envisioned the world to be divided into *Dar al-Islam* (house of peace) and *Dar al-Harb* (house of war), despite the fact that such a distinction does not exist in the Quran. *Siyar* deals with *jihad* within this context. Although these rules and regulations were considered to be a part of the Islamic *Shariah* in general, *siyar* acquired a distinct character and has become an analytical tool in the study and application of the *Shariah*. Sources of siyar include the Quran, the *Sunna* and the *Hadith*, practices of the four rightly guided caliphs, practices of the later caliphs, opinions of the educated, treaties and agreements, official instructions to military commanders and ambassadors, other state officials and customs. Juristic techniques, such as *ijtihad*, were utilized extensively to develop these rules.

Contrary to the general belief, *jihad*, which is often mistranslated as "holy war" against external forces, does not mean war with weapons, but literally means "striving" or "struggle" and refers to a commitment to "strive for the cause of God" (Q 22:78). More specifically, the Quran refers to *jihad* as struggling for the cause of God by means of speech, property, wealth or life. In another verse the Quran reads: "And if any strive (jahada) (with might and main), they do so for their own souls" (Q 29:6). In this context *jihad* becomes a spiritual path of salvation. However, it was also understood in terms of exerting an effort to repel the enemy. Based on these different connotations, Islamic scholars have articulated *jihad* in three distinct ways: to strive against a visible enemy; against the Devil; or against the ego or selfish interests. This is based on the *Hadith* issued after a military expedition: "We have returned from the minor *jihad* (war) to the major *jihad* (against the self)" (al Sobki 1968:158), which has been the basis for differentiating between these levels of *jihad* in the Islamic literature.

In the context of *siyar*, *jihad* means repulsion of aggression, protecting the faith, and defending the *Ummah* (the Muslim community). In this sense, *minor jihad* becomes no different from fighting (*qital)* and waging war (*harb*) to defend the Muslim faith and community against its enemies. The Quranic discourse considers war an odious measure and an instrument that never ought to be used for individual aggrandizement or sport (Salmi et al. 1998:68). Nevertheless, the Quranic discourse also recognizes that under extreme conditions war may become a necessity for a state which is responsible for the wellbeing of its citizens. Similar to the Just War Theory of St. Augustine, the Islamic doctrine of Just War (*Jus ad bellum*) includes both a justifiable reason and the necessary formalities for prosecuting war. The Islamic Just War Theory, as articulated in *Siyar* in the 8th century, considers war just only when it is commenced and prosecuted in accordance with the necessary formalities required under the Islamic system of law, or waged for justifiable reasons in accordance with the tenets of the religion or the mores of Muslim society (Khadduri 1955:57). Islam outlaws any kind of war except the war permitted by God, *jihad*, and the most obvious just cause according to Islam is self-defense. The Islamic tradition emphasizes that war can only be justified if it is in accordance with the sanction of religion and the implied orders of God, and launched by a legitimate Islamic leader. For jihad to be legitimate, those who wage war must also have the right intention, as fighting for the sake of material gains or conquest is not permitted. Still before waging war Muslims must offer Islam as a token of peacefulness and offer reconciliation or the conclusion of a peace treaty. War is permitted if the opponent insists on war.

Although war is permitted, it is also restricted in many ways and Muslims are warned against transgressing limits set by God as it is stated in the Quran: “Fight against those who fight against you in the way of God, but do not transgress, for God does not love transgressors” (Q 2:190). So *siyar* lays down strict regulations regarding acts that were not allowed when waging war (*Jus in bello*). *Siyar* clearly prohibits the killing of noncombatants, such as women, children, the blind, the old, monks and hermits, the insane or delirious, those who are physically incapable of actual fighting, and servants.

Islam also calls for a just and good treatment of war prisoners as the Prophet instructs: "Fear God regarding prisoners of war" and "Take care of prisoners of war". Also the Quran states “as to the righteous... they feed, for the love of Allah, the indigent, the orphan, and the captive, we feed you for the sake of God alone: no reward do we desire from you, nor thanks” (Q 76:8,9). Hence Islam forbids the killing of war prisoners and a majority of jurists agree that prisoners cannot be held liable for damage they inflicted on Muslim life and property while being combatants (Hamidullah 1961:214). They are to be given adequate food, shelter and medical care. A well-known example of such conduct is Saladin Ayyubi’s treatment of his enemies. He gave medical aid to his opponent Richard the Lion-Hearted of England, when he became seriously ill during the Crusades. Despite the fact that Crusaders slaughtered seventy thousand Muslims, including women, children, and the elderly, Saladin sent his own doctor and personally supervised Richard's treatment until he recovered.

Other Muslim leaders also followed the Prophet's example. For instance, Abu-Bakar instructed his soldier by saying:

> "Stop, O people, that I may give you ten rules to keep by heart! Do not commit treachery, nor depart from the right path. You must not mutilate, neither kill a child or aged man or woman. Do not destroy a palm-tree, nor burn it with fire and do not cut any fruitful tree. You must not slay any of the flock or the herds or the camels, save for your subsistence. You are likely to pass by people who have devoted their lives to monastic services; leave them to that to which they have devoted their lives. You are likely, likewise, to find people who will present to you meals of many kinds. You may eat; but do not forget to mention the name of Allah." [Khadduri 1955, fn 12:102]

Siyar records that Islam forbids using prisoners as shields or compelling them to fight their own army, or using poison. It also states that Islam does not allow the violation of mutual agreements on what to avoid in wartimes,[5] as well as any retaliation against the enemy neither when they kill Muslim women, children, the aged and hostages, nor for acts of mutilation. *Siyar* is also clear in stating that adultery and fornication with female captives, killing hostages as well as massacring innocent people, even if the enemy has resorted to such actions, is not allowed. *Siyar* also enunciates that unnecessary devastation of the enemy lands, destruction of animal stocks, harvest and cutting trees, especially fruit trees are not permissible (Salmi et. Al 1998; Kadayifci-Orellana 2007 and 2009; and Khadduri 1955).

Clearly many of the conflicts and methods employed by Muslim militants such as acts of decapitating hostages, attacking civilians, causing death by fire when flying planes into buildings, utilizing bombs that will mutilate bodies, and raping of prisoners, do not comply with Islam according to *siyar*. Individuals such as Osama bin Laden do not have the legitimate authority to wage war, and neither do they have Islamically sound and legitimate causes to do so. Yet they still employ Islamic sources to justify their conduct and conflicts. How is this possible?

Conclusion: Constructive Responses to Conflicts in the Muslim World

As in many other religious traditions, the goal of Islam is peace. However, the rise of violence and conflict in the name of Islam since the 1990s and especially recent terrorist attacks have created an image of Islam as a violent and barbaric tradition in the minds of many. Muslims themselves disagree on the 'correct interpretation' of Islam in terms

5 Quran states "Fulfill the Covenant of Allah when ye have entered into it, and break not your oaths after ye have confirmed them; indeed ye have made Allah your surety; for Allah knoweth all that ye do." (Q 16:91.).

of peace and conflict resolution. Recent studies in the field of peace and conflict resolution demonstrate that religio-cultural traditions inform conceptions of peace, conflict, and conflict resolution processes as well as providing them with legitimacy – a critical ingredient for transforming negative enemy images and establishing lasting peace. Religion in particular, as "a powerful constituent of cultural norms and values", is deeply implicated in individual and social conceptions of peace, as it addresses some of the most profound existential issues of human life, such as those concerning freedom/inevitability, fear/security, right/wrong, sacred/profane, etc. (Said and Funk 2002:37-38). For peace to be sustainable and long lasting, peacebuilding initiatives must be rooted in the religio-cultural traditions of the communities involved. Accordingly, conflict resolution and peacebuilding initiatives in the Muslim world must take into consideration religio-cultural traditions derived from Islamic sources.

As this paper displayed, Islam has a wealth of traditions and principles that emphasizes peace and if consistently and systematically applied, they can transcend all levels of conflict. These values and principles instruct Muslims with a wide range of attitudes and behavior models applicable in different situations (Abdalla 2000-2001:167). They emphasize the importance of the common good, social and divine harmony, justice, social responsibility, and accountability. There is a strong sense of community and solidarity as well as a collaborative understanding of freedom that is embedded in the notion of *Ummah,* the community of Muslims. Consequently the society and the common good comes before the individual, and the individual has obligations vis-à-vis the community. Because conflict is viewed as harmful to both divine and communal harmony, Islam instructs Muslims to take action to resolve conflicts and restore harmony peacefully and nonviolently (Q 49:9).

As Muslims aspire to model their behavior after the Quran and the *Sunnah* (sic), it becomes the task of Muslim conflict interveners to raise awareness of conflicting parties about the misperceptions and negative practices that for long have influenced their lives by focusing on traditional Islamic principles. There are many Muslim actors, such as religious leaders, nongovernmental organizations and other civil society institutions who work in their communities in order to resolve conflicts, build peace, encourage reconciliation and strengthen interfaith dialogue. Although Muslim peacebuilding actors in different parts of the world respond to the unique requirements of their own social, historical and political contexts and situate their peacebuilding activities within the cultural traditions of their communities, they still derive their inspiration from and base their practices on the same Islamic sources. Religious leaders, who know the conflicting parties, the history of the conflict and the Islamic tradition well, are legitimate authorities to intervene, either upon being called to do so, or on their own initiative. These actors are in an adequate position to identify the needs of their communities and know the social, political, religious, and cultural contexts of the conflicts they strive to resolve. Thus they have a better understanding of the constraints and possibilities of various peace initiatives in these communities. In order to address conflicts in the Muslim world it is critical that these Muslim peacebuilding actors are empowered and supported.

References

Abdalla, Amr (2000-2001): Principles of Islamic Interpersonal Conflict Intervention: A Search Within Islam and Western Literature. In: Journal of Law and Religion 15:1 and 2, 151-184.

Abu-Nimer, Mohammed (2003): Nonviolence and Peace Building in Islam: Theory and Practice. University Press of Florida, Florida.

Abu-Nimer, Mohammed and Kadayifci-Orellana, Ayse S. (2008): Muslim Peace-Building Actors in Africa and the Balkan Context: Challenges and Needs. In: Peace & Change 33:4, 549-581.

Ahmed, Akbar (2003): Islam Under Siege: Living Dangerously in a Post-Honor World. Polity Press, Cambridge.

Al Hakim, Suad (1998): Islam and Peace. Paper presented at the symposium "Islam and Peace in the 21st Century" in Washington DC, February 6-7. Translated by Tara Aziz and Karim Crow.

Appleby, Scott (ed.) (1997): Spokesmen for the Despised: Fundamentalist Leaders of the Middle East University of Chicago Press, Chicago.

Asad, Muhammad (1961): The Principles of State and Governance in Islam. University of California Press, Berkeley.

Avruch, Kevin (1998): Culture and Conflict Resolution. USIP Press, Washington DC.

Bouta, Tsjeard; Kadayifci-Orellana, Ayse S. and Abu-Nimer, Mohammed (2005): Faith Based Peacebuilding: Mapping and Analysis of Christian, Muslim and Multi-Faith Actors. Netherlands Institute for International Relations "Clingandael" in cooperation with Salam Institute for Peace and Justice, The Hague and Washington DC.

Chittick, William C. (1990): The Theological Roots of Peace and War According to Islam. In: The Islamic Quarterly 34:3, 145-163.

Esack, Farid (2006): The Contemporary Democracy and the Human Rights Project for Muslim Societies. In: Abu-Nimer, Mohammed; Said, Abdul Aziz and Sharify-Funk, Meena (eds.): Contemporary Islam: Dynamic not Static. Routledge, London, 117-128.

Funk, Nathan C. and Said, Abdul Aziz (2009): Islam and Peacemaking in the Middle East. Lynne Rienner Publishers, London.

Gopin, Marc (1997): Religion, Violence, and Conflict Resolution. In: Peace & Change 22:1, 1-31.

Hamidullah, Mohammad (1961): Muslim Conduct of State. Sh. Mohammad Ashraf, Lahore.

Huda, Qamar-UL (ed.) (2010): Crescent and Dove: Peace and Conflict Resolution in Islam. USIP Press, Washington DC.

Huntington, Samuel (1996): Clash of Civilizations and the Remaking of World Order. Touchstone, New York.

Jabri, Vivienne (2007): War and the Transformation of Global Politics. Palgrave, London.

Kadayifci-Orellana, Ayse S (2005): "Islamic Nonviolence Paradigm" in Islamic Peace Paradigms. Abdul Karim Bangura eds. Nova Science.

Kadayifci-Orellana, Ayse S. (2007): Standing on an Isthmus: Islamic Narratives of War and Peace in Palestinian Territories. Lexington Books, Lanham.

Kadayifci-Orellana, Ayse S. (2009): Muslim Perspectives on War and Peace. In: Abu-Nimer, Mohammed and Augsberger, David (eds.): Peace-Building By, Between, and Beyond Muslims and Evangelical Christians. Lexington Books, Lanham.

Kadayifci-Orellana, Ayse S. (2011): "Exodus in the Quran: Mercy, Compassion and Forgiveness" in Freedom Journeys: The Tale of Exodus and Wilderness Across Millennia by Arthur Ocean Waskow, Rabbi Arthur Waskow, Rabbi Phyllis Berman. Jewish Lights Publishing, Woodstock, Vt.

Kalin, Ibrahim (2010): Islam and Peace. In: Huda, Qamar-UL (ed.): Crescent and Dove: Peace and Conflict Resolution in Islam. USIP Press, Washington DC.

Khadduri, Majid (1955): War and Peace in the Law of Islam The Johns Hopkins Press

Khan, Maulana Wahiduddin (1998): Non-Violence and Islam. Paper prepared for the symposium "Islam and Peace in the 21st Century" in Washington D.C., February 6-7.

Mamdani, Mahmood (2004): Good Muslim, Bad Muslim: America, the Cold War, and the Roots of Terror. Three Leaves Press (Random House), New York.

Pickthall, Muhammad Marmaduke William (1930): The Meaning of the Glorious Qur'an, London

Qurashi, M. M. (1991): The Concept of Islamic Jehad. In: Islamic Thought and Scientific Creativity 2:1, 57-71.

Razvani, Sara in Quran Times available at http://www.literature.freeservers.com/image_islam/islamictranslation3.html.

Said, Abdul Aziz and Funk, Nathan C. (2001): Peace in the Sufi Tradition: An Ecology of the Spirit. In: Said, Abdul Aziz; Funk, Nathan C. and Kadayifci-Orellana, Ayse S. (eds.): Peace and Conflict Resolution in Islam. University Press of America (Rowman & Littlefield Publishing Group), Lanham, 247-262.

Said, Abdul Aziz; Funk, Nathan C. and Kadayifci-Orellana, Ayse S. (2001): Peace and Conflict Resolution in Islam: Precept and Practice. University Press of America (Rowman & Littlefield Publishing Group), Lanham.

Said, Abdul Aziz and Funk, Nathan C. (2002): The Role of Faith in Cross-Cultural Conflict Resolution. In: Peace and Conflict Studies 9:1, 37-50.

Said, Abdul Aziz; Funk, Nathan C. and Kadayifci-Orellana, Ayse S. (2002): Islamic Approaches to Conflict Resolution and Peace. In The Emirates Occasional Papers No 48. The Emirates Center for Strategic Studies and Research.

Sa'id, Jawdat (1997): Peace- or Nonviolence- in History and with the Prophets. Paper written for a conference on "Islamic Values for Change" in Bi'r Ajam, Qunaytra (Syria), April 3. Translated by Dr. Abduhu Hammud al-Sharif, revised with notes by Karim Crow.

Salmi, Ralph H.; Majul, Cesar Adib and Tanham, George K. (1998): Islam and Conflict Resolution: Theories and Practices. University Press of America (Rowman & Littlefield Publishing Group), Lanham.

Satha-Anand, Chaiwat (2001): The Nonviolent Crescent: Eight Theses on Muslim Nonviolent Action. In: Said, Abdul Aziz; Funk, Nathan C. and Kadayifci-Orellana, Ayse S. (eds.): Peace and Conflict Resolution in Islam: Precept and Practice. University Press of America (Rowman & Littlefield Publishing Group), Lanham, 195-211.

Sharify-Funk, Meena (2001): Peace and the Feminine in Islam. In: Said, Abdul Aziz; Funk, Nathan C. and Kadayifci-Orellana, Ayse S. (eds.): Peace and Conflict Resolution in Islam. University Press of America (Rowman & Littlefield Publishing Group), Lanham, 277-298.

Smock, David R. (1992): Religious Perspectives on War. USIP Press, Washington DC.

The Quranic Arabic Corpus (2012): http://corpus.quran.com/translation.jsp?chapter=16&verse=91

Tibi, Bassam (1996): War and Peace in Islam. In: Nardin, Terry (ed.): The Ethics of War and Peace: Religious and Secular Perspectives. Princeton University Press, Princeton.

Tirmidhi, Daawat 109, (3537). Cited in Fethullah Gulen: Toward a Global Civilization of Love and Tolerance. (Somerset, New Jersey: Light 2004).

Troger, Karl-Wolfgang (1990): Peace and Islam: In Theory and Practice. In: Islam and Christian Muslim Relations No. 1, 12-24.

Troy, Thomas (1997): Prisoners of War in Islam: A Legal Inquiry. In: The Muslim World 87:1, 44-53.

Yusuf Ali, Abdullah (1934 und 1937): The Holy Qur'an: Translation and Commentary Lahore; Saudi Revision: The Holy Qur-an: English translation of the meanings and Commentary.

Managing Violence and Promoting Nonviolence: The Emerging Agenda of Christian Peacebuilding

Scott Appleby

> On the evening of that first day of the week, when the doors were locked, where the disciples were, for fear of the Jews, Jesus came and stood in their midst and said to them, "Peace be with you." When he had said this, he showed them his hands and his side. The disciples rejoiced when they saw the Lord. (Jesus) said to them again, "Peace be with you. As the Father has sent me, so I send you." And when he had said this, be breathed on them and said to them, "Receive the holy Spirit. Whose sins you forgive are forgiven them, and whose sins you retain are retained."
> John 20:19-23

> While they were talking about this, Jesus himself stood among them and said to them, "Peace be with you." They were startled and terrified, and thought that they were seeing a ghost. He said to them, "Why are you frightened, and why do doubts arise in your hearts?"
> Luke 24:36-39

> Then Simon Peter, who had a sword, drew it, struck the high priest's slave, and cut off his right ear. The slave's name was Malchus. Jesus said to Peter, "Put your sword into its scabbard. Shall I not drink the cup that the Father gave me?"
> John 18:1-4,10-11

In The Bridge Betrayed, Michael Sells writes:

"The northeast Bosnian town of Zvornik was known for its heritage of Bosnian Muslim poets, saints, rebels and mystics. From April through July of 1992 the Serb military killed or expelled the entire Muslim population. After all the mosques in the primarily Muslim town were dynamited and ploughed over, the new Serb nationalist mayor declared: "There never were any mosques in Zvornik." Destroyed with those mosques was the evidence not only of the Muslim heritage of Zvornik but also of five hundred years of shared living between Christians and Muslims. History could now be rewritten according to the desires of those who wished to claim that this land was always and purely Christian Serb. In May 1993, to celebrate Zvornik's new status as 100 percent 'pure' and cleansed of all Muslims, the mayor dedicated a new church, renamed a local, formerly Muslim village "Saint Stephen", and kissed a crucifix.

[…]

The violence in Bosnia was a religious genocide in several senses: the people destroyed were chosen on the basis of their religious identity; those carrying out the killings acted with the blessings and support of Christian church leaders; the violence was grounded in a religious mythology that characterized the targeted people as race traitors and the extermination of them as a sacred act; and the perpetrators of the violence were protected by a policy designed by the policy makers of a Western world that is culturally dominated by Christianity" (Sells 1996:4).

I. Nonviolence in the Scriptures and Christian Just War Theory

The Christ of the New Testament enjoined forgiveness of enemies, warned his followers against taking up the sword, and submitted to his executioners, beseeching his heavenly Father to forgive them even as they crucified him. Early Christians saw Jesus as a model of imitation – not as a special case or an exceptional individual, whose attitudes and actions were foreordained (though his ultimate destiny may have been). Indeed, the early church imitation of "The Crucified One" led Christians to embrace nonviolence as a defining mark of Christian identity and mission. Among his many titles, Christ came to be worshipped in the ancient liturgy as "the Prince of Peace". All the miracles he worked and healings he performed, the Evangelists are clear, were enactments of his true mission and greatest work of wonder: the reconciliation of human beings with one another and with their Creator.

Acknowledging all this, we must nonetheless admit that the passages from the gospels of John and Luke quoted above are challenging and indeed discomfiting. In the first two resurrection narratives, the risen Lord appears to his apostles, who are huddled in hiding, paralyzed by anxiety. They had reason to be frightened: the one in whom they had put their faith, the one they understood to be the Messiah, who would lead them to victory over the Roman occupiers as well as their Pharisaical co-religionists, had been crushed mercilessly after agonizing tortures, and they feared they might be next. The last thing they expected, we may presume, was to look up and see Jesus standing among them. Luke tells us that they "were startled and terrified, and thought that they were seeing a ghost". Jesus, in his typically cryptic way, wonders why they are frightened, an unfair question if ever there was one.

The Johannine account, displaying that gospel's unfortunate tinge of anti-Semitism, emphasizes the apostles' "fear of the Jews". They come to recognize the figure as Jesus when they gaze upon his wounds: this is the one whose brutalization we have witnessed. John, seeking immediate theological rewards, does not allow the apostles much recovery time; they rejoice, almost instantaneously, upon recognizing him, and he responds by imparting his holy Spirit and his most significant power, namely the authority to forgive sins and reconcile men and women with the Father in heaven.

That the apostles recognize Jesus through the marks of his suffering raises a fateful question. Yes, it is through his wounds that we are healed. But must we, too, enter into the divine victimhood?

In both accounts, peace is the first word uttered by the risen Lord. In Luke's perhaps more realistic pacing of the narrative, the apostles are not impressed by this greeting but dumbfounded. They might well have responded: "Peace?! There you are – a ghost, in your risen glory – while we remain firmly stuck here in this vale of tears. Our suffering has not been redeemed; our wounds are not glorified."

The blessing of peace bestowed by Jesus in both accounts, in short, is clearly of the eschatological variety. It is the peace which passes all understanding, the final peace enjoyed by the saints as they dwell in the eternal now of God's reign. It is the time of fulfillment, experienced proleptically in the risen Christ. And thus it seems and seemed fair to ask: Is this kind of peace the basis of an ethic for the here and now, for the world of unjust violence and wanton suffering? Must we, too, forgive our enemies, turn the other cheek, renounce the sword – or was that behavior only required of the Lord, only possible for the Lord, who rebuked Peter for drawing his sword not, it seems, out of revulsion to an act of self-defense, but because it would stand in the way of Jesus drinking the cup the Father had prepared for him.

A measure of ambiguity toward violence, in short, is found in the scriptures themselves – and less ambiguously, of course, in Christian history after Constantine. Citing what they see as the unambiguous teaching and example of Jesus, Christians have chosen to imitate Christ's nonviolence and reconciliation; other Christians have concluded, however, that Christ's command to love the enemy is an unrealistic ethic for this earth, and in any case not intended for all Christians, being possible only at the eschaton, and perhaps for those rare virtuosi who, like Jesus, are capable of proleptic embodiment of the redeemed state of being. For the majority, however, mired in a fallen world, Christians must do what is necessary to preserve the holy tradition. In this view, the peace that passes all understanding is reserved for a place and time that passes all understanding. The City of God is not to be confused with the City of Man. As St. Augustine ruefully details, we can chart the progress of the saints, but we can also chart the progress of the devil. And we must battle the devil, by bloody warfare if necessary, as long as we find a way to render it "just".

In such a world as ours, then, many of those who have claimed to be followers of the Crucified One have sought a different kind of peace – a version of the Pax Romana. Today peace scholars call this reality "negative peace", a set of conditions in which open warfare and violence are contained or controlled by a comprehensive ruling authority or rule of law. A dingier version of this type of peace through conquest and absolute sovereignty occurs when the ethnic or religious other is marginalized, defeated or annihilated on the road to peace. One thinks of the elimination of the LTTE in Sri Lanka today, or of the attempted genocide against the Bosnian Muslims, analyzed as such by Michael Sells.

The Croatian Catholic and Serbian Orthodox treatment of the Bosnian Muslims is an instance of the distressingly familiar religiously inspired violence that continues to be committed or legitimated by Christians – often by Christians who have hitched their fortunes to state power, or to violent revolution against the state. Is the ideology legitimating such Christian violence? How can it possibly be Christian? "Whether such an ideology reflects the Serb Orthodox faith or is instead a perversion of it, is a question that Serb tradition will answer", Sells responds. Yet it remains a fact, he asserts, that "Serb religion, history, literature, art, and culture have been used to justify a crime the true proportions of which the world has yet to grasp."

The path from Golgotha to Srebrenica, in short, is not as obstructed by Christian discipleship as one would hope. It runs through the state, or through the church, whenever the church claimed or shared imperial power. For a minority, such as a persecuted sect, nonviolence is a plausible as well as a virtuous option. For a Christian state, however, it is decidedly inconvenient, and was thus quickly abandoned. Stooping to the occasion, bishops and theologians less nuanced than Augustine developed ramifying theories and ethics of "just" warfare. Evil must be eradicated, if the Church is to prevail. By this logic Christians have justified the persecution of nonbelievers or heretics "for their own good" as well as in protection of the orthodox community. They, too, retrieved scripture: He comes "not to bring peace but a sword."

Does this selective retrieval of scripture, this partial, narrow and thus distorted rendering of the Christian experience somehow make its practitioners non-Christian? Does the assumption that such interpretations of the Christ event are clearly flawed imply that they are inauthentic for the same reason? Elsewhere I have argued at length that the answer to both of these questions must be no. Bad theology and bad religion do not let Christianity off the hook; they still somehow inspired these bad theologians and bad priests. To put it differently, the numinous power of the sacred is pre-moral; the experience of an encounter with the sacred precedes ethics and interpretation. Even second-rate theologians and high priests are religious, as indicated by their ability to draw upon, and to unleash, the peculiar powers of the religious imagination and the human soul.

We might call this type of theology "demonic" in its consequences, but it nonetheless reached into the depths of those who, following it, became demons. And their successors have a precedent to draw on from within the tradition. Augustine's followers have caused a lot of mischief, all in the name of orthodox Christianity. Even the followers of St. Francis of Assisi have not contained themselves in their mutual contempt – or, in Bosnia, in their malevolent behavior against the religious and ethnic other.

In the modern period imperial power continues to be wielded not by the Christian emperor or the pope but by the nation-state – including nation-states that remain firmly rooted in Christian epistemological premises and values. No matter how much they have been influenced by the path to Enlightenment. France, Britain, and Germany served as surrogates for Christianity, or as allies in its colonizing global mission long after the churches had emptied. In America, our churches are relatively full and the missionizing zeal was in full force during the previous presidency. So entrenched is the identification of Europe and North America with a Christian civilizational project that the right to "religious freedom", as promoted by liberal states, is viewed with suspicion by Africans and Asians as a cloak for proselytism by Christian missionaries and post-Christian capitalists.

II. The Scope of Christian Peacebuilding

Given this dismal legacy, what needs explanation is not the phenomenon of violence inspired or committed by Christians; structures and justifying theologies abound. What needs studying is the phenomenon of Christian nonviolence and, particularly, nonviolent peacebuilding. How and under what conditions do modern Christians (bishops as well as laity, men as well as women) form social movements, inspire congregations and communities, staff nongovernmental organizations and assume the roles of mediators, negotiators, educators, reconcilers and instruments of transitional justice – roles that are actually not natural to religious actors, and especially not to religious leaders.

The study of these religious peacebuilders is in its infancy, owing in large part to the fact that religious peace*building* – as opposed to peacemaking, peacekeeping etc. – is a relatively new phenomenon, dating back in its current incarnation to the aftermath of the revolutions of the 1980s: People's Power in the Philippines, the Velvet Revolution in the Czech Republic, Solidarity in Poland. Peacebuilding is increasingly recognized as a long-term continuous effort at providing and sustaining the conditions of what scholars call a positive peace which addresses the whole of the conflict cycle – conditions such as access to education, economic growth, self-governance, a robust regime of human rights and toleration, and other structural elements essential to integral human development and authentic human flourishing. Education for peace, prevention and early warning, conflict management, conflict resolution, inter-faith dialogue and collaboration, secular-religious dialogue and collaboration in creating the network and organizations essential to a vital civil society – and also, post-accord violence control, transitional justice and social reconstruction: Each and every one of these areas of ongoing conflict transformation, areas that require more than good intentions and pious platitudes from religious actors but actual technical skills, social analysis and cultural leadership, constitute peacebuilding. Given that such a huge research agenda looms before us, what are its necessary foundations?

III. The Emerging Agenda

1. Resources for Christian Peacebuilding: First, scholars must be devoted to the question of resources, internal as well as external, for specifically Christian peacebuilding. It is necessary, of course, first to grapple with the unavoidable legacy of violence legitimated by Christians, often operating as Christian nationalists. The fact of deadly violence deployed by American, European and other putatively "Christian" nations and armies, as well as explicitly Christian militias and movements, is a gross reality which no peacebuilder may ignore; nor can these episodes of violence be judged categorically; their motivations and outcomes are both ambiguous and troubling in that such violence has at times been undertaken in the belief that the cause is just, and that the ends justify the means. The just war theory is one thing; its misapplication and distortions another – and both are called to account for the 21st century, viewed under a hermeneutic of suspicion. Is mass violence or even targeted, strategic or tactical violence, ever justified for the peacebuilder? Can it ever be an appropriate method within a larger, multilayered approach that could rightly be called "peacebuilding"? These questions are far from resolved; and thus the ethicist of the use of force and the moral philosopher do have a certain influence on the putative Christian peacebuilder.

As for internal resources, ideas or intellectual resources, there are a variety of Christian precepts, theologies, doctrines, ethical and symbol systems, that demand as much consideration as their concrete applications in practice. While we do have studies of the historical practice and theory of Christian nonviolence, and while there are important studies of the selective and limited use of violence to resist or oppose unjust or even demonic regimes, these experiences and the insights gained from them have not been integrated into a theory of Christian peacebuilding. For example, what are we to do with a figure like German theologian, Lutheran pastor and Christian martyr Dietrich Bonhoeffer, with his strident denunciation of a watered down cultural Christianity and insistence on the discipleship of the cross, who abruptly terminated his privileged research position at the Union Theological Seminary in New York City in order to return to Germany and clandestinely join a plot to assassinate Hitler? Bonhoeffer is often cited by moral theorists as an example of how Christians can undertake violent actions for a just cause and how occasionally Christians are compelled to break laws for a higher purpose. These are positions also held by one of Bonhoeffer's colleagues at the Union Theological Seminary, Reinhold Niebuhr, also invoked by Ben Mollov. Niebuhr wrestled with what we have identified as one of Christianity's oldest ethical problems: when is it permissible to use violence on behalf of a righteous cause? Niebuhr began his career as a pacifist, but in time grudgingly began to accept the position that a Christian, acting for the sake of justice, could be violent. Niebuhr showed the relevance of the just war theory by fusing it to what he regarded as the biblical Christian duty to fulfill the requirements of social justice. Viewing the world through the lens of "realism", Niebuhr was impressed that moral suasion was not sufficient to combat injustices, especially when they are buttressed by corporate and state power. For this reason, he explained in a seminal essay entitled "Why the Christian Church Is Not Pacifist" (1940), it was at times necessary to abandon nonviolence in favor of a more forceful solution. Building his case on Augustine's understanding of original sin, Niebuhr argued that righteous force was sometimes necessary to extirpate injustice and subdue evil within a sinful world, and that small strategic acts of violence were occasionally necessary to deter large acts of violence and injustice. If violence is to be used in such situations, Niebuhr explained, it must be used sparingly and as swiftly and skillfully "as a surgeon's knife".

For those who are currently developing an ethic for peacebuilding in the violence-drenched Christian-majority settings where it has emerged – in post-apartheid South Africa, in Great Lakes Africa, in Colombia, in Mindanao – the questions of resistance, pacifism, just war, and the selective use of violence for defensive purposes are very much alive. How might figures like Bonhoeffer and Niebuhr, no less than nonviolent exemplars like King and Gandhi, serve as retrievable figures for an ethic of Christian peacebuilding?

Similarly, contemporary experience, grafted into Christian theological and ethical sensibilities, has clearly become a stimulus for the development of peacebuilding as a self-conscious, intentional Christian way of life, vocation, or set of practices. Can we study this process comparatively and systematically, rather than observe it anecdotally? The process – the ongoing evolution of a distinctively Christian peacebuilding – is a complicated mix of historical experience, collectively reserved and institutionalized; direct experience of people on the ground; and fruitful encounter with the other, even the other within the religious tradition. Take, for example, the relatively recent emergence of peacebuilding within Roman Catholicism. That event must be situated in the context of the remarkable evolution of the host religious tradition during the modern period which started with the papal denunciations of religious freedom in the nineteenth century; and evolved further through the emergence of a discernible body of Catholic social teaching which outlined the Christian responsibility to the social order, and placed Catholics squarely in solidarity with the suffering sisters and brothers around the world, limiting state power to its proper sphere, and condemning the nuclear arms race. This trend found its remarkable culmination in the Second Vatican Council and the Declaration of religious freedom and the decisive abandonment of concordats with state power by the Church in order to focus on civil society and, not least, the momentum toward nonviolence and away from US war in the pronouncements of recent popes. Then, the evolution of peacebuilding within Catholicism must be tied, further, to concrete historical experiences, such as CRS in Rwanda and the emergence of the lay movement Sant'Egidio and its own internal evolution from social solidarity to explicit conflict mediation and transformation. And all along the way, there was the Catholic borrowing from the Christian peace churches.

How have the confessional churches evolved their own resources? What of the American evangelicals, what of Christians in Kerala or East Timor, or the Philippines? How have larger economic and political trends and developments, from democratization to the global economic crisis provided openings and opportunities as well as obstacles? These questions demand the active involvement and commitment of historians, theologians, economists, and social scientists.

Finally, in this category of intellectual and symbolic resources, we must address the key question of patterns of education and formation, and how these contribute to or impede the evolution of peacebuilding in a Christian mode, with peacebuilding understood not as the occupation of a few virtuosi or specialists but as the central vocation of every Christian. It is not enough to speak of the rich symbols and doctrines alone – of the Cross and the Cradle, of forgiveness and reconciliation, of the lamb that was slain for our sins, of the mercy and compassion of the Father who condescended to become fully human. Not only are these symbols broken and in need of reconstruction – broken by patriarchy, by colonialism, by racism, by cowardice; they must be reappropriated in each generation. It is now a commonplace for peace researchers to spout the words: "peace education and Christian formation for nonviolent social change" as their mantra in response to the theoretical and excruciatingly practical question: What turns one Christian toward race hatred and genocide, another toward resistance to such demonization, another toward the building of cross-cultural positive peace? We must go deeper, using the tools of the disciplines to implement and test religious education programs; to plumb the depths of spiritual formation and its relation to identity formation and attitudes toward the other, to chart the relations between ethnic and religious influences in community formation.

2. Practices of Christian Peacebuilding in a Globalized World: The second research cluster on the peacebuilding agenda focuses on actual interventions, their nature, and their consequences. Specifically, have Christians advanced the processes begun by secular actors, made their own distinctive contributions or, conversely, have essentially gotten in the way? We can cite examples of all three cases. We know most about Christian peacebuilding from the West, as it were, in which Christian theological doctrines have been transmuted as foundations for western legal and juridical institutions and practices. For example, Truth and Reconciliation commissions in Latin America, South America and ones proposed for parts of Europe and the UK, basically have complemented secular political and legal processes. Where tribal or ethnic practices have been preserved alongside Christian impositions, as in gacacca courts in Rwanda, the goals, metrics and outcomes are different. We know less about the evolving practices of Christian peacebuilding in an era in which Christianity is no longer a western phenomenon but thoroughly globalized and thus in constant interaction and contact with alternative cultural formations as well as non-Christian influences. Christianity's steady movement from a Eurocentric religion towards becoming more and more an authentically global religion in the modern age raises the challenges of such non-theological realities as colonialism (and its complex relationships to modern Christian missionary efforts) and globalization (and its positive and negative complexities) for Christian peacebuilders as well as for Christians more generally; such realities complicate this welcome movement towards a global multicultural, multi-racial, international explosion of Christianity in many new non-European indigenous forms. One only needs to recall that various kinds of Pentecostalism are the fastest growing form of global Christianity. Indeed, most forms of Christianity (especially Roman Catholicism, Anglicanism, and Protestant Evangelicalism) are also expanding exponentially in the southern hemisphere (in Asia, Melanesia, Latin America, and especially in Africa), even as some countries in Europe, all of North America, Australia, and New Zealand seem to become more and more secular.

This extraordinary move from a Eurocentric religion to a global religion (the most important shift in Christian history since its first century transformation from Jewish Christianity to Gentile Christianity) will mean that peacebuilding in its Christian forms will be increasingly diverse and heterogeneous.

3. Peacebuilding and its Impact on Christianity: The third cluster of questions concerns the way peacebuilding is transforming the already fluid and evolving reality we know as Christianity or Christianities. How is it transforming gender roles within the religious communities? In Catholicism, for example, women play a prominent role as peacebuilders. Likewise, peacebuilding on the ground is an inherently ecumenical, inter-religious and religious-secular enterprise. Here theology is lived, doctrines yield to and emerge from praxis, and praxis evolves in rapid response to changing realities on the ground. Is peacebuilding a source of renewal for communities? For the recruiting of youth, for example?

IV. Conclusion

Christian peace activists and scholars point almost triumphally to the nonviolent revolutions of the 1980s and 1990s – in Eastern Europe (Poland and the Czech Republic) and in the Philippines in particular – as indicators that nonviolence is now clearly the wave of the future, and war is obsolete. Yet the wars in Iraq and Afghanistan, Pakistan, the DRC and Israel/Palestine as well as in over three dozen other settings across the globe make this claim contestable even from within the peace camp.

More insidiously, nonviolence, like other historically contingent human acts, may have unintended consequences. The historian Judith Brown entitled her critically acclaimed biography "Gandhi, Prisoner of Hope" in order to reflect her thesis that Gandhi's religious worldview and ardent commitment to nonviolence ultimately undermined progress toward concrete political goals that might have led India closer to an actual experience of communal nonviolence. Brown also argues that the British would have withdrawn from India in any case, as they realized after the wars that they were hopelessly overextended; Gandhi's nonviolent campaign was less a trigger than the lore has it (Brown 1989). Similarly, the former New York Times journalist Chris Hedges, among others, has argued that the Christian advocates of nonviolent revolution in Eastern Europe – the so-called peacemakers in East Germany and the Czech Republic were irrelevant at best, and often feckless (Hedges 1999).

My point here is not to dismiss the political effectiveness of nonviolence, merely to note that it can be of limited efficacy and that the Christian commitment to it does not promise empirically specifiable results or an absence of sacrifice and often brutal suffering on the part of the practitioners. Sells also cautions:

"In the case of religious genocide, moral distinctions are particularly difficult to maintain; the basis of much moral thinking is to be found within religions, but in religiously motivated violence, religions are being manipulated to motivate and justify the evil. One response is to reform religions from within, in dialogue with other religions. Religious leaders of each tradition need to better understand and more clearly explain the full humanity of those who embrace other religions and the variety and richness within other traditions. Another response is to begin with a basic premise – that needless, willfully inflicted human suffering cannot and should not be explained away. The two responses may complement one another." (Sells 1996:144)

References

Brown, Judith M. (1989): Gandhi, Prisoner of Hope. Yale University Press, New Haven.

Hedges, Chris (1999): Response: Religion as an Antidote to Peacemaking. Harvard Divinity School, Center for the Study of World Religions. Unpublished remarks.

Niebuhr (1940): Why the Christian Church Is Not Pacifist. Student Christian Movement Press, London.

Sells, Michael A. (1996): The Bridge Betrayed: Religion and Genocide in Bosnia. University of California Press, Berkeley.

Peace and Violence in Hinduism: Gandhi – Beacon of Peace

Joseph Prabhu

This essay will elaborate on the resources for peace that exist within the Hindu religious and ethical traditions. I have chosen to focus on a single figure – that of Mahatma Gandhi – for a number of reasons: (1) in the space of a short essay it is impossible to summarize or survey a tradition of 5000 years;[1] (2) in Gandhi we see an interesting case study of the dialogue between tradition and modernity, where an ancient tradition is adapted to contemporary circumstances; (3) but by far the most compelling reason is that Gandhi is the modern Indian whose life and thought have most caught the world's imagination. His ethics of non-violence, though not particularly original in its theoretical underpinnings, is striking in its practical force. It represents the most significant development of Hindu ethics in the 20th century. His successes and failures point to some of the challenges now facing Hindu ethics in the 21st century.

Gandhi is fundamentally concerned with practice rather than with theory or abstract thought. The philosophy he applied was meant to reveal its "truth" in the crucible of experience, hence the subtitle of his autobiography "The Story of my Experiments with Truth".

The experiments refer to the fact that the truth of concepts, values, and ideals is fulfilled only in practice. Prior to that practical fulfillment they remain spectral and abstract. Furthermore, Gandhi's ethics are inextricably tied up with his religious beliefs, which itself is unconventional. Though an avowed Hindu, he was a Hindu in a philosophical rather than a sectarian sense, and there was much Hindu ritual and practice that he subjected to critique. In accordance with this religio-philosophical ideal, his understanding of religion could be described as the life of the self attempting to realize itself as Self, and thus achieving *moksha* or spiritual liberation. But *karma yogi* that he was, self-realization had to be expressed through work in the world and the details of daily life rather than through renunciation of the world. Gandhi's own ethics have a decidedly spiritual cast, but by taking pains to express them in a neutral philosophical manner, he intended them to have general validity. Thus, when he switches from affirming that God is truth to saying that truth is God, his rationale was that the latter is a more general statement which has resonance even for unbelievers. This is a testament to Gandhi's innate sense of tolerance and inclusiveness: he believed that his ideals of truth and nonviolence are accessible even to those who do not share his religious metaphysics.

1 According surveys can be found in other writings: Prabhu 2005, 2007.

Truth for Gandhi is not merely, or even primarily, the property of statements, though Gandhi does not deny the importance of factual truth or the correspondence between propositions and states of affairs in the world that either confirm or refute them. Rather, his multifaceted notion of truth emphasizes ontological, moral, and existential aspects. Ontologically *satya* is derived from *Sat*, the essence of self-existence, both the is and the ought of reality. It was this derivation that often led Gandhi to say "Nothing exists in reality except Truth, everything else is illusion." Beyond the illusory temporal flux of phenomena lies the eternal truth, what Gandhi also called "absolute truth". We humans with our finite capacities however can only have access to relative truth, an assertion Gandhi uses to justify epistemological humility and tolerance. All our perceptions of truth are inevitably partial and therefore claims of cognitive absoluteness are both unwarranted and dangerous.

While the ontological aspect of truth points to a more objective notion, the moral and existential aspects move in the direction of a more subjective, almost Kierkegaardian, notion of truth as subjectivity, the deeply personal intuition of truth which can be experienced only through action. Raghavan Iyer brings out the duality between the subjective and objective aspects of truth:

> "Gandhi could not regard truth either as solely the object of reason or as simply the product of human decision. For him [...] truth is nothing less than the splendor of reality and cannot be gained without an understanding of the Eternal Law of Nature, but when it is perceived and seized it must be acted upon. In this sense truth must be both discovered and created, found and enacted [...] In this activist view of truth [...] it is not enough for thought to be based upon truth; the life of the thinker must express it, must represent it visibly in his actions" (Iyer 1973:154).

As already intimated, this idea of truth for Gandhi found its fullest expression in the field of politics which, in accordance with his moral outlook, he regarded as the arena for doing good on the largest possible scale. The idea that Gandhi used to encapsulate this moral conception of politics was *satyagraha.* This was conceived as a practical experiment to introduce truth and nonviolence into the political field. Gandhi adopted this idea early in his political career when he chose *satyagraha* as the name for his resistance movement against the repressive South African government. Explaining his decision, Gandhi wrote: "Truth [*satya*] implies love and firmness [*agraha*] and therefore serves as a synonym for force. I thus began to call the Indian movement *satyagraha*, that is to say, the force which is born of truth and love of nonviolence" (Gandhi 1938:172). The forceful and activist character of *satyagraha* should correct a common misperception, namely that it denotes a passivity of resistance, a mere turning of the other cheek. Although Gandhi insisted that violence be met with love and understanding, the nonviolent means chosen should not obscure the powerful end of establishing justice and truth. In fact, he is on record to have said that if the choice were between the passive acceptance of injustice and violent resistance to it, he would choose the latter. He was convinced, however, that nonviolent resistance was superior to both alternatives.

Satyagraha begins with reasoning with one's opponent or adversary in an attempt to arrive at a just solution, recognizing that no party has a monopoly on the truth, or is wholly in the right. The purpose, therefore, is to work out a rational compromise that will be agreeable to both sides. It is only when such processes of reasoning, persuasion, and compromise have been tired and have proved unsuccessful that one adopts the direct action techniques of *satyagraha. Satyagraha* involves performing actions such as noncooperation like strikes, boycotts, lockouts, fasts; civil disobedience such as nonpayment of taxes, disregard of specific laws or injunctions; publicizing one's cause through marches, rallies, picketing, and other forms of peaceful protest; and constructive programs like low-cost housing, education, health facilities, cooperative banks for the poor. A big part of such nonviolent resistance is *tapas* or the willingness to suffer for one's cause. As Thomas Pantham puts it: "It is the assumption of *satyagraha* that when reasoning fails to move the head, the argument of suffering by the *saatyagrahis* helps move the heart of the oppressor or opponent. Self-suffering, moreover, is the truthserving alternative to the truth-denying method of inflicting violence on others" (Pantham 198:292-310).

Contained in this idea of *satyagraha* is the question of means and ends, which for Gandhi are two sides of the same coin. Gandhi strongly disagrees with the conventional political idea that the ends justify the means. To the contrary, he held that immoral means taint and distort potentially good ends and accordingly placed at least as much, if not more, emphasis on the means, which he described as ends in actions. "The means may be likened to a seed, the end to a tree; and there is just the same inviolable connection between the means and the end as there is between the seed and the tree" (Gandhi, CWMG, vol. 10:431)

The forceful and activist character of *satyagraha* naturally leads to the idea of nonviolence. Gandhi is obviously invoking the Jain precept of *ahimsa,* implying the prohibition to deliberately cause injury or harm to any being, but he takes the precept far beyond its merely negative formulation to encompass the largest love, the greatest charity. "If I am a follower of *ahimsa,* I must love my enemy or a stranger as I would love my wrong-doing father or son. This *ahimsa* necessarily includes truth and fearlessness" (Gandhi 1916 quoted in Iver 1973:180).

Ahimsa then is the deployment of moral force to persuade one's opponent or adversary. It differs from violence in that it respects the autonomy and dignity of the other. It differs from violence in the perpetual willingness to dialogue and negotiate with the other and, as far as it is consistent with rightness, to come to a compromise. Given that one's grasp of the truth is at best partial, it is imperative to see and appreciate the truth in the position of the other and to try and achieve a higher or dialectical reconciliation of conflicting ends. This negotiated compromise has the opposite effect of violence, which involves vanquishing and putting down one's opponent that inevitably sets up a cycle of resentment, ill-will, and further violence. Rather, the search for truth becomes a shared quest based on epistemological humility and mutual respect, notwithstanding the differences that still remain after the effort of mutual understanding.

Of course, Gandhi was not so naïve as to think that such moral persuasion would come about easily. He was all too aware that people who exercise power over others are not likely to give it up without some pressure being exerted. All the means of *satyagraha* mentioned above should then be adopted as a way of morally coercing one's opponent to negotiate. It is true that coercion is being exerted, but it is a coercion that still respects the moral agency and dignity of the other, not least by the willingness to undergo self-suffering.

The strategy presupposes that the opponent does have a minimal openness to such moral appeal, a trait that Gandhi was willing to grant to most people. However, he also recognized that there are madmen and tyrants, rapists and aggressors who would not fall within that category. In those extreme cases Gandhi was willing to use physical force for the purpose of self-defense, as for example when he sanctioned the use of military force to drive back the Pakistani Army in what he considered to be the invasion of Kashmir in 1947-1948.

The three concepts I have discussed, *satya*, *satyagraha,* and *ahimsa,* might give us some idea of the texture of Gandhi's ethical thought. The ideas of truth and nonviolence are certainly to be found in the Jain, Buddhist, and Hindu traditions, but there is a big difference between Gandhi's conceptualization of these ideas and traditional ones. The high standards of moral and spiritual discipline that Gandhi invokes were traditionally part of the *sadhana* of monks and saints, but decidedly not of people in political life. To the contrary, political thinkers like Manu and Kautilya sanctioned the use of physical force both for self-defense and for purposes of political order. Gandhi by contrast considerably softens the traditional dualism between religion and politics. Instead, he attempts to forge a non-dual relationship between the two, where religion, seen as reverence for and service to life, necessarily leads to politics, the arena for the greatest potential public service; and where politics in turn are saved from power-mongering and conflicting factional interests by the moral purification involved in religion at its best. It is very important to distinguish Gandhi's highly moral notions of both religion and politics from the ideological conceptions of them all too common in our time. Certainly the rise of religious fundamentalism and right-wing religious groups would make any peace-loving person nervous about the marriage of religion and politics. However, it should be clear from what I have written that the moral checks and balances that Gandhi exercised over religion and politics purified both domains and offered the world a far different and more noble conception of them that we have yet to measure up to.

Yet these principles of Gandhi represent only one aspect of his ethics – his ethics of love. But love, for Gandhi, was not a simple sentimental matter, a benevolence towards all, demanding as that ethic might be. Love in the full sense incorporates justice, treating people fairly, if not always equally. It was both these elements of love and truth on the one hand, and justice and fairness on the other, that constitute his comprehensive philosophy of peace. What warrants its claim to comprehensiveness is that it tackles overt and structural violence, the violence that is all too visible, and the more subtle and less visible violence contained in unjust practices and institutions. Peace, for Gandhi, was not simply a narrowly conceived moral and spiritual matter; it encompassed a holistic way of life that includes economic and social concerns as well.

As early as 1909 Gandhi wrote "*Hind Swaraj*", a book that was in many ways the foundation for his subsequent thinking. In it, he criticizes the western path of modernization as fundamentally unstable and alienating. It is materialistic, exploitative of nature and human beings, unrestrained, and lacks a sense of direction of moral purpose. The key factor responsible for this state of affairs is the conception of human beings and of human nature that underlies it. Instead of seeing humans as essentially moral and spiritual beings, western modernity basically regards them as consumers driven by greed and self-indulgence. Thus the goal of the modern economic system is to endlessly produce goods in response to the ever-increasing demand of consumers, continually driven and inflamed by modern advertising. Modernity confuses material production for progress, restlessness for vitality, acceleration for efficiency, and consumer satisfaction for an improved quality of life.

From his critique of western modernity we can guess the character of Gandhi's alternative modernity. It is based on a picture of human beings as moral, spiritual, and culturally creative. From this basic conception of human nature, Gandhi derives some regulative principles that should govern a good society. First, it should be informed by the spirit of what Albert Schweitzer called a "reverence for life". Because human beings are not the masters or owners, but are instead the caretakers and trustees of creation, they should organize their affairs in such a way that they respect nature's integrity, diversity, and rhythm, and adjust their demands accordingly. Second, because human beings are interdependent, a sound social system should discourage all forms of exploitation, domination, and inequality, and instead promote the values of love, truthfulness, cooperation and solidarity. Third, because human beings are creative and spiritual in nature, a good society should encourage them to develop these capacities, and in particular, their capacity for *swaraj* (moral self-rule). When Gandhi applied these principles to the social and economic spheres, the ideas he emphasized were those of decentralization, regional development, local self-sufficiency, and the creation of a technology adapted to the needs and resources of a particular area as well as to the creativity of people. He insisted that economic growth should proceed in harmony with nature and between people, even if such growth is slower and more gradual than that brought about by heavy industry and high technology.

A word of explanation may be necessary to justify the choice of the expression "alternative modernity" in connection with Gandhi's socio-economic vision. He is very often seen as a staunch traditionalist, indeed often a reactionary, who wanted to take his country back to a primitive way of life, marked by the spinning wheel and voluntary poverty. One cannot deny either Gandhi's personal asceticism or his desire for a way of life that is characterized by the values of simplicity, harmony, wholeness, and face-to-face relationality. But it would be false to think that he projected his personal asceticism as a social ideal for all, just as it would be inaccurate to characterize simplicity and restraint as merely traditional ideals. Gandhi had nothing against wealth or productivity; indeed he was in contact with many of India's leading industrialists and business people. His point was that the production of wealth should be regulated by a set of moral values rather than being an end in itself.

Gandhi's critique of modernity by no means implied a complete rejection of modernization. On the contrary, he greatly valued the scientific temper of modernity and its emphasis on investigation and experimentation. Gandhi also valued the spirit of Enlightenment with its valorization of independence, critical thinking, and moral autonomy. Conversely, there were many aspects of his tradition that Gandhi was very critical of, from caste and untouchability to the oppression of women. By the same token, modernity for Gandhi did not imply a wholesale rejection of tradition and an embrace of the new for its own sake. Rather he sought to assimilate the best of tradition and modernity, as measured by his own evolving standards. To that extent, I believe we can justify Gandhi's vision as being in tune with the spirit of openness and independence of thought betokened by modernity.

In 1948 Gandhi was assassinated by a fellow Hindu – a rabid nationalist who feared that he was betraying Hinduism. The dialogue that he had initiated between the past and the present and between tradition and modernity has continued since his time. India today, as a fully-fledged nation-state, grapples internally with a range of ethical problems from questions of distributive justice and minority rights to a uniform civil code for the diverse social and religious groups within its borders. At the same time, operating within the community of nations, and being the largest democracy in the world, it is faced with its share of transnational challenges, from the impact of globalization and global ecology, to problems of war and peace.

In meeting these challenges, Hinduism has a rich ethical tradition to draw on, with moral ideas that are deep and complex enough to allow for reinterpretation in new settings. Thus, to take a few examples, the idea of *dharma* with its cosmic, holistic, and ecologically-sensitive perspectives provides a counter-weight to the possessive individualism (to use C. B. Macpherson's evocative term), acquisitiveness and the nature-dominating features of modern and post-modern society. Likewise, the ethic of the *Bhagavad Gita* of doing one's duty selflessly and with inner detachment is one that has wide resonance. And Gandhi's ethic of nonviolence has long attracted the attention of groups in civil society working for peace, human rights, transnational distributive justice and ecological harmony. In an age of globalization, where nuclear and other weapons threaten to destroy the planet, it is heartening to read the comment of J. Duncan Derrett, a renowned scholar of comparative legal systems and of Hindu law in particular:

> "The [traditional] genius of India [...] is peaceful co-existence between groups, creative co-prosperity. India's harnessed the concepts of religion not to activity, nor to a meditative and self-absorbed stagnation, but to the creative co-prosperity of groups each recognizing the other's right to contribute to the whole. A balance of forces is still needed and because it favors it, Hinduism still dominates" (Smith 2003:202).

Flattering as this judgment might be, it nonetheless needs to be qualified. Any dispassionate student of Hindu ethics will readily admit that there are many urgent tasks ahead. There is a set of practical ethical challenges that India faces. One challenge surrounds toleration and pluralism. The peaceful coexistence of many different beliefs, practices, and institutions within Hinduism and its tolerant attitude towards non-Hindu traditions have been a hallmark from earliest times. There is at least a threefold basis for this tolerance: religions, philosophical as well as psychological grounds. The Vedic maxim "Truth is one, thought sages call it by different names" (*ekam sat vipra bahudha vadanti)* captures the pervasive sense of religious pluralism that Hinduism often espouses. The Jain doctrine of *Anekantavada*, the many-sidedness of truth, referring to the subjective quality of truth in general, signals the philosophical open-mindedness of Hinduism and the rejection of dogma. Psychologically, the idea of karma (moral cause and effect), together with the recognition of differences in personality, social station, and aptitude,, points towards a latitude of lifestyle and conduct. While there are indeed basic moral rules and norms (*sadharanadharmas)*, these are applied differently according to caste and one's stage of life (*varnashramadharmas).* This tolerance has merged with a general disposition in favor of nonviolence. It is both wrong and wrong-headed to coerce someone into agreement with one's particular moral standards, because that involves a violation of her or his moral integrity. This is a relativistic position, but one (a systematic ethics would show) that stops well short of a self-defeating relativism.

There are appropriate standards which can be justified, but the appropriateness is nuanced according to caste, class, state of life, etc.

All this is theoretical and like many theoretical pronouncements does not always translate into practice. In recent times, Indian Muslims and Christians have tested the limits of Hindu tolerance, and one cannot say that the results have been encouraging. Hindu-Muslim and Hindu-Christian tensions, alas, are fairly common and on the rise. This is a complex topic and the many causes of this development cannot be explored.

Suffice it to say that there is fault on all sides; suffice it also to say that many Hindus regret the chauvinism and fundamentalism that seem to be conspicuous features of their religion today. It is important for the future of Hindu ethics to distinguish the pluralism and genuine tolerance of Gandhi and Ramakrishna from inclusivism, which has often been mistaken for them. Inclusivism is the position in which one's particular tradition is taken to represent the final or ultimate truth, and other traditions are seen either as aspects of, or stages leading up to such final truth. It easily absorbs, assimilates or subordinates other traditions. The differentiation between pluralism and inclusivism reveals itself at a point where both ideologies have to deal with difference. Where inclusivism tends to neutralize difference and reduce it to the same, pluralism either celebrates difference as part of the infinite plenitude of being, or when differences harden into oppositions and celebrations is not possible, tries to live with such oppositions. Some, but by no means all, of Hindu tolerance has been of this inclusivist kind. Even that is an improvement compared to the exclusivism and marked intolerance that recent Hindu fundamentalism often displays.

I have attempted in brief to provide the ethical underpinnings of Gandhi's philosophy of peace. It is a matter of some concern that post-independence India has paid scant attention to that philosophy. The ongoing tension between Hindus and non-Hindus in India today represents a variation of Hinduism far different from the liberal Hinduism that he espoused and practiced. This diversity of interpretations of Hinduism is ironically part of the rich and problematic pluralism that contemporary India embodies.

References

Gandhi, M.K. (1938): Satyagraha in South Africa. S. Ganesa, Madras.

Gandhi, M.K. (1958-1994): The Collected Works of Mahatma Gandhi, 100 volumes, Government of India Publications Division, New Delhi, India (referred to as CWMG)

Iyer, Raghavan (1973): The Moral and Political Thought of Mahatma Gandhi. Oxford University Press, Oxford.

Pantham, Thomas (1987): Habermas's Practical Discourse and Gandhi's *Satyagraha.* In Bhikhu Parekh and Thomas Pantham *(eds.): Political Discourse: Explorations in Indian and Western Thought.* Sage Publications, New Delhi, 292-310.

Prabhu, Joseph (2005): Trajectories of Hindu Ethics. In: Schweiker, W. (ed.): *The Blackwell Companion to Religious Ethics.* Blackwell Publishing, Malden, 355-367.

Prabhu, Joseph (2007): Gandhi, Empire, and a Culture of Peace. In: Bilimoria, P. and Prabhu, J. (eds.): Indian Ethics: Classical Traditions and Contemporary Challenges. Volume 1. Ashgate, Burlington, 395-410.

Smith, David (2003): Hinduism and Modernity, Blackwell Publishing, Malden.

IV.
The Ambivalent Relationship of Religions towards Peace.
Empirical Evidence and Explanatory Approaches

Peacebuilding and Religious Constitutional Laws

Gerhard Robbers

Religion can bring out the best in people and can cause the most terrible wars. Time and again, religion has shown its immense community-building powers, as well as its ability to destroy communities. Faith and religion have a liberating power, but can also crush freedom. All attempts to overcome religion completely have failed; religion is something that cannot be abolished. It is part of humanity, just like love and hate, curiosity and infatuation, truth and error. Therefore it has to be acknowledged. Religion requires public attention.

Europe experienced the destructive power of religion during hundred years of religious wars that brought terrible devastation on the continent. The Thirty Years' War (1618-1648) is not that long ago that no passed-down memories are left of it. It took place less than 400 years ago. This time span equates to five eighty-year-olds with a grandchild on their lap, telling them about the old days when they used to sit on their grandmothers' laps. Collective memories do not fade in just five life times. During that span of time the generations following the Thirty Years' War have developed and reinforced institutions in which the power of religion could develop for the better.

The peace and freedom mission of religious law

The historical evolution of religious peace generally found expression and took place in the law. Ideally religious law is a law of conflict resolution and of conflict prevention. It builds on the principles of religious freedom and the equality of religions. It recognizes and supports the community-building and peacemaking power of religion. Attempts to reinterpret this law from a non-religious perspective in an attitude that casts aside religion do not only miss the basic principles of religious law, but ultimately endanger social peace. Understood correctly, religious law serves as the foundation and model for managing today's newly erupting religiously motivated conflicts. It must develop to do justice to the new demands placed on it. This applies particularly to the relationship to Islam. Islam must be given ample space to preserve its own cultural identity and values. If this fails, our religious laws will be at risk of losing, or will in fact lose, their libertarian and peacekeeping function. For this reason, it is absolutely appropriate that for instance imams are being trained at state universities in Germany, that religious instruction is being given at public schools and that – naturally – more and more mosques with minarets are going to be built.

The power of the values secured under constitutional law that have evolved culturally and developed and advanced within Christianity have to prove themselves when dealing with Islam; here it turns out whether we only ever talk about these values or whether Western democracies are open, tolerant, strong and self-confident enough to actually bring to bear the values of their constitutions in everyday life. But we must, of course, also ask how much variety, how much differentness a pluralistic, liberal-minded society can actually take, both practically and pragmatically; expecting too much in that respect is certainly not conducive to peace. Here, religious law is responsible for developing and strengthening the capacity for tolerance, and for finding forms and procedures to ensure that different views and ways of life and religions can coexist peacefully. After all, there is no alternative. Securing freedom also spells shaping the ambience, promoting tolerance and demonstrating calmness.

Religious law regularly expresses the deep-set basic structures of a society. In this view, it bears a high degree of its symbolic content. Religion transcends the respective statehood. The self-conception of a state-constituted community is visible in its religious laws as they appreciate religious lives. State and religion act towards one another in – and for – specific states and religions with their respective experiences, boundaries and perspectives. Religious law influences societies; it intensifies or limits their margins for tolerance, freedom and cultural development. Whilst nurturing or repelling religion, states touch life-expressions of particular strength and sensitivity. In so doing, religious law makes a substantial contribution to maintaining or endangering peace. For this reason, religious law must invariably incorporate the specific circumstances of the country in which it applies. Historic experiences, traditions and religious demographic conditions shape the effectiveness of religious law, and are crucial to its success or failure.

International variations

Religion has different functions for different state-constituted communities (Luckmann 1985:26 ff.; Spaemann 1985:9 ff.; Luhmann 1996). The evolution of nation-states was reflected particularly in the emergence of national state churches – such as in England. With all its shortcomings, laïcité in France is the nation's self-assurance. Last but not least, German statehood developed in a balancing act between two equally strong religious parties. Many peculiarities and sensitivities of religious law conditions in the United States of America may be explained by global immigration's need for integration. Today's renewed intensified nationalisation of Orthodox Churches in Eastern Europe is rooted in the quest for new community-building legitimacy. The European Union seeks a concrete definition of its reference to religion (Vignon 1996:43 ff.).

Today's religious demographic changes[1] create new conflicts: secularisation, which has reached its limits, restructuring institutionalised churchliness, migration, small new rapidly emerging religious communities and, above all, the spread and rise of Islam.

From the outset, the colonial background of France and the United Kingdom at least mitigated the impact of narrowing the European occidental horizon of main religions. In the legal discussion held in the United Kingdom, religion is described by joint worship,[2] dominant theistic starting positions are extended to enable exceptions for non-theistic convictions.[3] In France, laicist basic understanding, also shaped by Christianity in differentiating between God and the world,[4] makes it debatable whether state jurisdiction is at all authorised to define religion (Poulat 1997:101; Messner 1988a: 321 ff.). Only recently, the Lyon Cour d'Appel described elements of a legal concept of religion for the first time as an objective element of community, and with it a common faith as a subjective element, a ruling that was instantly dismissed by the French Cour de Cassation.[5]

Legal conceptions of religion consciously leave a back door open for exceptions and other developments (Odio Benito 1989:5; Robert and Duffar 1996:561-562; Duffar 1994:939-940). Evolutionary interpretation also characterise the individualising development of the term religion in the law of the United States of America, which identifies faith and religion.[6] There, concept formation is currently emerging *per analogiam*. Religion is defined analogous to the phenomena conventionally considered to be religion. At the same time, the contents of faith must concern ultimate questions,

1 See, for instance, the articles in: *G. Aijmer* (ed.) A Conciliation of Powers: The Force of Religion in Society, Göteborg: IASSA, 1992; *Robert Wuthnow* Rediscovering the Sacred: Perspectives on Religion in Contemporary Society, Grand Rapids/Mich.: W.B. Eerdmans Publishing CO, 1992; *Gilles Kepel* The Revenge of God: The Resurgence of Islam, Christianity and Judaism in the modern world, Cambridge: Polity Press, 1994; *Mark Juergensmeyer* Violence and the Sacred in the Modern World, London: Cass, 1992; *idem.* The New Cold War? Religious Nationalism confronts the Secular State, Berkeley: University of California Press, 1993; *Samuel P. Huntington* The Clash of Civilizations and the Remaking of World Order, London (et al.): Touchstone, 1998.

2 See *Anthony Bradney* Religions, Rights and Laws, Leicester: Leicester University Press, 1993, p. 124 ff.; *David Feldman* Civil Liberties and Human Rights in England and Wales, Oxford: Clarendon Press, 1993, p. 687 f.; on the definition of a place of religious worship: "a place of which the principal use is as a place where people come together as a congregation or assembly to do reverence to God. It need not be a God which Christians worship. It may be another God, or an unknown God, but it must be reverence to a deity. There may be exceptions. For instance, Buddhist temples are properly defined as places for meeting for religious worship" Lord Denning in *R v. Registrar General, ex parte Segerdal* [1970] 2 QB 697, CA, p. 707.

3 See also New Zealand High Court, *Centrepoint Community Growth Trust v. Commissioner of Inland Revenue* [1985] 1 NZLR, p. 673; Australian High Court, *Church of the New Faith v. Commissioner for Pay-Roll Tax* [1983] 57 ALJR 785, p. 796; *A. Bradney* (footnote 9) p. 125 f.

4 See Math. 22, 21; Mar. 12, 17; Luk. 20, 25.

5 CA Lyon, 28.7.1997, J.C.P. 1998, II, 10025; Cass. crim. 30.6.1999, *Eglise de Scientologie*, Juris-Data No. 003147.

6 See, for instance, *Malnak v. Yogi*, 592 F.2d 197 (3d Cir. 1979), *Founding Church of Scientology of Washington v. United States*, 133 U.S. App. D.C. 229, 409 F.2d, cert. denied, 396 U.S. 963 [1969].

they must be personal and important to the believer, and there must be a comprehensive system of beliefs. It is only as a confirming element that this law finally asks for formal signs resembling those of conventional religions, such as ceremonies or organisation (cf. Ariens/Destro 1996:947 ff.).

In interpretative adaptation, therefore, the legal regimes accept social developments and integrate them step by step. With a certain gain in time, which opposes the condition of seriousness of religion against ephemeral appearances, these new convictions open up a path to the freedom and status of religion. Legitimate legislative enactment must aptly incorporate the pre-judicial reality of religion. The self-conception of the freedom bearer is a main element of freedom-oriented legislative enactment. Dynamic and plural experiences of religion require a dynamic and plural law.

The theologically founded freedom of religion developed in accordance with human rights is brought to bear in all of today's constitutional states (Ibán/Ferrari 1998:4 ff.). Religion cannot be differentiated from faith and action; freedom of religion is therefore both freedom of thought and freedom of action. Freedom of religion bears the function of positive freedom. State law must provide space for the most comprehensive, unimpeded development of religious life.

State responsibility of freedom demands taking religious lifestyles seriously, for their own sakes, and not just promoting non-religious social considerations as to their usefulness or taking advantage of them as value providers.

However, state promotion of religion also serves other interests. Stabilisation of religion is in the interest of the state with regard to cultural preservation and social establishment of peace. For this reason, the integration capacity of new religions needs to be examined. The extent of freedom of religion and its consequences in the right of self-determination necessitate justified trust in the bearer of freedom by the legal regime.

The democratic state may and must, however, incorporate the understandings of life and structural expectations, and hence also the religiously motivated behaviours of the population, when shaping its legal regime. In so doing, pluralisation of religious conditions can lead to the culturally more acceptable pluralisation of the legal regime (Poulter 1998:25; Hamilton 1995:341). Germany already gained this role model-endowing experience in the wake of Protestant Reformation; in contrast, the result may not be the exclusion of the religious and the neutrality-violating preference of non-religious lifestyles.

The example of France

It has been shown that respectful cooperation between the state and religious groups and communities contributes considerably to the pacification of society. In their obligation to create peace and freedom, states are obliged to promote dialogue and respect between religions. The community-building strength of religion can make an important contribution to peacebuilding and peacekeeping.

I would like to cite the example of the peacebuilding function of religious law in France, not least in connection with the latest developments; I take France as an example because it is considered by many in Germany, Europe and the rest of the world to be a role model for strictly separating the state and religious communities, for being a system that drives back religion and crowds out religion from the public domain, and because this is precisely where there is a great deal of misunderstanding.

As written in its Constitution, France is a laicist republic, which is the sum of religious-political disputes that have been held since the beginning of the 19th century.[7] Laïcité was formerly an inflammatory term. Originally, it was the place of one's own laicist moral (Baubérot 1997:131 ff.; Morange 1995:130 ff.) that seeks expression in the Declaration of the Rights of Man and of the Citizen from 1789, and sets fundamental values against the basic values of the Catholic Church (Defois 1995:27 ff.; de Broglie 1964:123 ff.; Carbonnier 1993:17 ff.). It is based on an own republican holiness, and elements of a sacralisation of the republic survives in this ideology of laicism, something of the messianism of the French Revolution (Trotabas 1960:20; Bergounioux 1995:17 ff.).

The enemy stereotype of laïcité, as a type of latency term, is clericalism, defined as the claim of religion to exercise a moral magisterium over society (Baubérot 1990:225). The historic roots of laïcité, its major battles and social background, lie in opposition to the Catholic Church, which was dominant in France; it can be shortened to: the republican state versus the Catholic Church, "two Frances" against one another, the ideal of 1789 versus the syllabus errorum.[8] It is this latency that divides French laïcité from German neutrality. Hence laïcité stands for the pure privateness of religion and for a term of publicness marked by equality and republican indivisibility, without differentiation, that fights against intermediary powers and local peculiarities (Rosanvallon 1990; Braibant 1992:56). It therefore has a different focus to the understanding

7 I would like to thank Professor Dr. Brigitte Basdevant-Gaudemet, Université de Sceaux, for material she provided and for the intense discussions held with her; see also Article 1 Clause 2 of the Constitution of 1958, Preamble of the Constitution of 1946; Article 10 of the Declaration of the Rights of Man and of the Citizen from 1789. Regarding the body of standards, see *Bernard Jeuffroy/ François Tricard* (eds.), Liberté religieuse et régime des cultes en droit français. Textes, pratique administrative, jurisprudence, Paris: Les editions du Cerf, 1996; *Jean Boussinesq* La laïcité française, Paris: Editions du Seuil, 1994; on the history of religion in France, see *Christian Modehn* Religion in Frankreich, Gütersloh 1993; *Jean Gaudemet* Eglise et cité, Paris 1994, p. 141 ff.; *Jacques Le Goff/René Rémond* (eds.), Histoire de la France religieuse, 4 Bde, Paris 1992; *Jean-Marie Mayeur* La séparation des Eglises et de l'Etat, Paris: Éd.Ouvrières, 1991; see also the articles in: *Jean Gaudemet et al.* Administration et Eglise, Du concordat à la séparation de l'Eglise et de l'Etat, Geneva: Droz, 1987.

8 On the Protestant content of laïcité, see for further details: *J. Baubérot* (1997 p. 115); *A. Frhr. von Campenhausen* (1962) p. 5 f.

of publicness characterised by German law, with its term of general law as a place of importance, of valuable things, that is by no means a stranger to particularity and that seeks religious balance.

The primary juridical content of laïcité is unfolded, backed by the Constitution, in the Law of Separation of 1905, the climax of the French culture clash: freedom of conscience, the separation of the state from the Church, the prohibition of state financing of religious communities[9] (Basdevant-Gaudemet 1995:127 ff.; 1998:23 ff.; 1999; Barbier 1995; Durand 1999:427 ff.; Audibert et al. 1960; Bost 1990; de Naurois 1982:257 ff.; Metz 1977:21 ff.).

The geometry-ridden concept of strict separation, the 19th century dream, however, has been giving way for a long time to the positive acceptance of religious needs (Morange 1988:53 ff.; Rivero 1949:137 ff.; Freiherr von Campenhausen 1962; Metz 1983:1109 ff.; Baubérot 1994:57 ff.). Laïcité as a legal principle means neutrality and tolerance, that the state makes no difference between individual beliefs and does not intervene in religious institutions (*Boyer* 1993:105 f.).

State-constituted community, constituted in freedom, must have ready forms of organisation that are commensurate with the self-conception of the religious and its social importance. For this, France has an exceedingly complex, needs-oriented system of forms of religious associations, the original restrictive traits of which are now receding.

For want of an own legal personality, religious communities can establish cult associations, associations cultuelles[10] (Basdevant-Gaudemet 1990:101 ff.; Gueydan 1987:117 ff.; Basdevant-Gaudemet/Messner 1994:115 ff.), which act as their asset holders.[11] After 1905, the Catholic Church were allowed to form diocesan associations,

9 See *Brigitte Basdevant-Gaudemet* Staat und Kirche in Frankreich, in: Gerhard Robbers (ed.), Staat und Kirche in der Europäischen Union, Baden-Baden, 1995, p. 127 ff.; *Maurice Barbier* La laïcité, Paris: L'Harmattan, 1995; *Jean-Paul Durand* Droit public ecclésiastique et droit civil ecclésiastique français, in: Patrick Valdrini et al., Droit canonique, 2nd edition, Paris; Dalloz 1999, p. 427 ff.; on development, see the articles in: *A. Audibert et al.* La laïcité, Paris 1960; *Hubert Bost* (ed.), Genèse et enjeux de la laïcité, Geneva: Labor et fides, 1990; *Brigitte Basdevant-Gaudemet* Droit et religions en France, in: R.I.D.C. 1998, p. 23 ff.; *op. cit.* La jurisprudence constitutionnelle en matière de liberté confessionnelle en France. Régime juridique des cultes et la liberté confessionnelle. Rapport établi sur la demande du Conseil constitutionnel pour la conférence des Cours constitutionnelles de Varsovic, 1999 (unpublished); *Louis de Naurois* La non-confessionnalité de l'Etat en droit français, L'année canonique 1982, p. 257 ff.; *René Metz* Eglises et Etat en France, Paris: Ed. Du Cerf, 1977, p. 21 ff.; see also the articles in: Faut-il modifier la loi de 1905?, Les petites affiches 1.5.1996, p. 1 ff.

10 See Loi de la séparation of 9 December 1905 with amendments by the Laws of 2 January 1907, 13 April 1908 and 31 December 1913; see *Brigitte Basdevant-Gaudemet* A propos des associations cultuelles. Etapes d'une législation, in: L'année canonique 33/1990, p. 101 ff.; *Jean Gueydan* Les religions face au droit d'association français, in: Praxis juridique et religion 1987, p. 117 ff.; *Brigitte Basdevant-Gaudemet/Francis Messner* Statut juridique des minorités religieuses en France, in: European Consortium for Church-State Research (ed.), The Legal Status of Religious Minorities in the Countries of the European Union, Thessaloniki: Sakkoulas Publ./ Milano: Giuffre Editore, 1994, p. 115 ff.

11 For details, see *A. Boyer* 1993, p. 90; Law No. 87-571 of 23 July 1987.

associations diocésaines, to counteract liberalist cult associations. Diocesan associations in particular preserve the theologically required bishop's right to make the final decision[12] (Baubérot 1990:85; Rognoni 1923:119 ff.).

There is also the added possibility to establish general associations[13] (all kinds of variations with a less advantageous position with regard to property law and tax law) (*Boyer* 1993:88).

To become fully legally recognised, cult and diocesan associations[14] must prove that their religious community has existed for a certain time, that it has a large number of members and fixed organisational structures. They must also respect the freedom of the individual, the principles of society and the legal regime. They may not breach public morality or public order, nor may they be for-profit.[15]

Some of these requirements go beyond those leading to the recognition of religious communities as public bodies in Germany. Due to this, associations culturelles and diocésaines possess a special dignity (*Boyer* 1993:91). To all intents and purposes, and unlike the status of a public body in Germany, they are now reserved for Catholic, Protestant and Israelite religious communities,[16] which were recognised in the 19th century concordat system. In practice, the system enables the state to financially influence religious communities by granting tax advantages and state allowances; its handling contributes to the stabilisation of existing religious demographic conditions (*Boyer* 1993:104).

12 See Enzyklika Vehementer Nos of 11 February 1906; Gravissimo officii of 10 August 1906; Enzyklika Maximam Gravissimamque of 18 January 1924; Avis d'assemblée du Conseil d'Etat, 13.12.1923, in: B. Jeuffroy/F. Tricard 1996, p. 321 f.; *Jean Baubérot* Vers un nouveau pacte laïque? Paris: Éd. du Seuil, 1990, p. 85; on the legal position of the orders, see Law No. 505 of 8 April 1942; *A. Boyer* 1993, p. 168 ff.; contemporary crit. *Pierre-Jean Rognoni* Du statut légal de l'Eglise en France, Paris: Jouve 1922, p. 119 ff.

13 According to the Law of 1901; *B. Basdevant-Gaudemet* Staat und Kirche in Frankreich 1995, p. 127 ff.; see Cass. com., 17.3.1981, *Institut musulman de la Mosquée de Paris c/Lahoucine*, D. 1983, p. 23.

14 Article 4 of the Law of 9 December 1905.

15 *A. Boyer* 1993, p. 132; CE 1.2.1985, *Association chrétienne des Témoins de Jéhovah*, R.D.P. 1986, p. 274; CE 14.10.1985, *Association de l'Etude de la nouvelle Foi*, Lebon, p. 284; CE 17.6.1988, *Union des athées*, D. 1988, I.R., p. 197; CE 29.10.1990, *Association cultuelle de l'Eglise apostolique arménienne de Paris*, Lebon, p. 297; CE sect. 9.10.1992, *Commune de Saint-Louis c/Association "Siva, Soupramanien de Saint-Louis"*, D. 1992, I.R. p. 252; CE 24.10.1997, *Association locale pour le culte des Témoins de Jehovah de Riom*, D. 1997, I.R. p. 256.

16 CE 1.2.1985, *Association chrétienne des Témoins de Jéhovah*; *A. Boyer* 1993, p. 143.

The right to church buildings[17] in France marginalises the prohibition of state financing of religion (Lonjou 1992:25 ff.; Durand 1995:65 ff.; Flores-Lonjou 1995:41 ff.). The state owns all Catholic church buildings that were built before 1905[18] and is responsible for their maintenance.[19] They are placed at the Catholic Church's disposal free of charge.[20] Priests receive compensation for overseeing state church buildings; thus they receive an additional salary directly from the state.[21]

The state may not grant any financial allowances for the construction of new cult buildings. However, it can act as guarantor for religious communities to borrow funding, and grants building leases at a symbolic interest rate.[22] Allowances are extensive for cultural establishments beyond actual cult rooms, such as for church halls affiliated to cult rooms. This differentiation between cult and culture (Steiner 1983:9) enabled considerable public allowances to be granted as early as in 1921 for the construction of Paris Mosque, and recently for Evry Cathedral and Rennes Mosque. The laicist reduction of the religious to the cult opens up unexpected scope for the state promotion of religion, which is consistently exploited (*Boyer* 1993:131, 158).

Last but not least, this dynamic limitation of the ban on subsidies from the positively construed freedom of religion serves the purpose of balancing out a hidden de facto inequality[23] vis-à-vis those religious communities that did not possess any cult buildings in France in 1905, the doctrine of a new compensatory laïcité, satisfactory, regulatory and integration-oriented (Flauss 1990:10).

Laïcité lives from diversity. The situation in the three départements of Alsace-Lorraine differs in many respects (Boyer 1993; Messner 1997:61 ff.; 1988b:60 ff.). Here,

17 See *Magalie Lonjou* Les lieux des cultes, in: Actes, les cahiers d'action juridique, No. 79/80, "Les religions en face du droit", April 1992, p. 25 ff.; estimates yield over 38,000 Catholic churches, 1,200 Protestant churches, 1,600 mosques and Islamic prayer rooms – 8 large mosques with a minaret – almost 500 synagogues and Jewish places of worship, over 100 Buddhist pagodas; see *A. Boyer* 1993, p. 125 ff., 152; Le Monde, 14 April 1999; *Jean-Paul Durand* Lieux de cultes en droit français – Cultes affectataires –, in: L'année canonique 37/1995, p. 65 ff.; *Magalie Flores-Lonjou* Le statut des édifices cultuels en droit français, in: Revue de droit canonique 45/1995, p. 41 ff.

18 Circulaire du ministre de l'Intérieur, 13.8.1959, No. 388.

19 Article 5 of the Law of 13 April 1908 and the Law of 25 December 1942; CE 22.1.1937, *Ville de Condé-Sur-Noireau*; CE 26.10.1945, *Chanoine Vaucanu*, Lebon, p. 212.

20 Article 5, 1 of the Law of 20 January 1907; Article L 131-2.2° Code des communes; Article 26 of the Law of 1905.

21 On compensation for monitoring church buildings, see Circulaire of 7 February 1990.

22 Law of 25 December 1992; Réponse ministère de l'Intérieur, JO, Débats Assemblée nationale, 18.4.1988, p. 1674; Article 11 of the Law of 29 July 1961; Rapport Marchand (Rapport d'information déposé en application de l'article 145 du règlement sur l'intégration des immigrés), Assemblée nationale, No. 1348, 2e session ordinaire, 1989/90, p. 77.

23 See CE 12.2.1988, *Association des résidents des quartiers Portugal-Italie*, J.C.P. 1989, II, 21257; *A. Boyer* 1993, p. 131.

local law applies, coined by the Napoleonic concordat of 1801.[24] The President of France appoints the Bishops of Strasbourg and Metz. The Catholic, Lutheran and Reformed Church and the Jewish Community are recognised religious communities that constitute public bodies, organised by state act. Their clergy are paid directly by the state; the crucifix is being displayed in public schoolrooms, as well as both on and in other public buildings.[25]

Laïcité, accepted to pluralise religious conditions, is pluralising itself. France has seven different religious law systems (Damien 1995:82; Durand 1999:492 ff.); immediate payment of only the Catholic clergy by the département in Guyana on the one hand and state appointment of the Muslim mufti in Mayotte on the other are reminiscent of colonial rule and cultural mission.[26]

Today, such peculiarities can no longer be deemed merely tolerated exceptions. Their compatibility with the Constitution has been only rarely questioned (Flauss 1992:1625 ff.; Poulat 1997:102). French laïcité is open to definitive changes; above all, it has overcome its original hostility to the Catholic Church. Laïcité by all means acknowledges the political clause in the appointment of Catholic bishops[27] and – more than that – the approach of an *invocatio dei* in the Declaration of the Rights of Man and of the Citizen of 1789, which is part and parcel of the Constitution (Celerier 1991:15 ff.; Turpin 1994:100). The new laïcité was spoken about in diverse and even contrary nuances mentioning positive or neutral laïcité in particular[28] (Chablis 1990:683 ff.; Poulat 1997:63 ff., 102; Rémond 1995:7; Madiot 1995:79 ff.; Baubérot;

24 Together with the Organic Articles of the Catholic Church and of the Protestant Church of 1802, adopted unilaterally by Napoléon, as well as the provisions on the Jewish religious communities, primarily the French Religious Laws applicable prior to 1871, in addition to numerous German modifications from the time when Alsace-Lorraine belonged to the German Empire from 1870/71. On the development of the concordat, see *Brigitte Basdevant-Gaudemet* Le jeu concordataire dans la France du XIXe siècle, Paris 1988; *Jean Julg* L'Eglise et les Etats – Histoire des concordats, Paris: Ed.Nouvelle Cité, 1990, p. 81 ff., 133 ff.

25 Kaiserliche Verordnung of 22 April 1902 in conjunction with the décret of 26 November 1919; *A. Boyer* 1993, p. 192.

26 See, in particular, the Mandel Decree of 16 January 1939 and 6 December 1939; *A. Damien* 1995 p. 85; Ordonnance of 27 August 1827; Ordonnance royale of 12 November 1828; CE 9.10.1981, *Beherec*, Lebon, p. 358.

27 Aide mémoire de la Secrétairie d'Etat relatif à la promotion des évêques en France, 20.5.1921; see *Jean-Paul Durand* Le modus vivendi et les diocésaines (1921-1924). L'hypothèse d'un accord diplomatique en forme simplifiée, L'année canonique, 35/1995, p. 199 ff.; *A. Boyer* 1993, p. 97; *A. Damien 1995,* p. 88.

28 Well-tempered separation: *Eric-Rémi Chablis* Une séparation bien tempérée – Le droit des cultes en France, Etudes, 05.1990, p. 683 ff.; *René Rémond* La laïcité et ses contraires, in: La laïcité, Pouvoirs 1995, No. 75, p. 7; *Yves Madiot* Le juge et la laïcité, in: La laïcité, Pouvoirs 1995, No. 75, p. 79 ff.; described as a path to a new agreement of laïcité: *J. Baubérot* 1990; concordance without concordat: *A. Boyer* 1993, p. 145, 196; see also *Jacques Robert* La liberté religieuse et le régime des cultes, Paris: P.U.F., 1977, p. 36 ff.; *Jacques Zylberberg* Laïcité, connais pas: Allemagne, Canada, Etats-Uni, Royaume-Uni, in: La laïcité, 1995, No. 75, p. 37 ff.; *Anne-Marie Franchi* Laïcité: la parole à la défense, in: La laïcité, Pouvoirs 1995, No. 75, p. 85 ff.; *Hans Maier* Politik und Religion, in: P. Koslowski (1985 p. 136 ff.); *A. Frhr. von Campenhausen* (1962 p. 158 f.).

Boyer 1993:145, 196; Robert 1977:36 ff.; Zylberberg 1995:37 ff.; Franchi 1995:85 ff.; Mayeur 1991:136 f.; Freiherr von Campenhausen 1962:158 f.).

The guiding principle of laïcité is changing from conflict to consensus that has been set up already in elements of conciliation in the Law of Separation of 1905 and experienced in the trenches of Great War when the war volunteers of the French clergy suffered disproportionately high losses. The Catholic Church has adjusted to today's applicable law, which it actively shapes (d`Onorio 1990). The pluralistic claim of laïcité opens up to the right of say of religions and of religious experience. Where it has survived, the traditional anti-Catholic atheism has become an anti-religious attitude.

The obligation to tolerance laid down in religious laws

It generally applies that religion is more than a purely private matter (Drago 1993:222); it has a public impact and is relevant to public life (de Naurois 1962:241 ff.). Social rhythms of life, national holidays and the calendar reflect culturally shaping factors. Religion is an event that pervades all life contexts. Endeavours to reduce religion to a mere social phenomenon, essentially etatist, have failed in all legal regimes; religion invariably possesses a highly varied special legal status.

Altogether, it can be seen, particularly in the example of France, that cooperation between the state and religious communities is the key to peaceful existence; state law must respect theological needs, and must accommodate these needs. Flexibility of the law is consequently required, and is possible. The liberal state must enable freedom, also for religion. Needs-orientated law must accommodate the needs of citizens, as well as those of religion. The pluralistic state must act out plurality, also that of religion.

All this is an imposition, a demand; all this is difficult. The success of these endeavours reveals the culture of state-constituted community, its capacity for culture, its capacity for peace.

It can be seen again and again that openness towards the needs of religions is the safest way to keep the peace and shape freedom. The Organization for Security and Co-operation in Europe (OSCE) has an *Advisory Council for Freedom of Religion or Belief,* comprising independent members. Amongst other things, the members act in an advisory capacity in legislative projects on religious affairs in participating states, the Balkans, Central Asia, as well as in Western Europe and Turkey. Often it is not the actual governments that attempt to exclude religious groups in religious laws, to repel them or assert unjustified privileges. It is often the individual religious communities that attempt to strengthen their position by way of state law. This is quite acceptable as long as special laws are justified by special situations, when a religious community is of particular importance to the national identity, when it renders special services for the state community, both past and present, and therefore takes on special obligations and burdens, as long as this remains reasonable and not discriminatory. Religious law can accommodate these special situations. In so doing, it must protect everyone's needs for freedom and potential capacities.

The European Court of Human Rights issued a particularly emphatic warning. The issue in question was the state registration of the Christian Orthodox Metropolitan Church of Bessarabia in the Republic of Moldova. It formed after splitting from the general Moldovan Orthodox Church, which had several million followers. The government wanted only one Orthodox Church in Moldova, and refused its registration, which the schismatic church required to be able to act legally. The special situation was that the previous comprehensive Orthodox Church was subordinated to the Patriarchate of Moscow, whilst the seceded community – almost half of the population – was subordinated to the Romanian Patriarchate. The schism reflected the split in the population – from historic, ethnic, national, linguistic and religious perspectives. The government wanted a unified church to protect the union of the state and to ensure national peace; it seriously feared for the existence of the republic, not fully without reason.

However, the European Court of Human Rights condemned the Republic of Moldova for breaching the freedom of religion in accordance with the European Convention on Human Rights and explained that the state must remain neutral and impartial when it comes to religious communities. It is a matter here of preserving pluralism and of the functionability of democracy. One of its characteristic principles is that it offers the possibility to resolve a country's problems through dialogue, without recourse to violence, even if they are burdensome. Accordingly, it is not the role of state authorities to resolve the causes of tension by doing away with pluralism, but to ensure that rival groups tolerate one another.[29] In religious law, therefore, the state must promote peace and freedom. It must disseminate tolerance, for example by educating in state schools, and also, by all means, through the police and jurisdiction, through urban development, through the promotion of culture, through all of the many instruments available to the modern state to keep peace in freedom at home and abroad.

In so doing, cooperation is the cleverest way to proceed, also with those who do not seek cooperation. No religious law may be naive. With the community-building, peace-building strength of religion – this power must be the starting point – but with all this positive strength it is obvious how easily religion can be abused: cooperation is also the best instrument of control, control in freedom. If groups cooperate, they know about each other, they know of the others' intentions, how they think, what moves them, what

29 Metropolitan Church of Bessarabia and others v. Moldova, 45701/99, 13 December 2001; Hasan and Chaush v. Bulgaria [GC], No. 30985/96, § 78, ECHR 2000-XI; United Communist Party of Turkey and Others v. Turkey, judgment of 30 January 1998, Reports 1998-I, p. 27, § 57; Serif v. Greece, Nno. 38178/97, § 53, ECHR 1999-IX).

they feel – also at times when they are not so well-disposed towards one another. For this reason, it is right to strengthen the organisation of Islam in Germany, particularly to reign in the anarchical strength of this religion, and to show peaceful paths towards freedom and development.

References

Aijmer, Göran (ed.) (1991): A Conciliation of Powers: The Force of Religion in Society. IASSA, Göteborg.

Ariens, Michael S. and Destro, Robert A. (1996): Religious Liberty in a Pluralistic Society. Carolina Academic Press, Durham.

Audibert, A. et al. (1960): La laïcité. Presses universitaires de France, Paris.

Basdevant-Gaudemet, Brigitte (1988): Le jeu concordataire dans la France du XIXe siècle. Presses Universitaires de France, Paris.

Basdevant-Gaudemet, Brigitte (1990): A propos des associations cultuelles. Etapes d'une législation. In: L'année canonique 33:101 ff.

Basdevant-Gaudemet, Brigitte and Messner, Francis (1994): Statut juridique des minorités religieuses en France. In: European Consortium for Church-State Research (ed.): The Legal Status of Religious Minorities in the Countries of the European Union. Giuffrè, Milano.

Basdevant-Gaudemet, Brigitte (1995): Staat und Kirche in Frankreich. In: Robbers, Gerhard (ed.): Staat und Kirche in der Europäischen Union. Nomos, Baden-Baden.

Basdevant-Gaudemet, Brigitte (1998): Droit et religions en France. In: R.I.D.C.

Basdevant-Gaudemet, Brigitte (1999): La jurisprudence constitutionnelle en matière de liberté confessionnelle en France. Régime juridique des cultes et la liberté confessionnelle. Rapport établi sur la demande du Conseil constitutionnel pour la conférence des Cours constitutionnelles de Varsovic. (unpublished).

Barbier, Maurice (1995): La laïcité. L'Harmattan, Paris.

Baubérot, Jean (1990): Vers un nouveau pacte laïque? Éditions du Seuil, Paris.

Baubérot, Jean (1994): La France, "République laïque". In: Baubérot, Jean (ed.): Religions et laïcité dans l'Europe des douze. Syros, Paris, p. 57-68.

Baubérot, Jean (1997): La morale laïque contre l'ordre moral. Éditions du Seuil, Paris.

Bergounioux, Alain (1995): La laïcité, valeur de la République. In: Pouvoirs 75:17 ff.

Bost, Hubert (ed.) (1990): Genèse et enjeux de la laïcité. Labor et Fides, Geneva.

Boussinesq, Jean (1994): La laïcité française. Éditions du Seuil, Paris.

Boyer, Alain (1993): Le droit des religions en France, Paris, PUF.

Bradney, Anthony (1993): Religions, Rights and Law. Leicester University Press, Leicester.

Braibant, Guy (1992): Le droit administratif français. Presses de la Fondation nationale des sciences politiques, Paris.

Carbonnier, Jean (1993): La religion, fondement du droit? In: Archives de philosophie du droit "Droit et religion" 38:17 ff.

Celerier, Thibaud (1991): Dieu dans la Constitution. In: Les petites affiches 5 June 1991, 67:15-20.

Chablis, Eric-Rémi (1990): Une séparation bien tempérée – Le droit des cultes en France. In: Etudes 05:683 ff.

Damien, André (1995): Le statut juridique des Eglises reconnues en France. In: Esprit et vie 6:82 ff.

De Broglie, Guy (1964): Le droit naturel à la liberté religieuse. Beauchesne, Paris.

Defois, Gérard (1995): La laïcité, vue d'en face. In: Pouvoirs 75:27 ff.

De Naurois, Louis (1962): Aux confins du droit public et droit privé: la liberté religieuse. RTDC iv.

De Naurois, Louis (1982): La non-confessionnalité de l'Etat en droit français. In: L'année canonique 1982.

D`Onorio, Joël-Benoît (ed.) (1990): La laïcité au défi de la modernité. Téqui, Paris.

Drago, Roland (1993): Lagïcité, neutralité, liberté? In: Archives de philosophie du droit „Droit et religion" Volume 38.

Duffar, Jean (1994): La liberté religieuse dans les textes internationaux, R.D.P.

Durand, Jean-Paul (1995a): Lieux de cultes en droit français – Cultes affectataires. In: L'année canonique 37:65 ff.

Durand, Jean-Paul (1995b): Le modus vivendi et les diocésaines (1921-1924). L`hypothèse d'un accord diplomatique en forme simplifiée. In: L'année canonique 35:199 ff.

Durand, Jean-Paul (1999): Droit public ecclésiastique français. In: Valdrini, Patrick et al.: Droit canonique. 2nd edition. Dalloz, Paris.

Feldman, David (1993): Civil Liberties and Human Rights in England and Wales. Oxford University Press, Oxford.

Flauss, Jean-François (1990): Le principe de laïcité en droit français. Evolutions récentes. In: Le quotidien juridique 150:10 ff.

Flauss, Jean-François (1992): Droit local alsacien-mosellan et Constitution, R.D.P.

Flores-Lonjou, Magalie (1995): Le statut des édifices cultuels en droit français. In: Revue de droit canonique 45:41 ff.

Franchi, Anne-Marie (1995): Laïcité: la parole et la défense. In: Pouvoirs 75:85 ff.

Freiherr von Campenhausen, Axel (1962): Staat und Kirche in Frankreich, Göttinger Rechtswissenschaftliche Studien 41, O. Schwartz, Göttingen.

Gaudemet, Jean (1987): Administration et Eglise. Du concordat à la séparation de l'Eglise et de l'Etat. Librairie Droz, Geneva.

Gaudemet, Jean (1994): Eglise et cité. Cerf, Paris.

Gueydan, Jean (1987): Les religions face au droit d'association français. In: Praxis juridique et religion, 2, Vol. 4, p. 117 ff.

Hamilton, Carolyn (1995): Family, Law and Religion. Sweet & Maxwell, London.

Huntington, Samuel P. (1997): Kampf der Kulturen. Europaverlag, München.

Ibán, Iván C. and Ferrari, Silvio (1998): Derecho y Religión en Europa Occidental. McGraw-Hill, Madrid.

Jeuffroy, Bernard and Tricard, François (eds.) (1996): Liberté religieuse et régime des cultes en droit français. Textes, pratique administrative, jurisprudence. Cerf, Paris.

Juergensmeyer, Mark (1992): Violence and the Sacred in the Modern World. Frank Cass, London.

Juergensmeyer, Mark (1993): The New Cold War? Religious Nationalism confronts the Secular State. University of California Press, Berkeley.

Julg, Jean (1990): L'Eglise et les Etats – Histoire des concordats. Ed.Nouvelle Cité, Paris.

Kepel, Gilles (1994): The Revenge of God: The Resurgence of Islam, Christianity and Judaism in the modern world. Pennsylvania State University Press, University Park.

Le Goff, Jacques and Rémond, René (eds.) (1992): Histoire de la France religieuse. 4 volumes. Éditions du Seuil, Paris.

Lonjou, Magalie (1992): Les lieux des cultes. In: Actes, les cahiers d'action juridique 79/80:25 ff.

Luckmann, Thomas (1985): Über die Funktion der Religion. In: Koslowski, Peter (ed.): Die religiöse Dimension der Gesellschaft. Mohr Siebeck, Tübingen, p. 26 ff.

Luhmann, Niklas (1996): Funktion der Religion. Suhrkamp, Frankfurt a.M.

Madiot, Yves (1995): Le juge et la laïcité. In: Pouvoirs 75:79 ff.

Mayeur, Jean-Marie (1991): La séparation des Eglises et de l'Etat. Éditions de l'Atelier, Paris.

Messner, Francis (1988a): Peut-on définir juridiquement la religion? In: L'année canonique 31:321 ff.

Messner, Francis (1988b): Les associations cultuelles en Alsace-Moselle. In: Praxis juridique et religion 1988:60 ff.

Messner, Francis (1997): Le droit local des cultes alsacien-mosellan en 1996. In: European Journal for Church and State Research 1997:61.

Metz, René (1977): Eglises et Etat en France. Cerf, Paris.

Metz, René (1983): Das Verhältnis von Kirche und Staat in Frankreich. In: Listl, Joseph; Müller, Hubert and Schmitz, Heribert (eds.): Handbuch des katholischen Kirchenrechts. F. Pustet, Regensburg.

Modehn, Christian (1993): Religion in Frankreich. Gütersloher Verlagshaus, Gütersloh.

Morange, Jean (1988): Le droit et la laïcité. Revue d'éthique et de théologie morale. In: Le Supplement 164:53 ff.

Morange, Jean (1995): Le régime constitutionnel des cultes en France. In: Consortium européen: Rapports Religions-Etat (ed.): Le statut constitutionnel des cultes dans les pays de l'Union européenne. Litec, Milan.

Odio Benito, Elisabeth (1989): Elimination des toutes les formes d'intolérance et de discrimination fondées sur la religion ou la conviction. Nations Unies, New York.

Poulat, Emile (1997): La solution laïque et ses problèmes. Berg International, Paris.

Poulter, Sebastian (1998): Ethnicity, Law and Human Rights. The English Experience. Clarendon Press, Oxford.

Rémond, René (1995): La laïcité et ses contraires. In: Pouvoirs 75:7 ff.

Rivero, Jean (1949): La notion juridique de la laïcité. Dalloz, Paris.

Robert, Jacques (1977): La liberté religieuse et le régime des cultes. P.U.F., Paris.

Robert, Jacques and Duffar, Jean (1996): Droits de l'homme et libertés fondamentales. 6th edition. Montchrestien, Paris.

Rognoni, Pierre-Jean (1923): Du statut légal de l'Eglise en France. Jouve et Cie., Paris.

Rosanvallon, Pierre (1990): L'Etat en France de 1789 à nos jours. Éditions du Seuil, Paris.

Spaemann, Robert (1985): Über die Funktion der Religion. In: Koslowski, Peter (ed.): Die religiöse Dimension der Gesellschaft. Mohr Siebeck, Tübingen, p. 9 ff.

Steiner, Udo (1983): Kulturauftrag im staatlichen Gemeinwesen. In: Vereinigung der Deutschen Staatsrechtslehrer 42:9. De Gruyter, Berlin.

Trotabas, Jean-Baptiste (1960): La notion de laïcité dans le droit de l'Eglise catholique et de l'Etat républicain. Paris.

Turpin, Dominique (1994): Droit constitutionnel. 2nd edition. Presses Universitaires de France, Paris.

Vignon, Jérôme (1996): Europa eine Seele geben. In: Ökumenische Vereinigung für Kirche und Gesellschaft (ed.): Herausforderungen für Europa. Versöhnung und Sinn. Brussels, p. 43 ff.

Wuthnow, Robert (1992): Rediscovering the Sacred: Perspectives on Religion in Contemporary Society. Wm. B. Eerdmans Publishing, Grand Rapids.

Zylberberg, Jacques (1995): Laïcité, connais pas: Allemagne, Canada, Etats-Unis, Royaume-Uni. In: Pouvoirs 75:37 ff.

Court decisions

Australian High Court, Church of the New Faith v. Commissioner for Pay-Roll Tax [1983] 57 ALJR 785

Cass. com., 17.3.1981, Institut musulman de la Mosquée de Paris c/ Lahoucine, D. 1983

CE 22.1.1937, Ville de Condé-Sur-Noireau

CE 26.10.1945, Chanoine Vaucanu, Lebon

CE 9.10.1981, Beherec, Lebon

CE 1.2.1985, Association chrétienne des Témoins de Jéhovah, R.D.P. 1986

CE 14.10.1985, Assocation de l'Etude de la nouvelle Foi, Lebon

CE 12.2.1988, Association des résidents des quartiers Portugal-Italie, J.C.P. 1989, II, 21257

CE 17.6.1988, Union des athées, D. 1988, I.R.

CE 29.10.1990, Association cultuelle de l'Eglise apostolique arménienne de Paris, Lebon

CE sect. 9.10.1992, Commune de Saint-Louis c/ Assocation "Siva, Soupramanien de Saint-Louis", D. 1992, I.R.

CE 24.10.1997, Association locale pour le culte des Témoins de Jéhovah de Riom, D. 1997, I.R.

Cour d'Appel Lyon, 28.7.1997, J.P.C. 1998, II, 10025

Cour de Cassation: Cass. crim. 30.6.1999, Eglise de Scientologie, Juris-Data No. 003147

Founding Church of Scientology of Washington v. United States, 133 U.S. App. D.C. 229, 409 F.2d, cert. denied, 396 U.S. 963 [1969]

Hasan and Chaush v. Bulgaria [GC], no. 30985/96, ECHR 2000-XI

Malnak v. Yogi, 592 F.2d 197 (3d Cir. 1979)

Metropolitan Church of Bessarabia and others v. Moldova, 45701/99, 13.12.2001

New Zealand High Court, Centrepoint Community Growth Trust v. Commissioner of Inland Revenue [1985] 1 NZLR

R v. Registrar General, ex parte Segerdal [1970] 2 QB 697, CA

Serif v. Greece, No. 38178/97, ECHR 1999-IX

United Communist Party of Turkey and Others v. Turkey, judgment of 30 January 1998, Reports 1998-I

French laws and decrees

Aide mémoire de la Secrétairie d'Etat relatif à la promotion des évêques en France, 20 May 1921

Article 10 of the Declaration of the Rights of Man and of the Citizen of 1789

Avis d'assemblée du Conseil d'Etat of 13 December 1923

Circulaire du ministre de l'Intérieur, 13 August 1959, No. 388

Circulaire of 7 February 1990

Code des communes

Enzyklika Maximam Gravissimamque of 18 January 1924

Enzyklika Vehementer Nos of 11 February 1906

French Constitution of 1946

French Constitution of 1958

Gravissimo officii of 10 August 1906

Law of 9 December 1905

Law of 20 January 1907

Law of 13 April 1908

Law No. 505 of 8 April 1942

Law of 25 December 1942

Law No. 87-571 of 23 July 1987

Law of 25 December 1992

Loi de la séparation of 9 December 1905, amendments by laws of 2 January 1907, 13 April 1908 and 31 December 1913

Mandel Decree of 16 January 1939 and 6 December 1939

Ordonnance of 27 August 1827

Ordonnance royale of 12 November 1828

Rapport Marchand (Rapport d'information déposé en application de l'article 145 du règlement sur l'intégration des immigrés), Assemblée nationale, No. 1348, 2e session ordinaire, 1989/90

A Mixed Blessing: Religion, Violence and Peace in Sub-Saharan Africa[1]

Matthias Basedau, Georg Strüver and Johannes Vüllers

> Religion is like a knife: you can either use it to cut bread, or stick in someone's back.
> **Desmond Tutu**

1 Introduction

While the world was watching the World Cup final in South Africa on July 11, 2010, two bombs exploded in Kampala, Uganda, killing more than 70 people. The Somali Islamist group Al-Shabaab claimed responsibility for the attack. Religious violence in Africa[2] is not confined to Somalia or Uganda. In Nigeria, bloody clashes between Muslims and Christians have claimed hundreds if not thousands of victims in the last two years. Armed conflicts[3] in Ethiopia, Eritrea and Sudan are also connected to religion. While in these cases religion apparently plays an important role, quantitative research on conflict has failed to find evidence for a significant causal influence of religious factors in Africa and elsewhere (Dixon 2009; Hegre/Sambanis 2006). Moreover, research has failed to systematically account for the ambivalence of the sacred in Africa (Appleby 2000). Though evidence from case studies exists that shows faith-based peace efforts (see Weingardt 2010; Basedau/De Juan 2008), no systematic investigation of the religion-peace link exists.

Given this gap, it seems useful to take a closer look at the role of religion in conflict in the region. We have developed a new database on religion in sub-Saharan Africa (RSSA) that provides the basis for a more in-depth and systematic analysis and investigates how and to what extent religion is connected to violence and peace in Africa.

The paper proceeds as follows: First, we review the literature and show that research on the religion-conflict link suffers from a range of problems, particularly the lack of comprehensive studies on Africa and, closely related, the lack of adequate data. We

1 Research for this article was funded by the German Foundation for Peace Research in connection with the research project "Religion and Civil War: On the Ambivalence of Religious Factors in Sub-Saharan Africa." The authors are also indebted to Peter Körner and Jessica Haase for their indispensable support with coding as well as Håvard Hegre and Jeffrey Haynes for useful (and outspoken) comments.

2 If not indicated otherwise, "Africa" denotes the 48 countries of sub-Saharan Africa.

3 According to UCDP/PRIO, armed conflict is a "contested incompatibility that concerns government and/or territory where the use of armed force between two parties, of which at least one is the government of a state, results in at least 25 battle-related deaths." If not indicated otherwise, "conflict" refers to armed conflict.

then present the logic of our database including methodological aspects. A systematic description of how and to what extent religion is connected to conflict or peace in different dimensions (e.g. identities, ideas, organizations, behavior) constitutes the main part of the contribution. The paper demonstrates that religion matters for conflict (in Africa) and that many more countries are affected than previously detected. Religion and armed conflict or other types of violence are connected at different levels in many countries, particularly through warring factors varying by religious affiliation, religious incompatibilities, armed religious groups and events of religious violence. Religion is also frequently connected to peace, a finding exemplified by religious peace initiatives and inter-religious networks. The final section summarizes the findings and draws conclusions for policy and future research.

2 *Literature Review*

Over the last decade, there has been growing interest in research on the religion–conflict link (Huntington 1996; Juergensmeyer 2008). Today, the "ambivalence of the sacred" has been widely accepted: Religion may not only incite violence but also contribute to peace (Appleby 2000; Philpott 2007). Ambivalence also refers to the scope of impact. Sometimes religion plays a more important role, sometimes it is a less decisive factor. It seems plausible that the ambivalence of religion depends on the particular context (Basedau/De Juan 2008). Under certain religious and non-religious conditions, religion spurs conflict or fosters peace – or differs in regards to how much religion counts. Finally, it appears useful to consider different religious dimensions. "Religion" is a complex phenomenon and difficult to define precisely (Ter Haar 2005); we do not intend to solve this problem once and for all; we believe that for analysis in social sciences it is useful to distinguish between different dimensions of religion (Harpviken/Røislien 2008). There are different ways to typify these dimensions or factors (as we prefer to say) but it basically means that religion, is not, as often intuitively thought, solemnly about religious ideas (and respective discourse), but we will also include religious identity structures (e.g. demographic constellations), religious organizations (e.g. churches, networks) and related behavior of religious actors.[4]

2.1 Systematic-Descriptive Approaches

The relevance of religion for conflict can be demonstrated in two different ways. The first way can be labeled systematic-descriptive. Systematic-descriptive means that the

4 Please note that this paper conceptualizes religion in an abstract manner and does not primarily distinguish between different religious traditions like Christianity, Buddhism and Islam.

relevance is not demonstrated through evidence on causal relationships between variables but rather through the systematic identification of phenomena which in themselves demonstrate a connection. For this purpose, it makes sense to make use of various religious dimensions (Harpviken/Røislien 2008).

As mentioned above, religious variables cut into several dimensions and operate at different levels. Whenever conflict parties or warring factions differ by religious affiliation, this indicates relevance of religion in the identity dimension. In contrast, a common religious identity cross-cutting the differences between warring factions may be a resource for peacebuilding efforts. Religion is important for conflict in the ideological dimension, when religious ideas such as the introduction of religious laws or the domination of a particular religion in a given society are disputed among varying societal forces. Furthermore, conflict parties or religious actors can legitimize violence or peace with reference to religious ideas such as values and norms. The existence of armed groups with religious goals or inter-religious networks indicates the relevance of religion in the organizational dimension. Finally, the behavioral dimension includes certain forms of violence that can indicate the relevance of religion in conflict. Such events are attacks on clergymen or places of worship. In contrast, calls for peace or more pronounced activities such as peace initiatives or mediation approaches by religious actors can show their engagement for peace. Regarding empirical studies so far, none has captured all these (or possible further) religious dimensions. In fact, variables connecting religion and peace are not included in comparative or quantitative empirical studies. In regard to the religion-conflict nexus, two studies in particular extend beyond the (common) identification of different religious identities of conflict parties. For the period 1989–2003, Svensson analyzes 218 conflict dyads worldwide and identifies those dyads with different religious identities in 68 cases (31.3 percent) and a religious component in the incompatibility of the conflict in 43 cases (19.8 percent) (Svensson 2007). Such "religious" conflicts seem to occur at a below-average rate in Africa: Out of 87 African conflict dyads, only 11 cases show divergent religious identities between the conflict factions (12.6 percent) and in 13 cases a religious component in the conflict incompatibility is present (14.9 percent). Of the 48 sub-Saharan African countries, 23 have experienced civil war. Approximately one-third of those 23 countries had a religious conflict dimension.[5] Another study captures the ideological and behavioral dimensions (Croissant et al. 2009). The study defines religious conflicts as a subtype of cultural conflicts. Verbal or active references to religious people or symbols in conflict-related events (e.g. assassination of a religious leader or a disputed visit to a temple by the head of government) indicate religious conflicts. Of all global conflicts from 1945 to 2007, 11 percent were religious; sub-Saharan Africa's percentage was no exception, standing also at 11 percent.

5 Chad, Côte d'Ivoire, Ethiopia, Eritrea, Mali, Sudan and Uganda.

2.2 Causal Approaches

The second way to demonstrate the relevance of religion in conflict is to find theoretically plausible empirical evidence that religious variables and conflict are causally linked. The involved religious variables themselves – such as population-shares of religious communities – are not necessarily connected to violence. Theoretically, a number of hypotheses connect religious variables to conflict. Similar to ethnic and other social identities, diverse religious identities can result in escalating socio-psychological dynamics. Research demonstrates that people often privilege in-group members over out-group members (Seul 1999:565; Stewart 2009). As a result, it becomes easier for (religious) elites to mobilize such identities for conflict (Fearon/Laitin 2000; Hasenclever/Rittberger 2003). Furthermore, religious identities are connected to certain religious ideas. Such religious ideas are shared values and norms legitimized by a transcendental source, which are therefore assumed to be hardly subject to negotiation and compromise given their (accepted) supernatural origin. This can also entail a higher propensity towards violent behavior by religious actors. Non-believers and adherents to different religious traditions might be converted by force, especially if the religion in question claims universal validity. Furthermore, combatants might be motivated through specific religious rewards for participation in acts of violence (Toft 2007; Svensson 2007).

Empirically, there is no evidence that religious diversity as such increases the likelihood of conflict onset (Fearon/Laitin 2003; Tusicisny 2004). Furthermore, studies show mixed or non-significant results for more specific religious demographic structures. The results are consistent neither for a strongly fractionalized religious structure, nor for a so-called polarized structure, in which two more-or-less large religious groups coexist (Montalvo/Reynal-Querol 2005; Fearon/Laitin 2003). However, some studies find positive evidence that conflicts that are fought along religious boundaries may display a higher intensity and may endure longer than other conflicts that are not fought along such lines (Horowitz 2009:167–172; Svensson 2007; Toft 2007; Pearce 2005; Ellingsen 2005). Contested religious ideas as possible causes of conflict have not been systematically tested.

The peace dimension of religion in conflict is empirically and theoretically underdeveloped. The majority of theoretical works identifies religious peace norms as the only explanation of religious peace engagement (Gopin 2000; Butselaar 2005), neglecting material or institutional sources of religious communities and institutions of peacebuilding such as inter-religious networks. So far, empirical studies on religion and peace have yielded limited results regarding the structure and impact of religious peace initiatives (Little 2007; Appleby 2001).

2.3 Africa-Specific Approaches

The majority of studies on religion and conflict in sub-Saharan Africa are single case studies (Basedau/De Juan 2008:6). Comprehensive studies on religion and conflict are virtually non-existent. This comes as a surprise since religion has a high social relevance in Africa, and it has apparently increased in recent years (Pew 2010; Ellis/Ter Haar 2007; McCauley/Gyimah-Boadi 2009). The above discussed global descriptive studies find (below-) average relevance of religious dimensions in African conflicts. Africa-specific databases are basically non-existent. Large-N studies on the causal religion-conflict link in Africa find no evidence for a significant influence of religious diversity (Collier/Sambanis 2005; Elbadawi/Sambanis 2000). Instead, Collier and Hoeffler find that high ethnic and religious fractionalization decreases the likelihood of civil war onset in Africa (Collier/Hoeffler 2002). Haynes estimates that socio-economic and political factors better explain civil war (onset) value than ethnic and religious fragmentation (Haynes 2005). Basedau and Vüllers find initial support for a mobilization hypothesis (Basedau/Vüllers 2010). In particular, the overlap of religious and ethnic boundaries apparently makes armed conflict more likely (see also Stewart 2009).

The religion-peace nexus in Africa remains even more neglected than the religion-conflict link. The bulk of studies only discusses specific religious peace initiatives and gives no explanation for their occurrence, and at best anecdotal evidence of their impact (Haynes 2009; Abu-Nimer/Kadayifci-Orellana 2008). However, in the majority of conflicts, religion seems indeed to have an ambivalent influence, both in recent years (Basedau/De Juan 2008:17) and from a longer historical perspective (Møller 2006).

Summarizing the global and Africa-specific state-of-the-art, three observations are striking: Firstly, there is a contradiction between the findings of single case studies and the results of quantitative and cross-regional studies. While religion generally plays at best a minor role in armed conflict, religion evidently impacts armed conflict and its dynamics in particular countries such as Nigeria and Somalia. Secondly, the data available for large-N studies is extremely limited. Commonly, studies only measure the influence of religion with demographical constellations. Only a few studies go further and consider religious incompatibilities or the reference to religious symbols in conflict discourse. Thirdly and finally, the religion-peace link remains under-researched both empirically and theoretically.

3 The Database on Religion in Sub-Saharan Africa (RSSA)

The primary goal of the database we have built up as part of our research project on "Religion and Civil War: On the Ambivalence of Religious Factors in Sub-Saharan

Africa" is to fill at least one of the gaps identified in the previous section: to make data available that exceeds the kind of data commonly used in comparative and quantitative studies on linkage of religion to conflict or peace. The original contribution of the database[6] to the field consists of a compilation of some 30 religion-specific variables, which we believe are theoretically important. Following a multidimensional understanding of religion, we collected data referring to identities, ideational and organizational dimensions and how the behavior of actors relates to these dimensions (for more details on the variables see Basedau/Strüver/Vüllers 2011:27-28). Identity structures refer, for instance,[7] to the finding that in a given armed conflict, conflict parties significantly differ by religious affiliation. Ideational variables are religious incompatibilities in armed or other conflicts or the resorting to religious ideas in peace efforts. Organizational religious variables include the existence of armed religious groups or inter-religious networks. With regards to the behavioral dimension, we raised data concerning (principally peaceful) politicization, escalation and de-escalation by religious actors. We further coded for whether religious violence (e.g. clashes between different groups) occurred and asked whether religious actors incited violence, called for peace or even engaged in peace initiatives. If possible, we made use of existing data sources that are largely confined to religious demographics and the role of religion and the state (Fox 2004). Hence, for almost all religious variables presented in this paper we had to gather the data on our own.

The database covers the years 1990 to 2008 and includes all 48 countries of sub-Saharan Africa. Data were coded by year and we have a maximum of 909 observations per variable. Usually, variables were constructed either dichotomously or on nominal or ordinal scales. We were keen to maintain a uniform, consistent basis of sources in order to avoid distorted information. We used annual Africa Yearbook editions, Religious Freedom Reports and Human Rights Practices Country Reports (the latter two compiled by the U.S. State Department) as well as Economist Intelligence Unit (EIU) Country Reports published on a quarterly basis. The next section gives a systematic overview of our findings on religion and violence, taking a closer look at four dimensions: identity, ideas, organization and behavior.

6 In its extended form the database also includes conflict data and non-religious independent variables (e.g. UCDP/PRIO; Hegre/Sambanis 2006).

7 We do not explain and discuss particular variables at this point. Variables will be explained within the text as soon as it becomes important to do so.

4 *Religion and Violence*[8]

In the following we look at three ways religion can be connected to armed and other violent conflict. First, we examine the role of religion in armed conflict according to the definition by UCDP/PRIO, capturing both the identity and the theological dimensions. Second, we look at the existence of religious armed groups. Finally, we look at actual behavior and investigate four types of violent events or acts in which the involvement of religion is evident and assess both its incidence and intensity.

4.1 Religion in Armed Conflict

When is an armed conflict a religious conflict? One possible answer is that the parties in armed conflicts differ with regard to their religious identity, e.g. one party is primarily Christian while the opponent is primarily Muslim. Another kind of religious armed conflict is that contested religious ideas are an incompatibility between the warring factions (Svensson 2007).

Warring factions differ by religious identity

In the database, we tried to identify constellations of armed conflicts, in which the conflict parties differed substantially according to their religious identities. Such parallel religious and conflict boundaries are present in more than half of the countries with incidences of armed conflict between 1990 and 2008 (56 percent of countries and 47 percent of conflicts). Remarkable exceptions are civil wars in Sierra Leone and Somalia, where religious identities have not separated the warring factions. In a cluster of ten country cases, violent conflict and religious boundaries do partially run parallel. In four cases, Congo-Brazzaville, Côte d'Ivoire, Nigeria and Sudan, we find that the boundaries between conflict parties mostly run parallel. All four countries are civil war cases and it comes as little surprise that Côte d'Ivoire, Nigeria and Sudan are notorious examples for such identity conflicts. Until the comprehensive peace agreement in Sudan in 2005, Muslim government forces fought the Christian and African traditional Southern rebels. Such a religious North-South divide is typical of many West African countries. In Côte d'Ivoire and Nigeria we find bloody conflict mostly between Christians and Muslims.

8 If not indicated otherwise, all information in the following sections derives from the above-mentioned sources in the database.

Religious ideas as incompatibilities in armed conflict

Religious ideas might be contested between the conflict parties. Such religious incompatibilities refer to the role of religion within the state (e.g. dominance of a particular religion) or the introduction of religious laws.[9] In the great majority of cases, religious ideas are apparently not contested between the conflict factions. However, in nine out of the 25 sub-Saharan countries with at least one incidence of armed conflict during the sample period (36 percent of countries, 20 percent of conflicts), we identify conflict episodes in which religious incompatibilities separated the conflict factions. Religious incompatibilities characterize armed conflicts mainly in central and north-eastern Africa (Chad, Congo-Brazzaville, DR Congo (DRC), Eritrea, Ethiopia, Nigeria, Somalia, Sudan and Uganda, see Table 2).[10] In Nigeria, Somalia, Sudan, Eritrea and Ethiopia, the (attempted) introduction of Islamic law, the *sharia*, played a role in the onset of armed conflicts. For instance, the Ethiopian rebels of the *Ogaden National Liberation Front* called for a holy war against the overwhelmingly Christian-Orthodox government, in order to liberate the Ogaden region and establish an Islamic state. In contrast, the attempt to re-establish a Bakongo state in the DRC was connected to the idea of an African-Christian Kingdom. The case of the DRC also reminds us of the fact that conflicts with such religious incompatibilities form only part of a more complex conflict structure within these countries. Main conflict cleavages in the DRC are not connected to contested religious ideas.

4.2 Where Do We Find Armed Religious Groups?

According to the database, armed religious groups are groups that are a) involved in violence (not necessarily an armed conflict in the UCDP/PRIO sense) and b) have self-declared religious goals (though not necessarily exclusively religious goals). The use of a religious term in the name of a given group is an insufficient indicator for an armed religious group.[11] Altogether, we identified such groups in more than 25 percent of all sub-Saharan countries (13 cases). Yet, important differences between these groups

9 Coding of contested religious ideas between the parties derives from the self-ascribed goals of conflict actors. Such an assessment does not include any statement as to whether these ideas were merely exploited by leaders or whether they result from truly religious convictions.

10 In Chad, UCDP/PRIO does not specifically count a confrontation between an extremist group and government in 2008 (see below). We assign this to the larger conflict.

11 For instance, we did not code the Malian rebel group Front Islamique Arabe de L'Azouad (FIAA) as an armed religious group because we could not find positive evidence of religious goals. We did not code the Mungiki Sect in Kenya as an armed religious group either because no pronounced religious goals could be detected. In essence, it is an ethnic secret society (Kagwanja 2003). In contrast, Uganda's LRA and ADF were coded as armed religious groups because some LRA and ADF leaders claimed religious goals in interviews (Farmar 2006; Hovil/Werker 2005).

exist in terms of their level of activity and their origin. Sometimes these groups did not emerge from the countries in which they were active. In Tanzania and Kenya, Al-Qaida activities were mostly confined to the attacks on U.S. embassies in 1998. In the Sahel from Mauritania to Chad, Al-Qaïda au Maghreb Islamique, the North African affiliate of Al-Qaida and former Groupe Salafiste pour la Prédication et le Combat (GSPC), has been active and clashed with security forces in Mauritania, Niger, Mali and Chad. Its origin is Algeria. The Ethiopian Al-Ittihad uses neighboring Somalia as a base for military operations. The Eritrean Islamic Jihad Movement operates from safe haven Sudan. Islamic armed groups with a (more) pronounced national basis are found in Chad, Nigeria, Somalia and Sudan. In particular, the Somali Al-Shabaab has engaged in fierce battles with African Union peacekeepers and government militias. In 2010, Al-Shabaab declared its affiliation to Al-Qaida. Armed groups are not an Islamic monopoly. Besides the Christian Lord's Resistance Army (LRA) in Uganda, we can identify in Congo-Brazzaville the Mouvement Nsilulu, which was led by Pasteur Ntoumi and which fought against the regime of President Denis Sassou-Nguesso from 1998 until a peace accord was reached in 2003.

4.3 Types and Intensities of Religious Violence

The behavioral dimension of religion in conflict may be best captured through the prevalence of religious violence. We define religious violence as any violent event or act in which the involvement of religious actors or organizations is evident. According to the understanding of the database, there are four types of such events:[12] assaults on religious targets, violent attacks by religious actors against non-religious targets, and violent clashes between religious communities and government security forces, as well as violent clashes between religious groups. The database codes both whether and how many such events occurred and also estimates how intense the events were in terms of casualties. Numbers of casualties were estimated according to the RSSA sources.[13] According to our understanding, the four types are disjoint. We coded any given event of religious violence only once, assigning this event to the main type of violence that occurred. For example, we counted clashes between religious communities exclusively as inter-religious clashes although security forces often intervene in these clashes in order to end the violence.

12 Mob justice against alleged "witches" is not counted as religious violence. We only coded violent events in which a minimum of political relevance is evident or religious groups were targeted as such.

13 Sometimes, sources were imprecise ("some", "several") or inconsistent. We estimated an equal minimum coding for this verbal quotation. All numbers of casualties are minimum estimates.

Assaults on religious targets

The first type includes assaults on religious targets such as clergymen, places of worship or other sacred objects. In the period under investigation we observed 301 assaults in 43 countries and a total of 3,493 casualties in 28 countries. Six countries were especially violent and responsible for 3,168 deaths. In three countries, namely Burundi, Côte d'Ivoire, DRC, assaults resulted in more than 200 deaths each, followed by Liberia and Somalia with more than 500 deaths each. Assaults on religious targets in Nigeria left more than 1,100 persons dead.

The causes of the attacks on religious targets were numerous and they depend on the specific socio-political context of the country. In the majority of cases, assaults on religious targets were isolated incidents. For example, 43 Christian students died in a fire in the Kilimanjaro region (Tanzania). The perpetrators were unknown but there were rumors that Muslims were responsible for the fire. In Cameroon's capital Yaoundé, a dispute over a building area for a mosque resulted in three deaths. In Côte d'Ivoire, the presidential elections in 2000 were marred by massive religious violence. Churches and mosques were set afire, and in the suburbs of Abidjan a mass grave was discovered with the bodies of more than 50 Muslims inside who had apparently been murdered by government forces.

Furthermore, assaults on religious targets in countries with an ongoing armed conflict seem to follow a rational logic. In Liberia, believers and churches were repeatedly targeted by the warring factions. In 1990, 600 refugees were slaughtered after they had sought refuge in a church in Monrovia. A second example is the armed conflict in northern Uganda. The LRA targeted clerics, especially in 2003 and 2004 in northern Uganda, after the Acholi Religious Leader's Peace Initiative (ARLPI) had tried to persuade some senior LRA commanders to leave the rebel group.

Attacks by religious actors against non-religious targets

A second type comprises assaults by religious actors[14] against secular targets. We observed 66 attacks in 18 countries, and 9,497 casualties in 12 countries. It makes sense to distinguish these attacks by the level of organization of the perpetrators. Attacks by rather unorganized religious fundamentalists in Africa were less violent. For instance, Muslim extremists attacked pork butcheries in spring 1993 in Dar es Salaam, Tanzania. In Guinea, an angry crowd of Muslims assaulted a police station after a local imam had been arrested in 1997. In neither case killings occurred.

14 In this paper, "religious actors" denote both individuals (e.g. clergymen, leaders of religious organizations) and collective actors such as (armed) religious groups.

The number of casualties has been much higher whenever organized armed groups have been involved. An exceptionally violent single event was the double attack against the U.S. embassies in Nairobi (Kenya; 253 casualties) and Dar es Salaam (Tanzania; 10 casualties) in 1998 by Al-Qaida. Two armed religious groups in one country are responsible for the majority of casualties for the whole period in Africa: the LRA and the Allied Democratic Forces (ADF) in Uganda. Over the years, their fight against the government resulted in at least 9,021 deaths in Uganda. Especially the LRA targeted the civil population in northern Uganda. The raids started after the failed peace negotiations in 1995 and continued until 2005. The LRA apparently followed its own rational logic in which attacks on civilians are necessary to recruit fighters through abduction (Bevan 2007). The Islamic ADF started its insurgency in western Uganda in 1996. Starting its raids in late 1997, the ADF attacked, for example, the Kichwamba Technical College in Kabarole district and killed 50 students in June 1998. Generally, the logic of the attacks resembles LRA tactics.

Clashes between religious communities and government security forces

Confrontations between religious groups and government security forces form a third type. Between 1990 and 2008, this type of religious violence occurred in 18 countries (69 clashes, 882 deaths in 13 countries). Mainly, the clashes were isolated incidents. In Chad in 2008, for instance, Sheikh Ahmet Ismael Bichara had called for a holy war against the government (and to conquer Denmark because of the Mohammed cartoons). Subsequent clashes between security forces and the group resulted in almost 70 deaths. In Mauritania in 2008, violent clashes between Islamic groups and government security forces left 16 persons dead. Nine persons died in a confrontation between the police and *Takfir wa Hijra*, an extremist Islamic group, near Wad Medani in Sudan in 1996. Christians also clashed with security forces. In Ethiopia in 1993, the Orthodox community in Gondar protested against the incursions by Muslims and Protestants into this traditionally Orthodox region. Thirteen people died in the subsequent violence between the community and security forces.

Nigeria and DRC show exceptionally high numbers of victims. In Nigeria, 14 clashes resulted in altogether 381 deaths. The majority of the clashes occurred due to the *sharia* debate. Other important events were the demonstrations of Muslims against the Mohammed cartoons in 2006. Subsequent fighting between Muslims and security forces claimed 130 casualties. In the DRC in 2007 and 2008, clashes between supporters of the *Bundu dia Kongo* (BDK) and the police resulted in at least 195 deaths. Prior to the 2006 elections, relations between BDK and the police took a turn for the worse. Members of the BDK continued in 2007 to call for resistance against the "illegitimate state authorities."

Clashes between religious groups

The fourth type refers to "intercommunal" confrontations between different religious communities. We observed 90 clashes between religious groups in 23 countries, and a total of 5,915 casualties in 15 countries. This type of religious violence covers inter-religious confrontations (e.g. Muslims vs. Christians) but also clashes within one denomination in which religious subgroups confront each other. However, most clashes happened between Christians and Muslims. One example is a clash in 2004 between Christians and Muslims in the southern Chadian town of Bebedja, which left 12 people dead. More than elsewhere clashes (19) and casualties (5,706) occurred in Nigeria. Besides a few intra-communal clashes, violent attacks mostly happened between Christian and Muslim ethnic groups in Nigeria's Middle Belt and north, at least partially caused by disputes over the introduction of *sharia*. Arguably, these intercommunal conflicts are equally based on economic and political incompatibilities. Clashes in Nigeria often have their origins in conflicts about land rights and political representation. In the forest region of Guinea, a land dispute in 2000 resulted in a confrontation between Christians and Muslims leaving at least 30 people dead.

Similarly, hostilities between religious subgroups occurred due to theological incompatibilities, economic rivalries or power struggles. In Guinea-Bissau, members of the mainstream Muslim communities and of the Ahmadiyya sect clashed in February 2005. The Muslim crowd beat and detained Ahmadiyya members. In Nigeria, conflicts were reported that took place within religious groups. In 2005, for example, violent clashes between Shia and Sunni Muslim sects in Sokoto caused seven casualties. Similar power struggles were also observed in Christian communities. For example, in Nairobi (Kenya) fighting between factions of the Buru Buru Church of God resulted in numerous injuries in 2000.

Table 1: Casualties of Religious Violence in Africa, 1990–2008

Casualties	Country
>9000	Uganda
>7000	Nigeria
500–999	Liberia, Somalia
100–499	Burundi, Chad, Côte d'Ivoire, DR Congo, Ethiopia, Kenya, Sudan
25–99	Eritrea, Guinea, Mali, Niger, Tanzania
1–24	Angola, Benin, Burkina Faso, Cameroon, Central African Republic, Congo-Brazzaville, Djibouti, Ghana, Madagascar, Malawi, Mauritania, Mauritius, Mozambique, Rwanda, Senegal, Sierra Leone, South Africa, Swaziland, Zimbabwe
0	Cape Verde, Comoros, Equatorial Guinea, Gabon, Gambia, Guinea-Bissau, Seychelles, Togo

Source: Authors' compilation.

Table 1 shows the violence intensity according to cumulative casualties of the four types of religious violence for the whole period of investigation.[15] In sum, we could identify such events of religious violence in all but five countries from 1990 to 2008 (Botswana, Lesotho, Namibia, São Tomé and Príncipe, Zambia). Frequency and intensity, however, differ substantially. In two-thirds of the countries, either no casualties occurred or violence resulted in less than 25 estimated deaths. In five cases the death toll caused by religious hostilities was between 24 and 100 while in seven countries respective violent action led up to 499 casualties. In Liberia and Somalia violent clashes claimed between 500 and 1,000 lives. Uganda (9,057 casualties) and Nigeria (7,370) show by far the highest death toll connected to religious violence. In Uganda, religious armed groups, the LRA and ADF, were responsible for the bloodshed, while the Nigerian death toll is mainly due to inter-religious clashes.

4.4 Religion and Violence in Sub-Saharan Africa: A Summary

Summing up our descriptive findings on the role of religion in armed conflict and religious violence, we find in at least 22 cases a substantial link between religion and violence (see Table 2). Furthermore, in 19 out of the 25 countries with an ongoing armed conflict in the sample period – i.e. in 40 percent of all sub-Saharan nations – we discovered one or more religious dimensions, in 50 percent of the armed conflicts we found one or two religious dimensions (see Table 2). These results suggest that religion plays a more important role in armed conflict than previously assumed (Croissant et al. 2009; Svensson 2007).

Yet, the picture has to be differentiated. In only six cases are religion and conflict connected in all four dimensions (identity, ideology, organization and behavior): Chad, Eritrea, Ethiopia, Nigeria, Sudan and Uganda. Congo-Brazzaville, DRC and Somalia show three affected dimensions. Five countries – Côte d'Ivoire, Kenya, Liberia, Niger and Tanzania – have two dimensions. The remaining seven countries show just one of the factors. Remarkably, none of these eight cases (and none of the countries with two affected dimensions either) displays a finding in the ideological dimension. Positive findings at the ideological level usually coincide with problems at all levels.

In geographical terms, African regions also differ substantially. Seriously affected countries are mainly found in northeast and central Africa, partly in western Africa, but not in southern Africa. To a certain extent, religion as a conflict driving factor is more likely in areas close to the Arab world, suggesting that the traditionally moderate African Islam has undergone a certain infection by Muslim extremists from the Arab

15 Please note that casualties in armed conflicts in which conflict factions differ according to religious identity or in which religious incompatibilities exist (such as in Sudan) are not automatically counted as religious violence. In any incident, the religious character has to be proven.

world. We have no evidence, however, that a religion-conflict link is a purely Muslim phenomenon. Although little points to a strong connection between Pentecostal and evangelical Christianity and violence, we have found a considerable percentage of events and phenomena in which (mainline) Christians are involved in violence, too. Interestingly, we have detected almost no link between African traditional religion (ATR) and organized conflict. Presumably, ATR is rather connected to ritual violence at an individual level.

Looking at the dynamics from 1990 to 2008, no significant patterns for the whole region or prominent single variables could be identified (Basedau/Strüver/Vüllers 2011:29). In particular, we did not find any evidence that suggests a sharp rise in religious violence since September 11, 2001. Diverging religious identity boundaries and incompatibilities in conflict have remained rather stable, at least since the late 1990s. There is, however, a trend since 2006 that the activities of armed religious groups have become much more intense in the Sahel area and at the Horn of Africa. On the other hand, casualties caused by religious violence, as detailed above, result mainly from "religiously inspired" rebel group activities in Nigeria and Uganda. No substantial evidence has emerged showing that Africa will be the future battleground of a clash between Christian and Muslim civilizations. Though inter-religious confrontations occur overwhelmingly between these two groups, the number of these confrontations did not increase until 2008. Increased bloodshed after 2008 is again due to events in a particular country, namely Nigeria.

Table 2: Religious Dimensions of Armed Conflict and Violence in Africa, 1990–2008

Country/Dimension	Identity[a]	Ideology[b]	Organization[c]	Behavior[d]
	Conflict parties differ by religion	Religious incompatibility in conflict	Armed religious groups	High intensity of religious violence
Chad	X	X	X	X
Eritrea	X	X	X	X
Ethiopia	X	X	X	X
Nigeria	X	X	X	X
Sudan	X	X	X	X
Uganda	X	X	X	X
Congo-Brazzaville	X	X	X	
DR Congo	X	X		X
Somalia		X	X	X
Côte d'Ivoire	X			X
Kenya			X	X
Liberia	X			X
Niger			X	X

Country/Dimension	Identity[a]	Ideology[b]	Organization[c]	Behavior[d]
	Conflict parties differ by religion	Religious incompatibility in conflict	Armed religious groups	High intensity of religious violence
Tanzania			X	X
Angola	X			
Burundi				X
Central African Republic	X			
Guinea				X
Lesotho	X			
Mali			X	
Mauritania			X	
Senegal	X			
Total (rounded percent Africa)	14 cases (29 percent)	9 cases (19 percent)	13 cases (27 percent)	15 cases (31 percent)

Notes: [a] Conflict parties in armed conflict differ by religious affiliation. / [b] Religious ideas as incompatibility in armed/violent conflict. / [c] Existence/activity of armed religious group. / [d] At least 25 deaths in incidents of religious violence (see Table 1).
Source: Authors' compilation.

5 *Religion and Peace*

As already mentioned, religion may not only contribute to violent conflict but also to peace processes (Smock 2006). The following section will look at two pertinent phenomena in which religion is clearly connected to peace.

5.1 Inter-Religious Networks

The database defines a religious network as an institution that refers to a more-or-less institutionalized cooperation of different religious communities (e.g. Christians and Muslims).[16] Cooperation includes at least (more-or-less regular) meetings for dialog but can also include more sophisticated activities. The database captures their sheer existence but also probes for the degree of institutionalization (informal/formal) as well as its regional coverage (local/regional vs. national). Instances of regional and informal networks are relatively rare. In the Central African Republic, for example,

16 In case one the religious community comprises more than 90 percent of the population, we also code networks as "inter-religious" in which different denominations below that level (e.g. different Muslim brotherhoods or Christian churches) are included.

the Catholic Commission for Justice and Peace (CCJP) was the driving force behind an informal inter-religious network (2000-2005). The CCJP co-conducted educational and developmental programs with other religious groups throughout the country. Mostly, however, inter-religious networks have a rather formal and national character. Commonly, the major religious communities in the countries participated in these networks (e.g. Rwanda, Liberia). The activities of the inter-religious networks were often limited to common prayer ceremonies and talks between the religious leaders (e.g. Tanzania). Contrarily, some inter-religious networks were also very active in civil society and in politics (e.g. Angola, Côte d'Ivoire and Kenya). The Inter-Religious Council in Sierra Leone, for example, supported anti-corruption campaigns from civil society groups and supported reconciliation and rehabilitation efforts in the peace process after the end of the civil war in 2000.

Looking at the whole period from 1990 to 2008, we found such inter-religious networks in more than 75 percent of all cases. Their number increased constantly since 1990 (Basedau/Strüver/Vüllers 2011:29). However, there is little initial evidence that inter-religious networks contribute to substantially avoiding armed conflict. In more than half of all cases where inter-religious networks operated, conflict also occurred (see Table 3).

5.2 Religious Peace Initiatives

Inter-religious networks must not be equated with (religious) peace initiatives. Peace initiatives differ as they necessarily aim to maintain or promote peace. The database defines a religious peace initiative as an enterprise by religious actors aiming to promote peace and exceeding a singular call for peace. Examples are mediation, education of local peace-promoters or lobbying for awareness of the conflict on national and international levels. A peace initiative should be explicitly (and mainly) established in order to maintain or promote peace. The promotion of peace is the main raison d'être. For example, the Acholi Religious Leaders Peace Initiative was very active in the peace process in northern Uganda. It educated local peace-promoters and lobbied on the national and international levels for a conflict settlement. A successful religious peace initiative was the People-to-People Peace Process of the New Sudanese Council of Churches. The peace initiative organized several local conferences between the warring ethnic factions in Southern Sudan.[17] In addition, we coded for whether the participation of religious actors contributed to the success of the peace initiative – that means, whether the armed conflict in question was settled in the period of investigation.

17 The database also codes minor forms of religious peace initiatives if religious actors participate in a peace initiative founded by or mainly comprising secular actors.

Table 3: Inter-Religious Networks and Religious Peace Initiatives in Africa, 1990–2008

Violent Conflict [a]	Existence of inter-religious networks and degree of institutionalization		
	No Networks	Informal Networks	Formal Networks
Yes	**Burundi** Comoros **Guinea-Bissau** **Somalia** **Togo**	**Central African Republic** **Chad**	**Angola** Congo-Brazzaville Côte d'Ivoire DR Congo Djibouti Eritrea **Ethiopia** Guinea **Kenya** Lesotho **Liberia*** **Mali*** **Mozambique*** Niger **Nigeria** **Rwanda** Senegal **Sierra Leone** **Sudan*** **Tanzania** **Uganda***
No	Burkina Faso Cameroon Cape Verde Mauritania São Tomé and Príncipe Seychelles	Benin Botswana Equatorial Guinea Gabon	Gambia Ghana Madagascar Malawi Mauritius Namibia South Africa Swaziland Zambia Zimbabwe

Notes: [a] Violent conflict denotes at least one active armed conflict (UCDP/PRIO) and/or religious violence which resulted in at least 25 deaths (see Table 1) in a given year. / Bold letters indicate a religious peace initiative. Cases of successful conflict settlement are marked by an asterisk (*).
Source: Authors' compilation.

Table 3 shows that such peace initiatives can be identified in 18 countries. It is no surprise that peace initiatives frequently coincide with armed conflict. Only in Kenya and Tanzania religious peace initiatives are active without an armed conflict as defined by UCDP/PRIO. In both cases, however, religious (and ethnic) violence occurred as we have shown above. In more than half of all conflict cases religious actors participated in peace efforts suggesting that religious peace initiatives have to be seen rather as an answer to violence than a proactive prophylaxis. But there is little evidence that these peace initiatives are particularly successful. In five countries only conflicts did end after the peace initiatives were established (Central African Republic, Mali, Mozambique, Sudan and Uganda). The most well-known example is the settlement of the civil war in Mozambique. The Catholic laymen organization *Sant'Egidio* brokered the peace agreement in 1992 (Haynes 2009). Although the relative contribution of *Sant'Egidio* to ending the war in general remains subject to speculation, a substantial impact is likely in this case.

6 The "Ambivalence of the Sacred": Calls for Peace and Violence

Religious peace efforts do not necessarily take the form of institutionalized efforts such as inter-religious networks and religious peace initiatives. We thus tried to find evidence whether religious actors issued at least one single call for peace in one case. In order to systematically account for the "Ambivalence of the Sacred" (Appleby 2000), we also captured the "dark side" of religion by asking for any evidence of calls for violence by religious actors and institutions. At least a religious actor had to legitimize violence in order to be coded.

The findings are presented in a matrix in Table 4 and confirm the "ambivalence of the sacred" – although this does not suggest that the calls had a substantial impact. In only eight cases we find neither pro-peace nor pro-violence verbal statements. In 15 cases, both escalation and de-escalation are present. In the Comoros and Eritrea, no calls for peace but rather calls for violence were identified. Cases that show exclusively pro-peace statements are much more frequent: Calls for peace but no conflict escalating statements form by far the biggest sample with 23 cases. Both forms of statements have increased since 1990 (Basedau/Vüllers/Strüver 2011:29).

Table 4: Verbal Escalation and De-Escalation by Religious Actors in Africa, 1990–2008

Verbal de-escalation by religious actors[a]	Verbal escalation by religious actors [b] Yes	No
Yes	Chad Congo-Brazzaville DR Congo Ghana Guinea Kenya Mauritania Niger Nigeria Rwanda Senegal Somalia Sudan Tanzania Uganda	Angola Benin Burkina Faso Burundi Cameroon Cape Verde Central African Republic Côte d'Ivoire Ethiopia Guinea-Bissau Lesotho Liberia Malawi Mali Mauritius Mozambique São Tomé and Príncipe Seychelles Sierra Leone South Africa Togo Zambia Zimbabwe
No	Comoros Eritrea	Botswana Djibouti Equatorial Guinea Gabon Gambia Madagascar Namibia Swaziland
Total	17	31

Notes: [a] Coded positive if national religious actors or institutions make isolated calls for peace. / [b] Coded positive if religious actors or institutions degraded (adherents of) other beliefs or non-believers, legitimized or incited violence or engaged actively in violence.
Source: Authors' compilation.

7 Conclusion

Despite the many religiously diverse societies south of the Sahara and the religious overtones in a number of African conflicts, little systematic research has been done on the religion–conflict nexus in Africa. Most global quantitative studies limit analysis to demographic variables. Comprehensive studies on Africa are completely absent. In-depth case studies focus on a limited number of countries. Thus, the question remains how and to what extent religion is connected to conflict or peace in Africa. This paper contributed to filling the gap by presenting the results of a new data inventory of all sub-Saharan countries for the period 1990-2008. The paper demonstrates that religion matters for conflict (in Africa) and that far more countries are affected than previously assumed. Religion and armed conflict or other types of violence are connected at different levels in many countries, particularly through warring factors varying by religious affiliation, religious incompatibilities, armed religious groups and events of religious violence.

Religion is also frequently connected to peace, a finding exemplified by religious peace initiatives and inter-religious networks. The results demonstrate not only the general relevance, ambivalence and multidimensionality of religion in Africa but also significant differences between countries. Twelve countries are particularly prone to religious violence, while more than half of the countries are not really affected by a religious dimension of violent conflict.

Thus, any policy recommendation must primarily refer to the country level (or below) where specific case conditions have to be taken into account. This does not mean that we have not detected more general patterns. In particular, a contagion of the sub-Saharan area by Muslim extremism should be closely watched in the future. Though evidence for a "clash of Christian and Muslim civilizations" is fairly limited, according to our findings (and beyond) the potential for escalation clearly exists.

Any impact on violence by religious factors, however, will most likely also depend on the general conflict dimensions outside the specific religious context; the knowledge about these conditions remains deficient. For this reason there are still manifold challenges for future research. Although even a preliminary causal analysis is beyond the scope of this paper, the database will be helpful for any research activities on the topic (Basedau/Vüllers 2010; Basedau/Strüver/Vüllers/Wegenast 2011). There is a multitude of research questions and methodologies such as logit regressions, configurational methods or comparative case studies that can make use of the database presented in this paper. It might be also very fruitful to expand the database regarding both the coverage of time and geography (e.g. other regions, sub-national georeferencing). In any case, it will be particularly promising to have a close look at the micro level in order to better understand how religion may contribute to violence or peace.

References

Abu-Nimer, Mohammed/ Kadayifci-Orellana, Ayse S. (2008): Muslim Peace-Building Actors in Africa and the Balkan Context. Challenges and Needs. In: Peace & Change 33:4, 549-581.

Appleby, R. Scott (2000): The Ambivalence of the Sacred. Religion, Violence and Reconciliation. Rowman & Littlefield, Lanham.

Appleby, R. Scott (2001): Religion as an Agent of Conflict Transformation and Peacebuilding. In: Crocker, Chester A./ Hampson, Osler/ Aall, Pamela (eds.): Turbulent Peace. The Challenges of Managing International Conflict. United States Institute of Peace, Washington D.C., 821-840.

Basedau, Matthias/ De Juan, Alexander (2008): The Ambivalence of the Sacred in Africa. The Impact of Religion in sub-Saharan Civil Conflicts. GIGA Working Papers 70. GIGA German Institute of Global and Area Studies, Hamburg.

Basedau, Matthias/ Vüllers, Johannes (2010): Religion and Armed Conflict in Sub-Saharan Africa, 1990 to 2008 – Results from a New Database. Paper prepared for presentation at the SGIR 7th Pan-European Conference on IR, Stockholm, 9-11 September 2010.

Basedau, Matthias/ Strüver, Georg/ Vüllers, Johannes (2011): Cutting Bread or Cutting Throats? Findings from a New Database on Religion, Violence and Peace in Sub-Saharan Africa, 1990 to 2008. GIGA Working Papers 159. GIGA German Institute of Global and Area Studies, Hamburg.

Basedau, Matthias/ Strüver, Georg/ Vüllers, Johannes/ Wegenast, Tim (2011): Do Religious Factors Impact Armed Conflict? Empirical Evidence from Sub-Saharan Africa.In: Terrorism and Political Violence 23:5, 752-779.

Bevan, James (2007): The Myth of Madness. Cold Rationality and 'Resource' Plunder by the Lord's Resistance Army. In: Civil Wars 9:4, 343-358.

Butselaar, Jan van (2005): The Promise of the Kingdom and the Reality of Sin. Christian Religion, Conflict and Vision for Peace. In: Ter Haar, Gerrie/ Busuttil, James J. (eds.): Bridge or Barrier. Religion, Violence, and Visions for Peace. Brill, Leiden, 121-152.

Collier, Paul/ Hoeffler, Anke (2002): On the Incidence of Civil War in Africa. In: Journal of Conflict Resolution 46:1, 13-28.

Collier, Paul/ Sambanis, Nicholas (eds.) (2005): Understanding Civil War. Evidence and Analysis, 1, Africa. World Bank, Washington.

Croissant, Aurel/ Wagschal, Uwe/ Schwank, Nicolas/ Trinn, Uwe (2009): Kultur und Konflikt in globaler Perspektive. Die kulturellen Dimensionen des Konfliktgeschehens 1845-2007. Verlag Bertelsmann-Stiftung, Gütersloh.

Dixon, Jeffrey (2009): What Causes Civil Wars? Integrating Quantitative Research Findings. In: International Studies Review 11:4, 707-735.

Elbadawi, Ibrahim/ Sambanis, Nicolas (2000): Why are There So Many Civil Wars in Africa? Understanding and Preventing Violent Conflict. World Bank Policy Research Paper.

Ellingsen, Tanja (2005): Toward a Revival of Religion and Religious Clashes? In: Terrorism and Political Violence 17:3, 305-332.

Ellis, Stephen/ Ter Haar, Gerrie (2007): Religion and Politics. Taking African Epistemologies seriously. In: Journal of Modern African Studies 45:3, 385-401.

Farmar, Sam (2006): I will use the Ten Commandments to liberate Uganda, in: The Times, June 28, 2006. Available at: www.timesonline.co.uk/tol/news/world/article680339.ece. Accessed on: 4.2.2010.

Fearon, James D./ Laitin, David (2000): Violence and the Social Construction of Ethnic Identity. In: International Organization 54:4, 845-877.

Fearon, James D./ Laitin, David (2003): Ethnicity, Insurgency, and Civil War. In: American Political Science Review 97:1, 75-90.

Fox, Jonathan (2004): The Religion and State Project, Version 1. Available at: www-theard-a.com/ras/downloads. Accessed on: 9.12.2010.

Gleditsch, Nils Petter/ Wallensteen, Peter/ Eriksson, Mikael/ Sollenberg, Margareta/ Strand, Håvard (2002): Armed Conflict 1946-2001. A New Dataset. In: Journal of Peace Research 39:5, 615-637.

Gopin, Marc (2000): Between Eden and Armageddon. The Future of World Religions, Violence, and Peacemaking. Oxford University Press, New York/Oxford.

Harbom, Lotta/ Wallensteen, Peter (2009): Armed Conflict, 1946-2008. In: Journal of Peace Research 46:4, 577-587.

Harpviken, Kristian Berg/ Røislien, Hanne Eggen (2008): Faithful Brokers? Potentials and Pitfalls of Religion in Peacemaking. In: Conflict Resolution Quarterly 25:3, 351-373.

Hasenclever, Andreas/ Rittberger, Volker (2003): Does Religion Make a Difference? Theoretical Approaches to the Impact of Faith on Political Conflict. In: Hatzopolous, Pavlos / Petito, Fabio (eds.): Religion in International Relations. The Return from Exile. Palgrave Macmillan, New York, 107-145.

Haynes, Jeffrey (2005): Religion in African Civil Wars. In: Brocker, Manfred/ Hildebrandt, Mathias (eds.): Unfriedliche Religionen? Das politische Gewalt- und Konfliktpotenzial von Religionen. VS Verlag für Sozialwissenschaften, Wiesbaden, 277-294.

Haynes, Jeffrey (2009): Conflict, Conflict Resolution and Peace-Building. The Role of Religion in Mozambique, Nigeria and Cambodia. In: Commonwealth and Comparative Politics 47:1, 52-75.

Hegre, Håvard/ Sambanis, Nicholas (2006): Sensitivity Analysis of Empirical Results on Civil War Onset. In: Journal of Conflict Resolution 50:4, 508-535.

Horowitz, Michael C. (2009): Long Time Going. Religion and the Duration of Crusading. In: International Security 34:2, 162-193.

Hovil, Lucy/ Werker, Eric (2005): Portrait of a Failed Rebellion. An Account of Rational, Sub-Optimal Violence in Western Uganda. In: Rationality and Society 17:1, 5-34.

Huntington, Samuel P. (1996): The Clash of Civilizations and the Remaking of World Order. Simon & Schuster, New York.

Juergensmeyer, Mark (2008): Global Rebellion. Religious Challenges to the Secular State from Christian Militias to al Qaeda. University of California Press, Berkeley.

Kagwanja, Peter Mwangi (2003): Facing Mount Kenya or Facing Mecca? The Mungiki, Ethnic Violence and the Politics of the Moi Succession in Kenya, 1987-2002. In: African Affairs 102:406, 25-49.

Little, David (ed.) (2007): Peacemakers in Action. Profiles of Religion in Conflict Resolution. Cambridge University Press, Cambridge.

McCauley, John F./ Gyimah-Boadi, E. (2009): Religious Faith and Democracy. Evidence from the Afrobarometer Surveys. Afrobarometer Working Papers 113.

Møller, Bjørn (2006): Religion and Conflict in Africa. DIIS Report 6, Copenhagen.

Montalvo, José G./ Reynal-Querol, Marta (2005): Ethnic Polarization, Potential Conflict and Civil War. In: American Economic Review 95:3, 796-816.

Pearce, Susanna (2005): Religious Rage. A Quantitative Analysis of the Intensity of Religious Conflicts. In: Terrorism and Political Violence 17:3, 333-352.

Pew Forum on Religion & Public Life (2010): Tolerance and Tension. Islam and Christianity in Sub-Saharan Africa. Available at: www.pewforum.org/uploadedFiles/Topics/Belief_and_Practices/sub-saharan-africa-full-report.pdf. Accessed on: 10.8.2010.

Philpott, Daniel (2007): Explaining the Political Ambivalence of Religion. In: American Political Science Review 101:3, 505-525.

Seul, Jeffrey (1999): Ours is the Way of God. Religion, Identity, and Intergroup Conflict. In: Journal of Peace Research 36:5, 553-569.

Smock, David R. (ed.) (2006): Religious Contributions to Peacemaking. When Religion Brings Peace, not War. United States Institute of Peace, Washington D.C.

Stewart, Frances (2009): Religion versus Ethnicity as a Source of Mobilisation. Are There Differences? MICROCON Research Working Paper 18.

Svensson, Isak (2007): Fighting with Faith. Religion and Conflict Resolution in Civil Wars. In: Journal of Conflict Resolution 51:6, 930-949.

Ter Haar, Gerrie (2005): Religion. Source of Conflict or Resource for Peace? In: Ter Haar, Gerrie/ Busuttil, James (eds.): Bridge or Barrier. Religion, Violence, and Visions for Peace. Brill, Leiden, 3-34.

Toft, Monica Duffy (2007): Getting Religion? The Puzzling Case of Islam and Civil War. In: International Security 31:4, 97-131.

Tusicisny, Andrej (2004): Civilizational Conflicts. More Frequent, Longer, and Bloodier? In: Journal of Peace Research 41:4, 485-498.

Weingardt, Markus A. (2010): Religion Macht Frieden. Das Friedenspotenzial von Religionen in politischen Gewaltkonflikten. Bundeszentrale für politische Bildung, Bonn.

War on Earth and Peace from Heaven: Preventing Religions from Instrumentalisation

Andreas Hasenclever

The issue of religions' potential for violence has triggered intense debate amongst academics and the public in recent years. In contrast, their potential for peace has been contemplated much less frequently, which is not least unfortunate because both issues are closely intertwined: religions can only bring about peace if they themselves have not become part of a violent conflict (Harpviken/Røislien 2008). To achieve this, however, in view of the widespread appropriation of religious traditions by political elites, it is necessary to prevent the instrumentalisation of faith. Otherwise religions' potential for peace will be wasted where it is needed most.

I will develop this reasoning in three steps. In the first step, I try to show that armed conflicts follow a secular logic. People – and not their gods – are responsible for wars. But it must not, secondly, be concluded from this that religions and violent conflicts have nothing to do with each other. In fact, adding religion to a political struggle can lead to its escalation, culminating in the all-out use of violence. At the same time, however, religions have been seen to foster peace time and again. This positive impact is only probable, though, if religions have not already been appropriated as a resource for mobilisation by the warring factions. For this reason, our reflections must, thirdly, concentrate on how to prevent the instrumentalisation of religious traditions. After all, if conflicts are a "secular phenomenon" and if political elites deploy religious differences from a greater or less degree of inner conviction to legitimise violence, then we ought to know how we can effectively engage in some sort of "instrumentalisation prophylaxis" in order to preserve the peace potential of religions. There is a great need for research into this area.

The secular logic of armed struggle

Many contemporaries believe there is a close connection between religion and violence (Assmann 2006; Beck 2008; Rapoport 2006). According to them, religions are attended by absolute claims to truth and validity that set religious people against one another, repeatedly driving them into a bloody rage. Or, as Ulrich Beck (2007:12) once put it pointedly: "Religion kills. Religion should not be handed out to youths under 18." This point of view is connected to the hope that a world without religions would be more peaceful. And if such a world is utopian, then the immanent potential for conflict of religions should at least be contained and defused by the rule of law (Kohlhammer 2002).

While it is undisputed that absolute claims to truth and validity play a central role for the legitimization of, and mobilization to, armed conflicts and that religions enunciate exactly such claims to truth and validity time and again, the converse argument – that if religions are domesticated or disappear altogether the virulence of claims to truth and validity would be eradicated – does not necessarily apply. By contrast, it might be argued that human nature and scarcity in themselves lead to conflicts in which groups feel disadvantaged to such an extent that they turn to violence against each other. Under these conditions, how they substantiate their claims appears to be of secondary importance. It is only important that the group members believe in the superiority of their own cause and in the moral inferiority and perniciousness of the opposing side. The disappearance of religions or the control thereof would have little effect on this fundamental social problematic – not least because it is not so much the gods that set people against one another but their mundane conflicts.

If we take a first look at present violent conflicts, the mentioned concerns regarding a genuine and close connection between religion and violence appears to be confirmed. The opponents of many armed conflicts indeed differ in accordance with their faith. We only need to think of the fighting in Afghanistan, India, Indonesia, Nigeria, Palestine, Sri Lanka, Thailand or Chechnya. In these cases, religious convictions undoubtedly have an identity-forming function (De Juan/Hasenclever 2011). Religion helps the warring factions to foster their own internal cohesion, to clearly distance themselves from the opponent, to justify violence in the name of the sacred and to enhance individuals' capacity for sacrifice. In addition, it is undisputed that violent conflict would soon collapse without such a collective identity (Staub/Bar Tal 2003). At the same time, however, the empirical evidence shows that there are collective identities capable of violence beyond religions. Ethnic, ideological and nationalist conflicts are no less brutal than conflicts between hostile communities of faith. Examples of this include the genocide in Darfur, Guatemala, Cambodia, Rwanda and Somalia. What is more, many other violent conflicts across the globe have been, and are being, waged with indescribable cruelty without any discernible religious differences. In other words, groups need a collective identity to draw social boundaries, to identify enemies, to deny people their dignity and to legitimise the most brutal violence. The content to which these collective identities refer is effectively of secondary importance. Rather, the power of differences in faith to incite conflict and to motivate violence can evidently be substituted by ethnic, ideological or nationalist differences (cf. also Schäfer 2009; Waldmann et al. 2011). In any case, a group's type of identity does not alter the pattern of conflict to a great extent.

It therefore comes as no surprise that, despite intense search, quantitative research has not yet found any robust correlation between religious differences and the risk of violent conflict (Hegre/Sambanis 2006; Croissant et al. 2009; Tusciziny 2004). There is also a lack of convincing evidence of the frequently expressed hypothesis that Islamic societies are particularly prone to violence (Fish et al. 2010; Sørli et al. 2005). In contrast, the major significance of economic and political factors becomes apparent again and again. Indeed, a country's risk of falling into civil war increases in direct proportion to economic crisis and the disintegration of the state. In addition, there has been a recent renaissance of research approaches that consider the discrimination of entire population groups – whether of an ethnic or religious nature – to be a major cause of violence (Gottwald 2009; Stewart 2005; Wimmer et al. 2009). Although only a small proportion of the world's excluded identity groups rebel, their discrimination nonetheless significantly increases a society's proneness to civil war and, as a risk factor, is on a par with economic crisis and the disintegration of the state.

Finally, comparative studies on religious movements in the Muslim world reveal that their conflict behaviour is marked more by political opportunities than by underlying religious convictions. Thus the diversity of active groups in the Near East alone suggests that there is no plausible correlation between Islam and violence (Albrecht/Köhler 2008; Hafez 2003). What is more, surveys indicate that support for religiously founded violence among the population decreased significantly between 2001 and 2007, with the exception of the Palestinian territories (Pew Global Attitude Project 2008). This applies above all for societies that have been the target of terrorist attacks. In this context, it is also striking that there are no significant dogmatic differences between the religious convictions of militant groups and those groups that repudiate the use of violence in the pursuit of their goals. This suggests that it is not so much religion but opportunity structures that may explain why Islamists in Jordan and Morocco, for example, pursue their goals without the use of violence, whilst movements such as al-Gamaa al-Islamiyya and the Islamic Jihad in Egypt and the Islamic Salvation Army or the Armed Islamic Group in Algeria advocate armed struggle against governments. According to Quintan Wiktorowicz, it therefore makes no sense to conceive militant Islamists as perpetrators of violence sui generis (Wiktorowicz 2004:3). In fact, compared to other violent movements, they behave frighteningly "normally".

A number of recent studies on the path of religious groups towards terrorism points in a similar direction. In any case, these radicalisation processes exhibit an astoundingly high degree of structural similarities with the radicalisation of secular groups (Kruglanski et al. 2009; McCauley/Moskalenko 2008; Smeulers/Hoex 2010). At any rate, no particular effectiveness of religious convictions is discernible. A German Federal Criminal Police Office (BKA) study by Saskia Lützinger on the radicalisation of young Germans from different milieus comes to the same conclusion. According to this study, the path to terrorism is characterised by many coincidental occurrences. At the most, politics and religion are reported to be of secondary importance. "The chief motive for entering an extrem(ist) clique was the quest for social support, understanding and structure" (Lützinger 2010:71).

All in all, the research therefore provides strong indications that the correlation between religion and violence is not nearly as clear as a number of contemporaries believe. What becomes apparent is only that groups prone to violence need a strong ideology and that religion, at least at first sight, can provide such an ideological foundation. In this case, however, it is debatable whether we are still dealing here with religion in a strict sense. Thus Wolfhart Pannenberg (1988:188-205), for example, distinguishes between a subjective and an objective side of religion. We can only speak of religion if both concur, i.e. if both form and content are consistent with one another. It is precisely this that usually fails in attempts to legitimise violence with religion. According to Wolfhart Pannenberg (1988:202), in such cases religion degenerates into magic. It reflects human needs and people's power of imagination, and no longer has anything in common with the intended truth of religion. It appears as a "form of decay of religion", and then in fact becomes an inner-worldly ideology amongst many others that merely differs from them in that it claims a relation to transcendence – which it, of course, cannot keep. I shall come back to this in the final section.

Religions' potential for peace

Whilst a lot is being written and controversially discussed about the correlation between religion and violence, the correlation between religion and peace continues to be given insufficient attention in academia and politics (Abu-Nimer/Kadayifci-Orellana 2008; Kadayifci-Orellana 2009; Weingardt 2010). And yet, time and again, political movements have emerged from the heart of the large denominations that have protested against injustice and repression using nonviolent means on the basis of their traditions. Such examples include the early Indian National Movement, the Pakistani Soldiers of God, the American Civil Rights Movement and the Tibetan liberation movement. There is no doubt that for the key figures of these movements, such as Mahatma Gandhi, Khan Abdul Ghaffar Khan, Martin Luther King and the present Dalai Lama, both their demands for more social justice and their strict adherence to nonviolent strategies of protect inevitably arose from their religious beliefs.

The commitment of the Catholic Church in the Philippines demonstrates that the efforts of religious actors to bring about nonviolent change need not be without effect. In the mid-eighties, it played a decisive role in the People Power Revolution against the Marcos regime and forced the dictator to leave the country following rigged elections, against the will of the American government. A further example is South Africa, where the South African Council of Churches, under the leadership of Desmond Tutu, was engaged in nonviolent protest against the apartheid regime from the end of the seventies. It is undisputed that not least the commitment of Tutu and his parishes saved the country from descending into bloody civil war at the end of the eighties.

Lasting religious commitment to peace in crisis situations is not limited to the Christian world. As Mohammed Abu-Nimer and S. Ayse Kadayifci-Orellana show, Muslim peacebuilders are perhaps often less visible because they are organised differently and have fewer resources at their disposal (Abu-Nimer/Kadayifci-Orellana 2008). And yet their contribution to the peaceful resolution of conflicts should by no means be underestimated. In their study, the two authors identify more than fifty organisations and movements in the Balkans and Africa alone that advocate interreligious understanding in conflict zones, negotiations between perpetrators of violence, the peaceful support of repressed minorities, and justice or peace education on the basis of their religious conviction. As the authors note, the 50 cases they mention are all relatively visible peacebuilders. It can therefore be assumed that Muslim commitment to overcoming political violence is considerably underrepresented even in this study.

Additionally, spiritual authorities and communities of faith from all the world religions repeatedly play an important role in putting an end to bloody conflicts and in the peace consolidation phase (Bercovitch/Kadayifci-Orellana 2009; Harpviken/Røislien 2008). They are capable of promoting the rebuilding of trust between the parties on the basis of common values; they are able to offer a neutral forum of negotiation and create a relaxed climate for negotiations and, thanks to their presence within society, can monitor compliance with the agreements reached. As not least the work of truth commissions shows, they are important protagonists in reconciliation processes.

In a comprehensive empirical study on religions' potential for peace in political violent conflicts, Markus Weingardt explored the issue of what qualifies faith-based actors to become peacebuilders and what gives them chances of success where secular mediators have failed (Weingardt 2010). In addition to having the necessary expertise, the cases he illustrates show that religious actors – if accepted as such – enjoy a high degree of credibility. The warring factions obviously have great trust in their "independence, fairness and discretion" (Weingardt 2010:399). In this context, it proves useful if both internal and external independence correspond; in other words, if religious mediators are not only perceived as altruistic persons, but also represent an independent community of faith.

The examples mentioned, however, should not hide the fact that religious commitment to peace in political conflicts is the exception rather than the rule. In too many cases, communities of faith either remain passive, let their traditions be instrumentalised for political purposes or even actively support a warring faction. It is therefore no coincidence that many of today's violent conflicts have a religious dimension; after all, alongside ethnicity and political ideology, religions are a highly potent identity and mobilisation resource. However, in the extent to which violent conflicts are religiously charged, religions become part of the problem and risk losing their potential for peace.

As the example of Bosnia-Herzegovina shows, religious antagonisms exist long after fighting has ended, preventing the sustainable commitment of religious communities in the field of reconciliation and peace consolidation (Clark 2010).

Reflections on instrumentalisation prophylaxis

Religions are concerned with human transience. They raise the issue of the endurability of repression and death, and respond to this issue by referring to the salvational effect of personal or non-personal superhuman powers (Hildebrandt 2005; Riesebrodt 2007; Schäfer 2009). To be able to keep their promise of salvation, however, the revered powers must be released from the constraints of human finiteness. They are only credible if they transcend our world and are not at its mercy. We do not want to be in the same boat as the gods for long. Religions express these expectations. We encounter them in the form of discursively composed systems of symbols in which the promise of superhuman powers becomes perceptible to believers.

As elaborated not least by Wolfhart Pannenberg, religions shall be conceived as a "double-sided dimension" (Pannenberg 1988:157). Their primary mission is to convey the "infinite with the finite", retaining an awareness of one's own finite nature. Religions organise a relation to transcendence for their believers and simultaneously and necessarily have a historical figure for the purpose (Pollack 1995). For this reason, they must always stand the test of appropriately expressing the promised salvation under the conditions of their time. In so doing, believers have no choice but to make use of their own reason. At the same time, in their search for answers they must always take account of "the temporary nature of human judgement in their situation relativity" (Pannenberg 1999:169). Religions therefore prove themselves by doing the greatest justice possible to their intended truth. At the same time, this intended truth is so vast that it can never be expressed fully on the horizon of finiteness. Religions, therefore, are an attempt to provide an appropriate response to the promise of salvation – in the knowledge that this response can only be temporary and is always riddled with finite restrictions. Whist, then, the promise of salvation is clear to believers, what it leads to for their lives on earth is anything but clear.

The promise of salvation by religions is generally accompanied by community-building (Kippenberg 2008). Believers distance themselves from non-believers, and develop their very own – even if necessarily temporary – ideas on how their lives in this world should be organised so as not to lose the offer of help from the next world. This leads to tension arising from the difference between the internal organisation of a community of faith and its relevant environment. This is normal, and corresponds to the "in-group/out-group" processes familiar in sociology. De facto, however, political elites manage again and again with the aid of this social difference to mobilise communities of faith to take up arms to defend or propagate their religion, pursuing highly secular goals in the process. A recent example in the heart of 20th century Europe is the Yugoslavian wars of succession (Mojzes 1998; Sells 1996). Not only did large sections of the Serbian Orthodox hierarchy bless weapons and justify war with reference to the "superiority" of Serbia within the history of salvation – Slobodan Milosevic was very opportunistic with the argument of superiority in the course of the conflict. The moment it became apparent that a negotiated solution was inevitable, Greater Serbia lost its halo and became a bargaining chip despite the high clergy's opposition to this.

In order for the instrumentalisation of religious communities of faith to be used successfully for political purposes, however, a number of prerequisites must be met that elites cannot control entirely (Benford/Snow 2000; De Juan/Hasenclever 2009). First of all, religious arguments must find resonance with their addressees. There is no point declaring a holy war in a secular society. Rather, religion needs to play an important role in everyday social life. Secondly, the arguments put forward to the addressees need to be plausible. Robert Benford (1993:692) refers to "empirical credibility" in this context. If, then, people subjectively feel their religion and religious identity are being threatened and consider this threat to be existential, then attempts to mobilise them on the basis of religious traditions are particularly promising. Finally, if possible, there should be no public protest by recognised authorities. Religious calls for violence become less convincing if they are rejected by a competent party.

The prerequisites for successful mobilisation illustrate that the instrumentalisation of religious traditions for political purposes is by no means a sure thing and can indeed fail. This was the case in South Africa, for example, when Nobel Peace Prize laureate Desmond Tutu brought his entire repute to bear to prevent an escalation of the anti-apartheid struggle. Similarly, Muslim rebels in Southern Thailand tried in vain at the end of the seventies to mobilise their fellow-believers to take up arms against Buddhist Bangkok (De Juan/Hasenclever 2009:195-198). The local clerics were divided, and the rebels failed to mobilise the necessary support of the public.

If conflicts can be exacerbated by the instrumentalisation of religious traditions and if this instrumentalisation is not an automatism, from the perspective of peace and conflict research, the question arises how religions can protect themselves from being appropriated by entrepreneurs of violence (Hasenclever/De Juan 2007; Svensson 2007). In this context, it makes sense to fall back on what religions aim to achieve, namely the temporary mediation between the infinite and the finite. If we take this mission seriously, then it becomes apparent that, beyond their clear promises of salvation, religions are intrinsically virtually *unable* to develop the dimension of political reification required to legitimise violence and to mobilise believers to take up arms. Justification of violence is a task of human reasoning and cannot be derived seamlessly from divine revelation. It is therefore no coincidence that an extreme reduction of the complexity of religious traditions is observed in the relevant literature when calls to war are declared in the name of the sacred. This has particularly been stressed recently with regard to Islamist terrorism whose followers are purported to have a very one-sided understanding of their holy traditions (Esposito 2002:16; Ranstorp 2010:7; Sageman 2008:41). This, of course, does not mean to say that Islamist terrorists are not religious people. The opposite is frequently the case. Only that to which they refer in their subjective religiousness has very little to do with the intended truth of their religion. To put it very simply, it could be said that in these cases the form and content of religion contradict one another and they have a magical understanding of what religion, in its temporary nature, should and, hopefully also can, actually express.

To prevent a further misunderstanding: it also cannot be denied that communities of faith have repeatedly developed teachings to legitimise dominance and violence. But this essentially runs counter to what religion precisely should be to people. Dominance and violence must be justified by humans or cannot be justified at all in the first place. At the most, religion can be accorded a critical function in this context because it broaches the issue of experiences of finiteness injustice, to which an answer is required.

Consequently, a successful instrumentalisation prophylaxis should sharpen believers' religious awareness of the necessary complexity of their own traditions – because there is no other way of talking about promises of salvation and their grounds. It goes without saying that this discussion is still in its infancy. However, there are indications that if a population enjoys a solid religious education, it is harder to instrumentalise their beliefs. Scott Appleby (2000), for instance, is convinced that the Serb and Croatian government was only able to justify its policy of conquest in the Bosnian conflict with religious arguments because the citizens had become "religious illiterates" under Tito (Scott Appleby). Most of them no longer had the competence required to recognise the abuse of their traditions and to contradict to their grotesque interpretations. The same applies to graduates of radical madrassas in Pakistan: "The students (…) are indoctrinated to move all doubts; the only truth is divine truth and the only code of conduct is that written in the Qur'an and the Hadiths as selected by the clerics. The teachings cannot be questioned; there is no debate and only one answer permissible" (Kortenweg et al. 2010:42). Precisely because an adequate understanding of religion requires an understanding of the complexity of its traditions, the Protestant Church in Germany (EKD 2007:31) advocates a hermeneutically reflected acquirement of sacred writings. It is otherwise difficult to prevent their abuse. In addition, "wherever militant or terrorist violence is legitimised, advocated or exercised using religious arguments, the official representatives [should] persistently and publicly contradict such acts and their religious substantiations" (EKD 2007:34). Protestants and Catholics are in total agreement concerning this point. Thus the German Bishops' Conference (Die deutschen Bischöfe 2011:36) also calls for churches and religious communities to clearly distance themselves from violence: "They must agree upon an interpretation of their traditions that makes it clear that any religiously substantiated incitement to enmity and hatred misuses truths of revelation."

Religious publicity has a similar effect of preventing violence as a suitable religious awareness (Hasenclever/De Juan 2007). Religious publicity refers to discussion contexts in which religious elites justify their interpretation of joint traditions before an informed audience and advertise for the audience's support by way of argumentation. Religious publicity may not be equated to religion – it evolves through communication about religion. If in the process we assume the fundamental complexity of religious traditions, then religious publicity serves the purpose of coping with complexity. On the one hand, it reflects the temporary nature of specific interpretations and, on the other, features the interpretations that have so far proven to be effective in argumentation. Here, too, research shows that mainly militant religious movements have a strong tendency towards isolating themselves from their environment (Dawson 2010:10; Endres/Jung 1998:106, Hafez 2003:111 f.). They incline towards a kind of social autism and usually evade all public debate of their extremely one-sided interpretations of religious traditions. Accordingly, Rem Korteweg and his colleagues observe the following in radicalisation processes leading to Islamist terrorism: "A primary factor contributing to radicalization is the lack of debate within the Islamic community concerning the interpretation of holy text, which has created the possibility for extremist views to proliferate" (Korteweg et al. 2010:31).

The political instrumentalisation of religious traditions by elites prepared to use violence is therefore not a foregone conclusion. It can be prevented if militant slogans are seen by the population to be what they often are: namely, an attempt to use religion as a conflict resource. In the process, instrumentalisation prophylaxis is important to control the escalation potential of religions, thus reducing the risk of violence. However, instrumentalisation prophylaxis is also crucial for communities of faith to be able to play an independent role in preventing violence, ending violence and consolidating peace.

References

Abu-Nimer, Mohammed/Kadayifci-Orellana, Ayse S. (2008): Muslim Peace-building Actors in Africa and the Balkan Context: Challenges and Needs. In: *Peace & Change* 33:4, 549-581.

Albrecht, Holger/Köhler, Kevin (eds.) (2008): Politischer Islam im Vorderen Orient. Zwischen Sozialbewegung Opposition und Widerstand. Nomos, Baden-Baden.

Appleby, R. Scott (2000): The Ambivalence of the Sacred. Religion, Violence, and Reconciliation. Rowman & Littlefield, Lanham.

Assmann, Jan (2006): Gesetz, Gewalt und Monotheismus. In: Theologische Zeitschrift 62:4, 475-486.

Beck, Ulrich (2007): Gott ist gefährlich. So human Religion auch scheinen mag: Sie birgt stets einen totalitären Kern. In: DIE ZEIT 52 (19.12.2007), 12.

Beck, Ulrich (2008): Der eigene Gott. Von der Friedensfähigkeit und dem Gewaltpotential der Religionen. Verlag der Weltreligionen, Frankfurt am Main.

Benford, Robert D. (1993): Frame Disputes within the Nuclear Disarmament Movement. In: *Social Forces* 71:3, 677-701.

Benford, Robert D./Snow, David A. (2000): Framing Processes and Social Movements: An Overview and Assessment. In: *Annual Review of Sociology* 26:3, 611-639.

Bercovitch, Jacob/Kadayifci-Orellana, Ayse S. (2009): Religion and Mediation. The Role of Faith-Based Actors in International Conflict Resoultion. In: *International Negotiation* 14:2, 175-204.

Clark, Janine N. (2010): Religion and Reconciliation in Bosnia & Herzegovina: Are Religious Actors Doing Enough? In: *Europe-Asia Studies* 62:4, 671-694.

Croissant, Aurel/Wagschal U./Schwank, Nicolas/Trinn, Christoph (2009): Kulturelle Konflikte seit 1945. Die kulturellen Dimensionen des globalen Konfliktgeschehens. Nomos, Baden-Baden.

Dawson, Lorne L. (2010): The Study of New Religious Movements and the Radicalization of Home-Grown Terrorists: Opening a Dialogue. In: Terrorism and Political Violence 22:1, 1-21.

De Juan, Alexander/Hasenclever, Andreas (2009): Das Framing religiöser Konflikte – Die Rolle von Eliten in religiöse konnotierten Bürgerkriegen. In: Bussmann, Margit/Hasenclever, Andreas/Schneider, Gerald (eds.): *Identität, Institutionen und Ökonomie. Ursachen innenpolitischer Gewalt.* VS Verlag für Sozialwissenschaften, Wiesbaden, 178-205.

De Juan, Alexander/Hasenclever, Andreas (2011): Die Ambivalenz religiöser Integration. Zur erzeugten Relevanz von Glaubensunterschieden in bewaffneten Konflikten. In: Ferhadbegovic, Sabina/Weiffen, Britta (eds.): *Bürgerkriege erzählen. Zum Verlauf unziviler Konflikte.* Konstanz University Press, Konstanz, 223-247.

Die deutschen Bischöfe (2011): Terrorismus als ethische Herausforderung. Menschenwürde und Menschenrechte. Sekretariat der deutschen Bischofskonferenz, Die deutschen Bischöfe: 94, Bonn.

EKD (2007): Aus Gottes Frieden leben – für gerechten Frieden sorgen. Eine Denkschrift des Rates der Evangelischen Kirche in Deutschland. Gütersloher Verlagshaus, Gütersloh.

Endres, Jürgen/Jung, Dietrich (1998): Was legitimiert den Griff zur Gewalt? Unterschiede im Konfliktverhalten islamistischer Organisationen in Ägypten. In: Politische Vierteljahresschrift 39:1, 91-108.

Esposito, John L. 2002: Unholy war. Terror in the name of Islam. Oxford University Press, Oxford.

Ferhadbegovic, Sabina/Weiffen, Britta (eds.) (2011): Bürgerkriege erzählen. Zum Verlauf unziviler Konflikte. Konstanz University Press, Konstanz.

Fish, M. S./Jensenius, Francesca R./Michel, Katherine E. (2010): Islam and Large-Scale Political Violence: Is There a Connection? In: *Comparative Political Studies* 43:11, 1327-1362.

Gottwald, Eva (2009): Horowitz ernst nehmen: Der Einfluss von Leidensdruck auf den Ausbruch von Bürgerkriegen. In: Bussmann, Margit/Hasenclever, Andreas/Schneider, Gerald (eds.): *Identität, Institutionen und Ökonomie. Ursachen innenpolitischer Gewalt.* VS Verlag für Sozialwissenschaften, Wiesbaden, 73-99.

Hafez, Mohammed M. (2003): Why Muslims Rebel. Repression and Resistance in the Islamic World. Lynne Rienner, Boulder, Col.

Harpviken, Kristian B./Røislien, Hanne E. (2008): Faithful Broker? Potentials and Pitfalls of Religion in Peacemaking. In: *Conflict Resolution Quarterly* 25:3, 351-373.

Hasenclever, Andreas/Juan, Alexander De (2007): Religionen in Konflikten. In: *Aus Politik und Zeitgeschichte* Vol. 6, 9-16.

Hegre, Håvard/Sambanis, Nicholas (2006): Sensitivity Analysis of Empirical Results on Civil War Onset. In: *Journal of Conflict Resolution* 50:4, 508-535.

Hildebrandt, Mathias (2005): Unfriedliche Religionen? Das politische Gewalt- und Konfliktpotential von Religionen, in: Hildebrandt, Mathias/Brocker, Manfred (eds.): Unfriedliche Religionen? Das politische Gewalt- und Konfliktpotenzial von Religionen. VS Verlag für Sozialwissenschaften, Wiesbaden, 9-35.

Kadayifci-Orellana, Ayse S. (2009): Ethno-Religious Conflicts: Exploring the Role of Religion in Conflict Resolution. In: Bercovitch, Jacob/Kremenyuk, Victor/Zartman, Ira W. (eds.): *The Sage Handbook of Conflict Resolution.* Sage Publications, Los Angeles, 264-284.

Kippenberg, Hans G. (2008): Gewalt als Gottesdienst. Religionskriege im Zeitalter der Globalisierung. Beck, München.

Kohlhammer, Siegfried (2002): Islam und Toleranz. Duldung, Ausbeutung, Demütigung. In: Merkur 56:639, 589-560.

Korteweg, Rem/Gohel, Sajjan/Heisbourg, Francois/Ranstorp, Magnus/de Wijk, Rob (2010): Background Contributing Factors to Terrorism: Radicalization and Recruitment. In: Ranstorp, Magnus (ed.): Understanding Violent Radicalisation. Terrorist and Jihadist Movements in Europe. Routledge, London, 21-49.

Kruglanski, Arie W./Fishman, Shira (2009): Psychological Factors in Terrorism and Counterterrorism: Individual Group, and Organizational Levels of Analysis. In: *Social Issues and Policy Review* 3:1, 1-44.

Lützinger, Saskia/Kraus, Benjamin (2010): Die Sicht der Anderen. Eine qualitative Studie zu Biographien von Extremisten und Terroristen. Luchterhand, Köln.

McCauley, Clark and Moskalenko, Sophia (2008): Mechanisms of Political Radicalization: Pathways Toward Terrorism. In: Terrorism and Political Violence 20:3, 415-433.

Mojzes, Paul (1998): The Camouflaged Role of Religion in the War in B&H. In: Mojzes, Paul (ed.): Religion and the War in Bosnia. Scholars Press, Atlanta, Ga.,74-98.

Pannenberg, Wolfhart (1988): Systematische Theologie. Vol. 1, Vandenhoeck & Ruprecht, Göttingen.

Pannenberg, Wolfhart (1999): Beiträge zur systematischen Theologie. Vandenhoeck & Ruprecht, Göttingen.

Pollack, Detlef (1995): Was ist Religion? Probleme der Definition. In: *Zeitschrift für Religionswissenschaft* 3:2, 163-190.

Ranstorp, Magnus (2010): Introduction. In: Ranstorp, Magnus (ed.): Understanding Violent Radicalisation. Terrorist and Jihadist Movements in Europe. Routledge, London, 1-18.

Rapoport, David C. (2006): Terrorism. Critical Concepts in Political Science. Routledge, London/New York.

Riesebrodt, Martin (2007): Cultus und Heilsversprechen. Eine Theorie der Religionen. C. H. Beck, München.

Sageman, Marc (2008): The Next Generation of Terror. In: *Foreign Policy* 165, 36-42.

Schäfer, Heinrich W. (2009): Zum Religionsbegriff in der Analyse von Identitätskonflikten: Einige sozialwissenschaftliche und theologische Erwägungen. In: *EPD-Dokumentation* 5/2009, 6-16.

Sells, Michael A. (1996): The Bridge Betrayed. Religion and Genocide in Bosnia. University of California Press, Berkeley, CA.

Smeulers, Alette/Hoex, Lotte (2010): Studying the Microdynamics of the Rwandan Genocide. In: *The British Journal of Criminology* Vol. 50, 435-454.

Sorli, Mirjam E./Gleditsch, Nils P./Strand, Havard (2005): Why Is There So Much Conflict in the Middle East? In: *Journal of Conflict Resolution* 49:1, 141-165.

Staub, Evin/Bar-Tal, Daniel (2003): Genocide, Mass Killing, and Intractable Conflict. Roots, Evolution, Prevention, and Reconciliation. In: Sears, David O./Huddy, Leonie/Jervis, Robert (eds.): Oxford Handbook of Political Psychology. Oxford University Press, Oxford, 710-751.

Stewart, Frances (2005): Groups and Capabilities. In: *Journal of Human Development* 6:2, 185-204.

Svensson, Isak (2007): Fighting with Faith: Religion and Conflict Resolution in Civil Wars. In: *Journal of Conflict Resolution* 51:6, 930-949.

Tusicisny, Andrej (2004): Civilizational Conflicts. More Frequent, Longer, and Bloodier? In: *Journal of Peace Research* 41:4, 485-498.

Waldmann, Peter/Sirseloudi, Matenia/Malthaner, Stefan (2010): Where Does the Radicalisation Process Lead? Radical Community, Radical Networks and Radical Subcultures. In: Ranstorp, Magnus (ed.): Understanding Violent Radicalisation. Terrorist and Jihadist Movements in Europe. Routledge, London, 50-67.

Weingardt, Markus A. (2010): Religion Macht Frieden. Das Friedenspotenzial von Religionen in politischen Gewaltkonflikten. Bundeszentrale für politische Bildung, Bonn.

Wiktorowicz, Quintan (2004): Introduction. Islamic Activism and Social Movement Theory. In: Wiktorowicz, Quintan (ed.): *Islamic Activism. A Social Movement Theory Approach*. Indiana University Press, Bloomington, 1-33.

Wimmer, Andreas/Cedermann, Lars-Erik/Min, Brian (2009): Ethnische Politik und bewaffnete Konflikte. Eine Konfigurationsanalyse eines neuen globalen Datensatzes. In: Bussmann, Margit/Hasenclever, Andreas/Schneider, Gerald (eds.): *Identität, Institutionen und Ökonomie. Ursachen innenpolitischer Gewalt.* VS Verlag für Sozialwissenschaften, Wiesbaden, 39-72.

Religions, Peace and Human Rights

Javaid Rehman

Religions and religious ideologies are capable of advancing an abundance of positive values, including those of social harmony, justice, equality and peace. Major religions claim to be vehicles of peace and fairness, and also take credit for having promoted human rights. However, and at the same time, there is also an equivocation over the content and application of many religious doctrines and values. Dependant on the power dynamics between religion and the state (or society), religious ideologies have also been used to advocate intolerance, discrimination and the violation of fundamental human rights. As exemplified in various historical and contemporary contexts, texts of religious scriptures have been interpreted to sanction religious wars, occupations, slavery, torture and genocide – the religious wars of the medieval and middle ages, the Crusades and the aggressive *Jihad* can be seen as products of this phenomenon. Following the terrorist attacks in New York, Madrid, Bali and London, especially the Islamic religion and Muslims have been subjected to increasing criticism. In particular, Samuel Huntington's *The Clash of Civilizations and the Remaking of World Order* is held up as an accurate depiction of Islam's incompatibility with perceived Western values (Huntington 1996). Huntington argues, "[t]he Koran and other statements of Muslim belief contain few prohibitions on violence, and a concept of non-violence is absent from Muslim doctrine and practice" (Huntington 1996:263).

This paper, while highlighting the equivocation built within religious ideologies, emphasises the importance of using contextual interpretations in order to promote the inherent and fundamental values of peace and human rights. A particular focus of the paper is upon Islam, therefore the role of Islam in advancing the precepts of fairness, peace and human rights will be discussed in depth. Initially, some preliminary observations regarding the relationship between the concepts of religion, peace and human rights will be accentuated and a number of contentious issues will be considered. Second, I will go on to consider the role of religion in promoting peace and human rights before outlining the negative impact that particular interpretations of religion may have on these ideals. Finally, I will draw together some key conclusions from the previous discussion.

Preliminary remarks

There are various understandings of the term "rights", in particular "human rights". Human rights are generally considered to be non-static in nature; allowing them to be contextualised in the light of recent developments and situations and leaving them open to vastly differing interpretations. In particular, recent debates have emphasised questions over religious and cultural relativism. Consequently, human rights in many ways can be considered to be hugely variable and inconsistent. In recent years the debate over human rights has undergone a shift in paradigm. Notably this shift informs and continues to inform religious, social and ethical values. Indeed, a similar point (about the relative nature) could be made (out) about our understanding of the concept of "peace". Thus, for example, the "peace" that emerged from World War I and II, was a peace envisaged and engineered by the victorious powers. Notions of equality, human rights and self-determination for all peoples was an ideal, but could not be realised in the immediate post-war arrangements.

In order to highlight the complexity and relativity in the debate on human rights, I shall advance a few examples. While the right to life and the debate on capital punishment are fundamentally human rights issues, they are also informed to a large extent by religion. If human rights are to be considered sacrosanct, then surely the right to life needs to be absolutely guaranteed. Yet, opinion on this is divided – international human rights treaties, while protecting the right to life, tend not to prohibit the death penalty. Shestack comments: "[S]ome of the civil and political rights [as provided in the International Covenant on Civil and Political Rights] are in the nature of immunities meaning that governments cannot derogate from them. But are there any absolute rights? Surely the right to life guaranteed by Article 6 (1) of the Covenant would seem to be so basic as to be considered absolute. Yet, Article 6 (1) only offers protection against 'arbitrary' deprivation of life. What is the effect of this qualification on the nature of the right involved? When we speak of inalienable rights, what do we mean? Do we mean a right to which no exceptions or limitations are valid? Or do we mean a 'prima facie' right with a special burden on the proponent of any defeasance? Or do we mean a principle which must be followed unless some other principle weighty enough to allow that abridgement arises? Must considerations which justify an exception be of the same moral category as those that underlie the right?" (Shestack 1984:71).

The International Covenant on Civil and Political Rights (ICCPR) recognises under article 6 (1) "Every human being has the inherent right to life. This right shall be protected by law. No one shall be arbitrarily deprived of his life". However, article 6 (2)-(5) recognise that while states are not obliged to abolish the death penalty, certain procedural safeguards must be in place, in particular the conditions demanding that the death penalty must only be used in instances of the most serious crimes (Article 6 (2) ICCPR) and may not be imposed on those under 18 or pregnant women (Article 6 (5) ICCPR). However, the death penalty is still frequently imposed on minors, even though the prohibition on the execution of minors has been held to be *jus cogens* by the Inter-American Commission on Human Rights (*Michael Domingues v. US,* Report No. 62/02, Merits, Case 12.285 Inter-American Commission on Human Rights). While the

Second Optional Protocol to the ICCPR seeks to abolish the death penalty, this has been ratified by less than half of the world's states indicating a lack of consensus on this issue. Furthermore, it is ironic that there is not only a lack of consensus amongst societies on the prohibition of capital punishment but also on the grounds on which to award capital punishment. While article 6 (2) prescribes that the "sentence of death may be imposed only for the most serious crimes in accordance with the law in force at the time of the commission of the crime", there remain wide and varied grounds for which capital punishment is awarded, including murder, rape, drug trafficking, offenses against the state, homosexuality and blasphemy. While offensive and hurtful comments towards a particular religion do not make a convincing case for criminal punishments, there are recent unfortunate examples of targeted killings of those opposing such draconian laws, such as the blasphemy laws (BBC 2011). This ambiguity regarding the imposition of the death penalty is also echoed in regional human rights treaties. The Arab Charter on Human Rights[1] dedicates three provisions to the death penalty. However, these provisions are similar to article 6 ICCPR:

> **Article 5**
> 1. Every human being has the inherent right to life.
> 2. This right shall be protected by law. No one shall be arbitrarily deprived of his life.
>
> **Article 6**
> Sentence of death may be imposed only for the most serious crimes in accordance with the laws in force at the time of commission of the crime and pursuant to a final judgment rendered by a competent court. Anyone sentenced to death shall have the right to seek pardon or commutation of the sentence.
>
> **Article 7**
> 1. Sentence of death shall not be imposed on persons under 18 years of age, unless otherwise stipulated in the laws in force at the time of the commission of the crime.
> 2. The death penalty shall not be inflicted on a pregnant woman prior to her delivery or on a nursing mother within two years from the date of her delivery; in all cases, the best interests of the infant shall be the primary consideration.

The right to life is protected in similar terms in the African Charter on Human and Peoples' Rights[2], the American Declaration on Human Rights[3] and the European Con-

1 League of Arab States, Arab Charter on Human Rights (22 May 2004) Reprinted in 12 Int'l Human Rts. Rep. 893 (entered into force 15 March 2008).
2 African [Banjul] Charter on Human and Peoples' Rights, adopted 27 June 1981, 21 October 1986 OAU Doc. CAB/LEG/67/3 rev. 5; 21 I.L.M. 58 (1982).
3 Signed November 1969; entered into force 18 July 1978. OASTS Official Records: OEA/SER.L/V/11.23,doc.21,rev. (1979); 9 ILM (1970) 67.

vention on Human Rights.[4] The Cairo Declaration on Human Rights in Islam,[5] in contrast proclaims:

> Article 2:
> (a) Life is a God-given gift and the right to life is guaranteed to every human being. It is the duty of individuals, societies and states to safeguard this right against any violation, and it is prohibited to take away life except for a Shari'ah prescribed reason.
> (b) It is forbidden to resort to any means which could result in the genocidal annihilation of mankind.
> (c) The preservation of human life throughout the term of time willed by Allah is a duty prescribed by Shari'ah.

The Protocols to the ICCPR and the European Convention on Human Rights have subsequently sought to completely prohibit the death penalty[6].

While all members of the Council of Europe – with the exception of Russia – have ratified Protocol 6 to the European Convention on Human Rights, the Second Protocol to the ICCPR has been less successful. The Second Optional Protocol only has 73 states parties, notably the USA, China, India and almost all members of the Organisation of the Islamic Cooperation (OIC) have not signed or ratified it. Furthermore, regional organisations outside of Europe have not attempted to prohibit the death penalty.

In addition to the disagreement over the use of the death penalty, other issues falling within the scope of the right to life include the controversy over the beginning of life and the permissibility of abortion and euthanasia. These issues are not purely legal issues but also have moral, religious and societal undertones. Further, a number of religions inform interpretations of fundamental human rights, for example both Islamic and Catholic states do not permit abortion on religious grounds. However, the Inter-American Commission on Human Rights found in *Baby Boy* that the abortion of a foetus did not lead to a violation of the American Declaration of the Rights and Duties of Man.[7] Consequently, while the right to life may, on the face of it, seem to be a fundamental right, in fact the wide range of standards and the continuing use of the death penalty reveal a lack of consensus. If there are irresolvable conflicts over the right to life, then it is hardly surprising to find a lack of agreement on other civil and political rights. These differences are further exacerbated in relation to economic, so-

4 Convention for the Protection of Human Rights and Fundamental Freedoms,, *entered into force* 3 September 1953; 213 UNTS 222.

5 Adopted on 5 August 1990, U.N. GAOR, World Conf. on Hum. Rts., 4th Sess., Agenda Item 5, U.N. Doc. A/CONF.157/PC/62/Add.18 (1993).

6 Second Optional Protocol to the International Covenant on Civil and Political Rights, aiming at the abolition of the death penalty, G.A. res. 44/128, annex, 44 U.N. GAOR Supp. (No. 49) at 207, U.N. Doc. A/44/49 (1989), *entered into force* 11 July 1991; Protocol No. 6 to the Convention for the Protection of Human Rights and Fundamental Freedoms concerning the abolition of the death penalty as amended by Protocol No. 11, adopted Strasbourg, 28 April 1983; entered into force 1 March 1985.

7 *Baby Boy,* Case No. 2141 (United States), Res. 23/81, OEA/Ser.L/V/II.54,Doc.9, rev. 1, Oct. 16, 1981. See further, Shelton, 1981, 309.

cial and cultural rights, as well as third generation rights such as the right to development and the right to self-determination.

The disadvantaged position of marginalised groups such as homosexuals, religious minorities, indigenous peoples, persons with disabilities and women has frequently been blamed on religion. However, in respect of women and women rights which forms a critical debate on religion and its approach towards women's rights it is hugely ironic that in the great revolutions of France, the United States and Russia, the champions of human rights and equality had a very limited vision on matters of women's rights and gender-based equality. Consequently, women's rights have not been a priority for the human rights movement until recently. Therefore, the violation of women's rights cannot be attributed entirely to the position of women in religions. A similar historical contextual remark could be made about those who championed human rights but also justified slavery or slave-trade.

While the violation of human rights has frequently been attributed to religion, states such as the USA, usually perceived as a protector and promoter of human rights standards, have increasingly violated fundamental rights in the name of the war on terror. Following the September 11, 2001 terrorist attacks, the United States have violated fundamental rights such as the prohibition on torture and cruel, inhuman and degrading treatment, the right to liberty and security of the person and the prohibition on arbitrary detention in Guantánamo Bay, Iraq and Afghanistan. Consequently, there is not necessarily a continuing trend of greater recognition of rights in western states – and blaming the lack of rights recognition and protection purely on religion would not be accurate. In conclusion, in a scenario of shifting human rights values, it would be unfortunate to accuse religion of consistently being at odds with human rights, when these 'anti-human rights' attitudes may reflect more widespread consensus.

Religions and the Value of Peace and Human Rights

As noted earlier, religions have the great capability of advocating values of justice, fairness and peace. Major religions have been great harbingers of solidarity and humanitarianism; they lay magnificent claims to universal human rights. I would argue that this, to a certain extent, is correct. If you consider the essence of Christianity, Judaism and Islam, they are replete with examples of peace and humanitarianism. In particular, examples of the life of Jesus Christ or Prophet Mohammad would affirm the view that religion serves to create peace and the respect of others.

However, there remain question marks over the content and application of many religious doctrines and values. Equally, religions have frequently served to justify wars, and acts of cruelty against adherents of other religions. Furthermore, a strict interpretation of religious norms may justify discrimination and intolerance. Islam provides some of the most familiar instances of the use of religion in order to justify human rights violations as Islamic history is littered with situations of violence and breaches of human rights. This is equally true, however, of the other monotheist religions, Christianity and Judaism. Thornberry notes: "The question of religion takes international law to the limits of human rights, at least in so far as the law functions in a community of states. It is quite meaningless, for example, to the adherents of a religion to have their beliefs or practices declared to be contrary to 'public morality'. To the believer, religion is morality itself and its transcendental foundation grounds it more firmly in terms of obligation than any secular rival, or the tenets of other religions. All religions are to a great or lesser extent 'fundamentalist' in character in that they recognise that theirs is the just rule, the correct avenue to truth" (Thornberry 1991:324).

However, it has been claimed that in relation to other religions and the context of the time, Islam provided more favourable rights for religious minorities than other monotheist religions (Evans 1997:59). Mayer notes that "conquered Christians and Jews were allowed to persist in their beliefs because Islamic law opposes compelled conversions" (Mayer 1995:126–127). Those known as the *ahal-i-kitab* (People of the Book) under strict *Sharia,* have the political status of *dhimmis.* Although *dhimmis* are subject to the *Sharia,* they are also permitted to follow their own rules of personal status and are tolerated. In return for such toleration *dhimmis* were required to submit to Muslim rule and also pay a special capitulations tax known as *jizya.* However, such tolerance was not afforded to those not belonging to a monotheist religion. The 'non-believers' – comprised of pagans or polytheist minorities – were essentially given the choice between converting to Islam or perishing. Khadduri asserts that: "no compromise is permitted with those who fail to believe in God; they have either to accept Islam or fight. In several Qura'nic injunctions, the Muslims are under the obligation to 'fight the polytheists wherever you may find them'; to 'fight those who are near to you of the polytheists, and let them find in you sternness'; and 'when you meet those who misbelieve, strike off their head until you have massacred them...'. In the *Hadith* of the Prophet Mohammad is reported to have declared: 'I am ordered to fight polytheists until they say: 'There is no god but Allah.' All the jurists, perhaps without exception, assert polytheism and Islam cannot exist together; the polytheists, who enjoin other gods with Allah, must choose between war or Islam" (Khadduri 1955:75).

It is widely acknowledged that religious scriptures have been interpreted to justify religious crusades, *jihad,* and the genocide of religious minorities. Nevertheless, I would neither deny the existence of these violations nor feel apologetic about them or shift the blame on other things. I am sure there are many examples; however, it is vital to look at the context in which these violations of rights took place. It is my view that even while taking these verses at their face value, and comprehending them in their entirety, they do not in fact advocate unconditional aggression and violence. The aforementioned pronouncements are accompanied by a number of caveats and moderating references (Rehman 2006:84). The *Quran* does not permit the indiscriminate use of force. Furthermore, within the Holy Book, there are many scriptures which propagate freedom of religion and love for humanity. In particular, the *Quran* clearly states: "Let there be no compulsion in religion. The right direction has become distinct from error" (The Quran 2:256) and "unto you your religion and me my religion" (The Quran 109:6). The tolerance initially granted by the *Quran* and the *Hadith* to the Jews and Christians has been extended to pagans and polytheist religions. The Muslim invasions of India and the subsequent peaceful co-existence between Islam, Hinduism and Buddhism provide an excellent example of the extension of religious tolerance to all faiths.

It is the human interpretations of the *Quran* and the *Sunna* that sanction religious intolerance and instruct followers to fight in the path of Allah. It is these interpretations that have led some jurists to claim that apostasy in Islam warrants the death penalty. Further, a huge amount of disagreement exists on the freedom to change one's religion or belief. Consequently, this has become a major obstacle to the drafting of a binding treaty on freedom of religion or belief. The issues of the succession to the Prophet Muhammad and the leadership of the Muslim *Ummah* have led to much violence and aggression within Islam since the Prophet's death. In fact three of the Caliphs were assassinated. This state of affairs resulted in the terrible tragedy of the Battle of Karbala which is considered to have contributed to the anguish and dissension between the majority Sunnis and minority Shias.

Deductions

We cannot deny that violence and breaches of human rights values stem in many instances from interpretations of religion and religious ideology. However, these violations and forms of aggression cannot be ascribed to any inherent antithetical views of religions towards human rights or humanitarianism. They have in fact been based on the specific contexts in which violence and aggression can be found. Religions do not function outside or independent of the societies in which they operate. In the historical context, their operation is determined by the dynamic of powers, societal relations and issues of governance. The examples of Islam above were dictated not by disregard of freedom of religion or the projection of aggressive war, but were determined by the power dynamics of the time. While *Meccan* verses of the Holy Quran are considered to be generously humanitarian, *Medinan* verses show strains of governance and state operations in the seventh century Arabia with its endemic violence, hostility and aggression. The difference between these verses must be considered in the context in which they were revealed. At the time of *Medinan* verses, the Prophet Mohammad and his followers faced extermination. They were forced to migrate to Medina in order to avoid persecution and ensure their continued existence (Weeramantry 1988:4-5; Rehman 1994:113). It was therefore in the context of persecution, betrayals, attempted humiliation and disregard for kinship and obligations on the part of the Quresh of Mecca that a number of these verses were revealed (Rehman 2006:84).

This context to a large extent explains the difference between the *Meccan* and *Medinan* verses. However, even the *Medinan* verses do not advocate indiscriminate violence. For example: "Warn the disbelievers of a painful chastisement, excepting those of them with who you have a pact and who have not defaulted in any respect, nor supported anyone against you. Carry out the obligations you have assumed towards them till the end of their terms. Surely Allah loves those who are mindful of their obligations. When the period of four months during which hostilities are suspended expires, without the idolaters having settled the terms of peace with you, resume fighting with them and kill them wherever you find them and make them prisoners and beleaguer them, and lie in wait for them at every place of ambush. Then if they repent and observe Prayer and pay the Zakat, leave them alone. Surely Allah is Most Forgiving, Ever Merciful. If any one of the idolaters seeks asylum with thee, grant him asylum so that he may hear the Word of Allah; then convey him to a place of security for him, for they are a people that lack knowledge" (The Quran 9:3-6). The ordinance to fight an aggressive war can be seen as the product of war, and primarily in the context of self-defence. The same points regarding power dynamics and governance can also be made about the endemic violence after the Prophet's death and on the issue of succession.

Conclusions

To conclude, violations of peace and breaches of human rights must be analysed carefully and this analysis must take into account historical and contextual aspects. Conflicts and indeed bloody conflicts and breaches of human rights would take place even if we take religion out of the equation. For contemporary and future societies, it seems that religion will continue to remain an important feature of life. Consequently, it is important to acknowledge that religions have a lot to offer in terms of promoting peace, harmony and human rights. While we cannot deny the equivocation and conflict-riddled histories of religions, at this stage of maturity we must focus on the positive humanitarian values *within* religions in order to promote the agenda of universal peace and human rights.

References

BBC (2011): Punjab Governor Salman Taseer Assassinated in Islamabad. Available at: http://www.bbc.co.uk/news/world-south-asia-12111831 4 January 2011 (6 January 2011). Accessed at February 28, 2012.

Evans, Malcolm D. (1997): Religious Liberty and International Law in Europe. Cambridge University Press, Cambridge.

Huntington, Samuel. P (1996): The Clash of Civilizations and the Remaking of World Order. Simon & Schuster, London.

Khadduri, Majid (1955): War and Peace in the Law of Islam. John Hopkins: Baltimore.

Mayer, Ann E. (1995): Islam and Human Rights: Traditions and Politics. Westview Press, Boulder.

Rehman, Javaid (1994): Self-Determination, State Building and the Mihaijirs: An International Legal Perspective of the Role of the Indian Muslim Refugees in the Constitutional Developments of Pakistan. In: Contemporary South Asia 3:2, 111-129.

Rehman, Javaid (2006): Conflicting Values or Misplaced Interpretations? Examining the Inevitability of a Clash between 'Religions' and 'Human Rights'. In: Ghanea, Nazila (ed.): Does God Believe in Human Rights? Martinus Nijhoff Publishers, The Hague, 65-88.

Shelton, Dinah (1981): Abortion and the Right to Life in the Inter-American System: The Case of "Baby Boy". In: 2 Human Rights Law Journal, 309-318.

Shestack, Jerome J. (1984): The Jurisprudence of Human Rights. In: Meron, Theodor (ed.): Human Rights in International Law: Legal and Policy Issues. Clarendon Press, Oxford, 69-113.

Thornberry, Patrick (1991): International Law and the Rights of Minorities. Clarendon Press, Oxford.

Weeramantry, Christopher G. (1988): Islamic Jurisprudence: An International Perspective. Macmillan, London.

Zafrulla Khan, Muhammad (1981): The Quran. Third Revised Edition. Curzon Press Limited, London.

Reconciliation as Religious Worship

Daniel Philpott

The Peace of Westphalia signed in 1648 marked the end of a 130 year period of violence motivated in large part by the warring claims of Catholics, Protestants, and different kinds of Protestants. The peace involved reconciliation, though it was what some theorists today are calling *thin* reconciliation. Falling far short of deep toleration, it was rather a *modus vivendi*, an agreement to live together and to respect the regional autonomy of religious populations.

Two trends during the past generation in global politics evoke memories of Westphalia. The first involves a reversal of a long historical trend that began during the long crisis that led to Westphalia. It is the increasing subordination of religious authority to the power of the nation-state. This trend began with the Erastianism of the sixteenth and seventeenth centuries, intensified with the French Revolution, and reached a peak in the mid-twentieth century with communism, Nazism, and post-colonial nationalism in Africa and Asia. The reversal consists of an assertive comeback of religious authority vis-à-vis the state over the past forty years within every religion and every part of the world (Toft/Philpott/Shah 2011).

The second trend is a global outbreak of peacebuilding efforts, by which I mean concerted political, cultural, and sometimes religious efforts to build peace and stability in the wake of genocide, civil war, and dictatorship. This, however, does not mean an outbreak of peace. Rwanda, Yugoslavia, Congo, and Timor Leste and so many other places defeated the hope of an imminent and enduring peace after deep conflict. We now know that civil war settlements break down within five years some 40 percent of the time (Call/Cousens 2008:5). What we are noticing, rather, is the outbreak of more than 33 United Nations (UN) peace operations since the end of the Cold War; more mediated settlements since the end of the Cold War than in the previous 200 years; some 40 truth commissions; two international criminal tribunals and now an International Criminal Court; the makings of a global regime of reparations; a rash of global apologies by world leaders; the building of museums and monuments; and acts of forgiveness. All of this – which together makes our time an "age of peacebuilding" – has been occasioned by the third wave of democratization and a wave of civil war endings and has been propelled by global communications and transportation and their enablement of imitation.

Rise of religion in the age of peacebuilding

The central claim of this chapter sits at the intersection of these two global trends – the rise of religion and the age of peacebuilding. My claim has to do with the involvement of religion in peacebuilding. The most distinctive, important, and interesting way that religion has contributed to peacebuilding, and perhaps to global politics in general, is through bringing the concept of reconciliation into politics around the world. The rise of reconciliation is still another trend of the past generation. Though reconciliation is not an exclusively religious concept it has been advanced disproportionately in politics by religious thinkers and religious doers.

Thinkers and doers: both sorts of people are responsible for the rise of reconciliation as a principle for politics. I wish to consider each of them separately in making the case that the religious have brought a new concept to peacebuilding.

First, the thinkers. During the age of peacebuilding, the globally dominant concept of peacebuilding – and by that I mean the concept that dominates the thinking of the United Nations, Western governments, international lawyers, human rights activists, and powerful global institutions like the World Bank – is what may be called "the liberal peace" (Paris 2004; Richmond 2006:291-314). It involves first securing a ceasefire or a peace agreement. But it is far more than such a negative peace. It also entails establishing the rule of law, human rights, democracy, free markets, and a free media, holding elections, and reforming institutions. With respect to the crimes of the past, the liberal peace finds close cousins in human rights activists and international lawyers who call for trials and disqualification from office, typically justifying these measures as valuable for building the rule of law and accountability. Certain other strands of peacebuilding, by contrast, liberals view with demurral, especially when they are applied publically: personal and spiritual healing, the transformation of emotions, interpersonal reconciliation, forgiveness, and religious language and ritual. All of these commitments find a pedigree in Locke, Kant, Mill, Wilson, and Roosevelt and their commitments to individual rights, democracy, and international law and institutions.

But during the same age of peacebuilding an alternative school of thought has arisen – reconciliation – and behind it has been a disproportionate concentration of religious thinkers. It is a remarkable development. In most of Christianity's history reconciliation and its close cousin forgiveness have been confined to the confessional or to personal relationships and have enjoyed scant place in politics. But in the nineteenth and early twentieth centuries lone voices in Christian theology began to think differently, applying concepts like atonement and reconciliation to political orders. Theologian John de Gruchy traces this trajectory, counting among these voices religious thinkers like Albrecht Ritschl, P. T. Forsyth, Karl Barth, Dietrich Bonhoeffer, and Jan Milic Lochman (De Gruchy 2002). Had he included Catholic sources he might have mentioned Pope John Paul II, who advocated mercy and forgiveness as political practices in his far too overlooked 1980 encyclical, *Dives in Misericordia*. Scholar Erik Doxtader has shown that South Africa was a particularly strong incubator of thought about reconciliation in politics, which anti-apartheid intellectuals as early as the beginning of the 1960s (Doxtader 2008). When Archbishop Tutu famously made reconciliation the central theme of South Africa's truth commission, he was drawing from a vibrant homegrown tradition. Today's leading theologians of reconciliation also include de Gruchy, Miroslav Volf of Yale University, New Zealand's Christopher Marshall, and other scholars (De Gruchy 2002; Volf 1996; Marshall 2001).

The Jewish and Muslim traditions arguably advanced reconciliation as a public concept far earlier than Christianity. In the thought of Moses Maimonides as well as in the practice of medieval Jewish communities we can find complex practices of reconciliation on the community level such as *teshuva* (the Hebrew word for "repentance" or "turning") that involve confession, apology, forgiveness, and restitution. Today, American Rabbi Marc Gopin has made it his life work to adapt such concepts to conflict in the modern nation state. Similar to the work of Gopin is the work of Abu-Nimer in the Muslim world, who has sought to tap concepts and rituals from the Quran, Hadith, and subsequent Islamic tradition for reconciliation and peacebuilding in modern states. He, too benefits from history, drawing from pre-modern Arab Islamic rituals of *sulh* and *musalaha*, which communities practiced in order to repair the effects of crime.

But if religious thinkers have advanced reconciliation as a concept for modern politics, what do they mean by it and how does it differ from the liberal peace concept? Reconciliation need not reject, and should incorporate, in my view, concepts like human rights, the rule of law, free markets, and accountability for war criminals. But in most versions reconciliation connotes a far wider, more holistic restoration of persons, relationships, and social orders. To the degree that reconciliation has a common meaning it can be summarized as restoration of right relationship. Along with establishing human rights and the like, most religious concepts of reconciliation also envision practices like the confession and repentance of perpetrators, the forgiveness of victims, empathetic acknowledgment of victims' suffering on the part of other citizens, and the overcoming of enmity.

The link between reconciliation and worship

Religious theorists of reconciliation root practices of reconciliation and restorative justice in the character, purposes, and actions of God.

It is here that the link between reconciliation and worship can be made. Worship is devotion or acclaim, especially when expressed towards what one views as supreme or ultimate. Even violence can be carried out in a spirit of worship when it is directed at an object that the performer of violence takes to be ultimate. Reconciliation is akin to worship insofar as it is conceived of as an imitation of, a response to, or even participation in God's own will to restore humanity – in contrast to the liberal peace which is rooted in forms of reason that have no explicit divine reference.

But the concept of reconciliation needs development. While Volf, de Gruchy, Tutu, and John Paul II achieved the central innovations that have made reconciliation relevant for politics, much remains to be said about how this concept can provide guidance for politics. When it comes to the justice of dealing with past injustices in hopes of building a more just future we have nothing that resembles what the just war theory provides for the morality of warfare, for instance. I wish to advance the project of religious thinkers a few meters forward by proposing a broad outline of a more applied ethic of reconciliation. It draws from the basic concepts in the three religious traditions of Judaism, Christianity, and Islam as well as the contemporary movement of restorative justice. I choose these schools of thought on the basis of familiarity and realism and invite others to extend the same framework to further traditions.

At the core of my outline is the idea that reconciliation is a concept of justice. Such an idea will ring strange in Western ears. Is not justice what the liberal peace says that it is – rights, law, and deserved punishment for crimes? Judaism, Christianity, and Islam indeed contain a different way of thinking about justice. In each of their scriptures justice commonly means "righteousness", understood comprehensively as right relationship between all the members of a community in all of their affairs. Such justice is not only a state of right relationship but also a process of restoring right relationship. Restoring relationships to a condition of right relationship is also what the three traditions mean by reconciliation or else by their close cognates of reconciliation. Reconciliation, then, can be understood as a concept of justice, one that means a comprehensive, holistic restoration of right relationship.

The idea of justice as reconciliation converges with these religions' understandings of peace. The Hebrew word *shalom*, the Greek word *eirene*, and the Arabic word *salam* all describe a peace of comprehensive right relationship, corresponding to the condition that reconciliation envisions. Justice understood as reconciliation converges, too, with how these religions understand the concept of mercy, namely as a will to restore to good all that is diminished, either by injustice or by involuntary suffering. Mercy corresponds to the process of restoration that reconciliation envisions.

It is not only in their scriptural concepts of justice, peace, and mercy that these three religions support an ethic of reconciliation but also in their broad narration of God's response to evil and injustice. In contrast to Enlightenment philosophy, which proposed various philosophical solutions to the "problem of evil", God's response is one of action. Here again arises the link between worship, an orientation to who God is and what God does, and reconciliation. The Jewish scriptures depict God restoring his covenant with the Jewish people variously through meting out recompense, forgiving, restoring justice for the poor, and commanding repentance. The New Testament builds on this justice and expands it into the atoning work of Christ. For its part, the Quran depicts Allah as willing to forgive the repentant but ready to punish the unrepentant, both acts of judgment that can be argued to entail a restorative purpose.

Religious and secular approaches

As I mentioned earlier, it is not only these three religious traditions, but also, among other schools of thought, the contemporary restorative justice movement, that conceives of justice, and by implication, of peace and mercy, along the lines of reconciliation. In fact, here the line between the religious and the secular is not so neat, for restorative justice arises from religious traditions, especially the Mennonite tradition, as well as from secular thought. While restorative justice arose in the 1970s as an approach to criminal justice, mainly in the English-speaking nations, by now several innovators, including Chile's Commission on Truth and Reconciliation, Tutu and others in South Africa, as well as a handful of scholars, have sought to adapt restorative justice to the context and scale of the nation-state.

How, then, does reconciliation as a concept of justice, peace, and mercy translate into political behavior in the affairs of states and relations between states? Two further concepts convey insight here: wounds and practices. Justice that involves a holistic restoration of right relationship must begin by identifying the range of ways in which political injustices wound persons and right relationship in the political order. There are at least six of these: 1) the violation of a victim's basic rights; 2) the range of harms to the person of victims', including to life, health, prosperity, and psychological well-being; 3) ignorance of the source and circumstance of political injustices; 4) the failure of members of the surrounding political community to acknowledge the suffering of victims; 5) what I call the standing victory of political injustices, or the sense in which their affront to victims' dignity continues to stand as a moral fact unless somehow defeated; and 6) the wounds that crimes inflict on perpetrators themselves. These wounds are destructive to human flourishing in themselves but also redound, through emotions of fear, hatred and revenge, to bring about further injustices, a dynamic that we can understand by looking only as far as Bosnia, Rwanda, Northern Ireland, and scores of other locales.

To this wide range of wounds, an ethic of political reconciliation responds with an array of practices. It is the practices that convey the core concepts of justice, peace, and mercy into practical action. Each aims to repair right relationship with respect to a different set of wounds in a different way and each involves a unique form of communication among victims, perpetrators, members of communities at large, and the state. Each mirrors the restorative action through which God responds to injustices. There are six of these practices. They include first, building socially just government institutions based on human rights and the rule of law. This is where reconciliation converges most with the liberal peace. It is important to mention because reconciliation without it is cheap. Second comes acknowledgment of the suffering of victims by the surrounding community. This is the work of truth commissions and other forums for remembrance. Reparations in the form of material compensation for victims are a third practice. Fourth comes political apology. A fifth practice is punishment, which might include national and international judicial courts, but is achieved especially restoratively through community forums that seek to reintegrate perpetrators into community life. Finally, forgiveness as performed by victims towards perpetrators of political injustice is a sixth practice. How each practice restores wounds of political injustice and the ethics that each practice involves demand far more explication than I can offer here. Such an explication though, would fill out with concrete content an ethic of reconciliation that both draws from religious roots and delivers a distinctive and practical guide to political orders recovering from genocide, civil war, and dictatorship. Above all, this ethic puts forth a form of justice that entails a holistic, restorative response to the manifold suffering that large scale injustices leave in their wake.

The role of religious leaders and activists

Now having dealt with thinkers and their understanding of reconciliation let us take a look at the doers. Religious leaders and activists, too, have driven reconciliation into prominence over the past generation. Of course, the line between thinkers and doers is not always a neat one. Figures like Tutu and John Paul II have been both. Still, for many religious leaders in many settings the main fruit of their advocacy of reconciliation has been some form of political action.

One of the settings in which this fruit has been most visible is that of societies making political choices about what sort of institutions to adopt in dealing with past injustices – a setting widely known as transitional justice. Shall a truth commission be conducted? Trials? A combination of both? Neither? Addressing political institutions, of course, is not the only way that religious actors wield an influence for reconciliation; I choose this setting only for focus and comparison.

In those locales in which religious actors have exercised strong influence they have almost always promoted truth commissions, with a few exceptions like Timor Leste and post-communist Germany, where certain religious leaders urged trials as well as truth commissions. Most dramatically, religious leaders have actually formed and conducted truth commissions. The Catholic Church in Chile and both Catholic and Protestant leaders in Brazil ferreted out the truth about torture and disappearances under the nose of dictatorships in the late 1970s and early 1980s and later forwarded this information to actual truth commissions in the wake of their countries' transition to democracy. In Guatemala, after a peace settlement brought three decades of civil war to an end, the Catholic Church, led by Archbishop Juan Gerardi, formed and conducted its own Recovery of Historical Memory Project (REMHI), which proved remarkable both for the number of human rights violations it uncovered and for the deeply personal way that it conducted its investigations, providing psychological, spiritual, and emotional support for victims. Other countries in which religious actors have shaped truth commissions include South Africa, East Timor, Peru, Sierra Leone, and Germany. They have exercised their shaping power through lobbying governments, advocating publicly for truth commissions, sometimes serving as truth commissioners, contributing a religious discourse to the proceedings of truth commissions, providing counseling for victims, and encouraging their members to participate.

But religious actors do not always exercise a strong influence on transitional justice. Sometimes they are very weak. In Rwanda, for instance, following the genocide of 1994 the large established churches – Catholic, Anglican, and Presbyterian – wielded little influence on the state's choice to stage trials of *genocidaires* or to conduct the *gacaca* courts at the level of villages. True, they encouraged their members to participate in *gacaca* and sometimes conducted the work of reconciliation at the community level. But as corporate bodies they far more typically struggled to come to terms with their own passivity and complicity in the genocide. The majority Catholic Church had little to do with the work of truth commissions in Argentina or El Salvador. Nor did Protestant or Catholic churches in the Czech Republic exercise much influence on their government's choice to undertake "lustration" of Communist collaborators. Yugoslavia is still another example where religious institutions were largely inefficacious towards transitional justice institutions. By and large, the Orthodox Church in Russia, Bulgaria, Romania, and Greece had little influence on the character of their states' transitional justice institutions either.

Determinants of success in reconciliation

What has characterized those religious actors who exercise a strong influence over transitional justice institutions versus those that have proven weak and ineffectual? Two factors, I argue. First, they have held a doctrine of reconciliation much like the one that I have described in the case of the religious thinkers. They view the central task of their society as one of reconciliation; they speak the language of reconciliation; and they seek to promote reconciliation in practical ways. Typically, too, reconciliation is widely held among the middle layers and rank and file of their religious body. Tutu may be the model here; his advocacy of reconciliation has received more attention than that of any other religious leader in settings of transitional justice. But other religious leaders have advocated reconciliation forcefully, too, including Gerardi in Guatemala and leaders in Chile, Peru, Sierra Leone, Timor Leste, and several other locales. By contrast, those religious bodies that exercised little influence on transitional justice were ones in which the idea of reconciliation was scarce at the time of transition. This could be said of major churches in Rwanda, Argentina, Poland, and the Czech Republic, as well as the Orthodox churches in Russia and Eastern Europe.

The second major factor characterizing religious bodies that influenced transitional justice was a history of institutional independence from their state government during the period prior to the transition – that is, the period of dictatorship or civil war. By institutional independence I mean autonomy from the state in governance, activities, finances, and personnel. This independence was by and large a conflictual one, maintained through resistance against a regime that wished to suppress this independence. From their position of relative independence, these civil society religious actors typically played a dissident role against an authoritarian regime or a mediating role in ending a civil war, a role that gave them great prestige and power following the transition. By contrast, religious actors like the Catholic Church in Rwanda, Argentina, and the Czech Republic or Protestant hierarchies in Rwanda or East Germany were closely linked to their regimes, either through cooperation or through being dominated, and thus had limited influence over transitions. In the case of the Orthodox churches, a history of close collaboration with state rulers robbed them of autonomy from Communist states during the Cold War.

It is not my view that doctrine and independence from the state are all that matter. The unity, size, and demographic makeup of a religious body all make an important difference, as do the leadership qualities of those who head it. It should also be noted that the vast majority of religious actors who have shaped transitional justice have been Christian. In part this fact is due to demographics: the vast majority of national efforts at transitional justice have occurred in Christian countries. But in some places Muslim leaders have supported truth commissions with an intent to reconciliation as well. In both South Africa and Sierra Leone, whose population is 60 percent Muslim, clerics have supported truth commissions and related reconciliation efforts. Morocco became the first country with an overwhelmingly Muslim population to carry out a truth commission. Muslim leaders in both Afghanistan and Iraq – Ayatollah Sistani, for example – have advocated reconciliation and in some cases also truth commissions.

At this point I can summarize my argument. Reconciliation is a profoundly important contribution religious actors have made to global politics in the past generation. Rooted in religious traditions, an ethic of reconciliation means a holistic restoration of right relationships. Developed further, it can be viewed as a concept of justice, peace, and mercy and is enacted through political practices that repair wounds inflicted upon persons, relationships and political orders. During transitions away from war and authoritarianism, religious actors have promoted truth commissions more than trials. Those who have done so mostly have carried an ethic of political reconciliation and were independent from state institutions in their authority.

Though it is difficult to measure precisely the political result of the rise of reconciliation, it is fair to say that reconciliation enjoys a strong position in global discourse and practice and that the religious have done a great deal to put it there. Reconciliation is eponymous for truth commissions in Chile, Peru, Ghana, East Timor, the Solomon Islands, Sierra Leone, Liberia, and Morocco. The concept motivates religious restorative efforts at the level of civil society, too. Even the 2006 Iraq Study Group in the United States used the word reconciliation 63 times in its report. Reconciliation has not overtaken the liberal peace in its prestige among the powerful, but it has become a viable alternative. As sociologist Jonathan Van Antwerpen comments, reconciliation can be thought of as "heterodoxy" to the liberal peace's "orthodoxy" – perhaps an irony for a concept for which religious orthodoxy is so profoundly responsible (Van Antwerpen 2010).

References

Call, Charles T./Cousens, Elizabeth M. (2008): Ending wars and building peace: international responses to war-torn societies. In: International Studies Perspective 9, 1-21.

De Gruchy, John W. (2002): Reconciliation: Restoring Justice. Fortress Press, Minneapolis.

Doxtader, Erik (2008): With faith in the work of words: the beginnings of reconciliation in South-Africa, 1985-1995. Michigan State University Press, East Lansing.

Marshall, Christopher D. (2001): Beyond retribution: a new testament vision for justice, crime and punishment. Eerdmans, Grand Rapids.

Paris, Roland (2004): At war's end: building peace after civil conflict. Cambridge University Press, Cambridge.

Richmond, Oliver P. (2006): The problem of peace: Understanding the 'liberal peace'. In: Conflict, Security & Development 6:3, 291-314.

Toft, Monica Duffy/Philpott, Daniel/Shah, Timothy Samuel (2011): God's Century. Resurgent Religion and Global Politics. Norton, New York.

Van Antwerpen, Jonathan (2010): Reconciliation as Heterodoxy. Unpublished manuscript. Social Science Research Council.

Volf, Miroslav (1996): Exclusion and embrace: A theological exploration of identity, otherness, and reconciliation. Abingdon Press, Nashville.

Index of Authors

Appleby, Scott, Prof. Dr., is Professor for History and Director at the Kroc Institute for International Peace Studies at Notre Dame University, Indiana. His research interests are religious motivated violence and religious motivated peace engagement. Appleby co-chaired the Chicago Council on Global Affairs' Task Force on Religion and the Making of U.S. Foreign Policy, which released the influential report "Engaging Religious Communities Abroad: A New Imperative for U.S. Foreign Policy" (2010). He is the author of the pioneering book "The Ambivalence of the Sacred: Religion, Violence and Reconciliation" (2000).

Basedau, Matthias, Dr., is a political scientist and the senior research fellow at the Institute of African Affairs of the German Institute of Global and Area Studies (GIGA), where he heads the Research Programme "Violence and Security". His research interests focus on the causes of violent conflict, particularly on ethnicity, natural resources, state institutions and religion in Africa.

Czada, Roland, Prof. Dr., is Professor of Government and Public Policy at the University of Osnabrück and chair of the Academic Council of the Osnabrück Peace Forum. His current research interests focus on societal interest intermediation, democratic governance and civic integration policies. Recently, he has published on issues such as societal power-sharing, non-majoritarian-government, cultural corporatism, and on religious governance.

Hasenclever, Andreas, Prof. Dr., is Professor of International Relations at the Institute of Political Science at the Eberhard-Karls-University of Tübingen. His main research interests are in the field of Peace and Conflict studies with particular reference to the analysis of the Democratic Peace, regime analysis, and the impact of religious traditions on political conflicts. On these topics he authored numerous articles and books.

Haynes, Jeffrey, Prof. Dr., is Associate Dean of the Faculty of Law, Governance and International Relations, and Director of the Centre for the Study of Religion, Conflict and Cooperation at London Metropolitan University, UK. His research interests are religion and international relations, religion and politics, democracy and democratization, development studies, and comparative politics and globalization.

Harvey, Peter, Prof. Dr. em., is Emeritus Professor of Buddhist Studies at the University of Sunderland, UK. His research focuses on early Buddhist thought and practices, and Buddhist ethics. He is author of various books about Buddhist history, practices and values.

Held, Thomas, Dr., is the Managing Director of the German Foundation for Peace Research in Osnabrück.

Kadayifci-Orellana, S. Ayse, Prof. Dr., is currently Assistant Professor in the field of Peace and Conflict Resolution at the School of International Service at American University, Washington D.C. She is also the one of the founding members and the Associate Director of Salam Institute for Peace and Justice. Dr. Kadayifci-Orellana's has authored "Standing on an Isthmus: Islamic Narratives of War and Peace in the Palestinian Territories" and co-authored the edited the volume, "Anthology on Islam and Peace and Conflict Resolution in Islam: Precept and Practice." Her research interests include religion and peace building, cross-cultural conflict resolution and mediation, interfaith and intra-faith dialogues, peacebuilding and development, Islamic sources of conflict resolution, Muslim women peacebuilders, Women and development, Muslim peace building actors in Africa and the Balkans, and education in the Islamic world.

Küng, Hans, Prof. Dr., is President of the Global Ethic Foundation in Tübingen. He held the professorship of Ecumenical Theology at the Eberhard-Karls-University of Tübingen from 1960 to 1996. Professor Küng founded in 1995 the Global Ethic Foundation and acts as its president. He was a member of the "Group of Eminent Persons" appointed by the Secretary-General Kofi Annan in 2001 to write a report on the dialogue of cultures. The report has been published under the title "Crossing the Divide".

Leggewie, Claus, Prof. Dr., is Professor for Political Sciences and since 2007 Director of the Institute for Advanced Study in the Humanities in Essen. Professor Leggewie is member of the German Advisory Council on Global Change and co-director of the Käte Hamburger Kolleg "Political cultures of the world society" at the University of Duisburg-Essen. His research focuses on cultural preconditions of modern societies' adaption to the impacts of climate change, preconditions and consequences of cultural and religious globalization, European conflicts of remembrance and history politics as well as political and scientific communication via digital media, democratization of non-western societies.

Little, David, Prof. Dr., was a member at Harvard's Faculty of Divinity since 1999. He retired in 2009. Professor Little writes in the areas of moral philosophy, moral theology, the history of ethics and the sociology of religion, with an interest in comparative ethics, human rights, religious liberty, and ethics and international affairs. He has published widely about religious conflicts in Sri Lanka, Tibet and Iraq.

Mollov, Ben, Prof. Dr., is member of the Faculty of the Interdisciplinary Department of Social Sciences and the Graduate Program in Conflict Management at Bar-Ilan University in Israel. He directs the University's Project for the Study of Religion, Culture and Peace. He is specialized in conflict management from an intercultural perspective and aspects of the Jewish political tradition.

Philpott, Daniel, Prof. Dr., is Associate Professor of Political Science and Peace Studies at the Kroc Institute for International Peace Studies at the University of Notre Dame. His research interests lie in reconciliation, religion and global politics, and ethics and international affairs. He is author of the recently published book "Just and Unjust Peace: An Ethic of Political Reconciliation" (2012).

Prabhu, Joseph, Prof. Dr., is Professor of Philosophy and Religion at California State University, Los Angeles and past President of the international Society for Asian and Comparative Philosophy. He has widely published on religious philosophy, the role of religions in their socio-cultural contexts and possibilities for cooperation within and between them in areas of civil society, human rights, economic organization, and peace and justice. He is also Trustee of the Parliament of the World's Religions, the Co-Chair of the Southern California Parliament for the World's Religions, and a participant in UN dialogues on Human Rights.

Rehman, Javid, Prof. Dr., is a Professor of Law and Head of the School of Law at Brunel University, London. He is the founding Director of the Collaborative Research Network/University Research Network, Security, Media and Human Rights, Brunel University (founded in 2008). He has been invited to provide legal opinions in a number of high profile cases and has written extensively on the subject of Islamic law, international human rights and minority rights.

Robbers, Gerhard, Prof. Dr., is Professor for Public Law at the University of Trier and Director of the Institute for European Constitutional Law and Director of the Institute for Legal Policy at the University of Trier. His research focuses are constitutional law, law regulating the relationship between church and state and comparative law. He is judge at the Constitutional Court of Rhineland-Palatinate and will be the President of the 34th German Protestant Kirchentag 2013.

Strüver, Georg, M.A., is a research fellow of the project "Contested Leadership in International Relations: Power Politics in South America, South Asia and Sub-Saharan Africa", financed by the Volkswagen Foundation, at the German Institute of Global and Area Studies (GIGA) in Hamburg.

Vüllers, Johannes, M.A., is a research fellow at the Institute of African Affairs of the German Institute of Global and Area Studies (GIGA) in Hamburg. His research interests focus on the role of religion in conflict, the determinants of peace engagement by religious leaders as well as the consequences of mediation and power-sharing agreements.

Weingardt, Markus, Dr., is a political and administrative scientist at the Global Ethic Foundation (Tübingen). His peace and conflict research focuses on the peace potentials of religions. As a research fellow at the Protestant Institute for Interdisciplinary Research/FEST in Heidelberg (2006-2011) he was also coordinator of the research network "Religion and Conflict" and co-organiser of the Religions and World Peace Symposium. He is the author of the pioneering book "Religion Macht Frieden" ("Religion Powers Peace") (2010) and editor of the series "Religion – Konflikt – Frieden" at Nomos-Verlag (Baden-Baden).

Name Index